He Came To Set The Captives Free

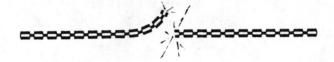

By Rebecca Brown, M.D.

Published by Chick Publications
P.O. Box 662, Chino, CA 91710
Printed in the United States of America

Published by Chick Publications
P.O. Box 662, Chino, CA 91710
Printed in the United States of America

Library of Congress Catalog Card No. 86-50833

ISBN 0-937958-25-5

Tenth Printing

195/G

TABLE OF CONTENTS

WARNING!

This will be one of the hardest books you have ever tried to read. **SATAN DOES NOT WANT YOU TO READ THIS MATERIAL!**

> Heavenly Father, I ask you to shield and protect the reader of this book and give him or her a clear understanding of all that you have directed us to say. I ask you for this, and thank you, in the precious name of your Son, Jesus Christ our Lord. Amen.

The purpose of this book is to show you the many ways Satan and his demons are at work in the world today, to show you how you can effectively fight against them, AND how you can be set free from bondage to Satan.

Satan will do everything he can to keep you from reading this. He will afflict you with overwhelming sleepiness, confusion, constant interruptions and many other things. FEAR is one of Satan's major weapons. He will use fear to try to stop you from reading this book. You simply need to rebuke fear directly and out loud in the name of Jesus Christ to overcome it. Also pray and ask for shielding as you read in order to understand this material.

My deepest appreciation goes first to the Lord, and then to Elaine. The writing of this book would not have been possible without the information given to me by Elaine, and the strength, guidance and encouragement given to me by the Lord.

All names have been changed to protect the people involved in this book. We pray earnestly that the Lord Jesus Christ will bless you richly with His salvation and understanding as you read the following pages.

> "And he [Jesus] came to Nazareth, where he had been

brought up: and, as his custom was, he went into the synagogue on the sabbath day, and stood up for to read. And there was delivered unto him the book of the prophet Esaias [Isaiah]. And when he had opened the book, he found the place where it was written,

> 'The Spirit of the Lord is upon me, because he hath anointed me to preach the gospel to the poor; he hath sent me to heal the broken-hearted, to preach deliverance to the captives, and recovering of sight to the blind, to set at liberty them that are bruised, to preach the acceptable year of the Lord.'

And he closed the book, and he gave it again to the minister, and sat down. And the eyes of all them that were in the synagogue were fastened on him. And he began to say unto them, this day is this Scripture fulfilled in your ears."   Luke 4:16-21

HE CAME TO SET THE CAPTIVES FREE!

CHAPTER 1

Enter Rebecca

From the first moment she crossed through the doorway into that building, she sensed that there was something different about the place. A hovering of darkness, as it were. Something she could not define, but knew was there. She knew also that it was something that she had never experienced before.

Rebecca is a doctor. She was just entering Memorial Hospital for the first time to begin her training in internal medicine. She had finished medical school the previous month and had now moved away from home really for the first time in the 30 years of her life. She had no idea that the tragedies she would see in that hospital would forever change both her and the course of her life. The brooding darkness she sensed in her spirit seemed to be watchfully waiting . . . waiting. Suddenly it would strike, plunging Rebecca into a series of events that would test to the utmost her commitment to her Lord and Savior, Jesus Christ.

The first test was quick to come — Rebecca had been working as a doctor at that hospital for about 2 months. One night while she was working in the Emergency Room, a man in his 30's was brought in about 2 A.M. Rebecca recoiled in horror as she viewed his mangled and torn body. She had 6 years of experience working in Emergency Rooms (E.R.) in large inner city hospitals as a Registered Nurse prior to becoming a doctor, but she had never seen anything like this! As she worked rapidly with the other personnel in the E.R. to save the young pastor's life, her mind raced. How could this be? Who would do such a thing? He had obviously been tortured. His body was partially skinned, he had multiple burns, stab wounds, lashes from whips, and most horrifying of all, holes in the palms of his hands from spikes being driven through them. He was unconscious and in deep shock.

After the initial medical care was done, the patient stabilized and then transferred to the Intensive Care Unit, Rebecca looked for the police officers who had brought him in. They had little to say other than the fact that this was a kidnapping case. They had found the body and at first thought he was dead. They refused to talk about the incident any further and left quickly, mumbling something about having to file their report.

Everyone else in the E.R. went on with their work as if nothing unusual had happened. No one seemed particularly surprised or upset about the condition of the patient. Again, Rebecca felt overwhelmingly that brooding darkness. She was greatly puzzled and concerned, but was, herself, quickly caught up in the pressure of the work at hand. Nothing in her background could possibly have prepared her for the shock of that young pastor's testimony of what had happened to him prior to coming into the Emergency Room that night. She did not know that the next blow would come to one of her own patients who was very dear to her.

But first, let us trace the training the Lord gave Rebecca to prepare her for all that was to happen.

Rebecca had the tremendous privilege and blessing of being born to faithful Christian parents who prayed daily for her. She had accepted Jesus as her Savior at a very young age, but knew nothing about a personal walk with Him. She was raised in a very tight and narrow religious group and was not permitted to form friends or interact with anyone outside the group. She was rejected both within the group and without — mocked and ridiculed at school and by the other members of the religious group; she grew up very lonely. She also had much illness, spending her childhood in and out of the hospital. Then as she got older, she was discovered to have an incurable and debilitating neuromuscular disease. But her loving parents provided stability in her life and their prayers surrounded and protected her, no doubt keeping her from entering the occult world that snares so many other young people with similar backgrounds.

During the first year of medical school she came to the point of finally committing her life to the Lord in all areas, making Jesus the *master* in her life as well as Savior. The four years of medical school were an intense struggle because of the neuromuscular illness and also because of the lack of finances. During those four years Rebecca learned to trust the Lord, to walk with Him day by day, to hear Him speak to her in her spirit, to follow His guidance, and to experience His provision for her every need.

Before medical school she had been a Registered Nurse for seven years. Then, as a result of the Lord's powerful working in her life, and a whole string of miracles, she left nursing, returned to school and then on to medical school.

At the time Rebecca entered Memorial Hospital she knew absolutely nothing about Satanism or of Elaine, a powerful witch who lived near by. Rebecca never dreamed that her walk with Christ in that hospital would cause such shock waves in the spirit world that the forces of darkness would become enraged. She became involved in a titanic struggle as Elaine, one of the top witches in the U.S., led an organized attack by many witches using all of their powers and skills of witchcraft to try to kill Rebecca.

The internship year is the first year of training that a doctor receives after graduating from medical school, if he or she is going to specialize in something. It is by far the most intense year of training, and the most frightening one. It was no different for Rebecca at Memorial than anyone else except that she was constantly aware of something so strange but undefinable about that hospital. No one else seemed to notice it, including her few Christian colleagues. From the first she found an overwhelming atmosphere of hatred, back-biting and fighting within the whole department, and indeed, within the whole hospital itself. It was an extremely cold atmosphere. This on top of the tremendous physical and emotional pressures of the year were used by the Lord to greatly increase her closeness to Him.

She found almost from the beginning that there was an unusual resistance to the gospel. Over and over people with whom she tried to share Jesus would flatly refuse to even listen. In fact, within six months of the start of her training at that hospital, the hospital administration had all the Gideon bibles removed from the patient rooms and a memo was posted on each nursing unit stating that the hospital would fire, on the spot, any employee who was caught "evangelizing" the patients. Also, any minister that was coming to the hospital to visit patients was not permitted to visit with anyone except their own private parishioners, and, if the nurses found them "evangelizing" other patients they were to have them escorted from the hospital by security and asked not to return again. A chaplaincy service was not permitted, which was also unusual. Indeed, it seemed as if an effort was being made to wipe away any mention of Christianity within the walls of the hospital.

Rebecca was first assigned to the intensive care unit and immediately was plunged into a whirl-wind of activities. She spent up to 120 hours per week working at the hospital. Because of this schedule she attributed the steady worsening of her physical condition to her exhaustion.

Then the Lord began steadily laying upon her heart that she must go into the hospital early each morning to spend an hour in prayer before work asking the Lord for that institution and that city, that the gospel would be proclaimed and bear fruit. As she began obeying the Lord and praying each morning an hour before work, repeatedly she found herself compelled by the Holy Spirit to pray asking the Lord to restrain the powers of darkness in that place. Again and again she found herself quoting Numbers 10:35 where Moses said:

> "Rise up, Lord, and let thine enemies be scattered;
> and let them that hate thee flee before thee."

She did not know why she was praying in this manner, and indeed sometimes thought that it was strange to do so, but over and over the Holy Spirit compelled her to pray in such a manner.

As the Lord steadily increased the burden on her heart for the souls in that place she began to pray daily asking the Lord to permit her to stand in the gap for the hospital and the city, as in Ezekiel 22:30-31:

> "And I sought for a man among them, that should make up the hedge, and stand in the gap before me for the land, that I should not destroy it: but I found none. Therefore have I poured out mine indignation upon them; I have consumed them with the fire of my wrath: their own way have I recompensed upon their heads, saith the Lord God."

She was not sure just what was involved in "standing in the gap" but asked the Lord to use her if He could.

During Rebecca's first few months at Memorial, God taught her a very valuable lesson in total dependance on Him in her medical work. Late one night a patient was admitted to the Coronary Care Unit with severe chest pain, high blood pressure and a possible heart attack. It was Rebecca's responsibility to examine the patient and care for him that night. He gave her a list of the medicines that he was taking and among them was a particularly good one to use for lowering blood pressure while simultaneously taking the work load off of the heart. He adamantly stated that he was taking a particular dose and Rebecca accepted his word. She elected to give him that dose in an effort to lower his blood pressure and to relieve the work load on his heart in hopes of preventing a heart attack. What she did not know was that that dosage is very dangerous to give unless she had herself gradually worked the patient up to that amount.

One hour later, the nurses called her and told her that the patient's blood pressure had dropped very low, that he was in shock and looked as if he were dying. Pure terror and dismay overwhelmed her. She called her superior and told him about the situation and asked what could be done to reverse the effects of the medicine she had given. He coldly told her that she had made a stupid mistake and that there was absolutely nothing that could be done, except to see if the patient lived or died. No medicine was available that could be used to reverse the effects of the one she had given. He went on to add that he, too, had made a similar mistake as an intern and that his patient had sustained greatly extended damage to his heart as a result of that period in shock and had nearly died.

Many thoughts were madly racing through Rebecca's head as she walked down the lonely, dark halls to the CCU (Coronary Care Unit) that night to see the patient. Guilt and fear and self-chastisement were uppermost amongst them. Cold sweat ran down her back as she anguished over the fact that in all probability she had killed the patient. Suddenly the Holy Spirit showed her the error of the thoughts uppermost in her mind. She had been thinking, "God made an orderly universe where cause and effect take place in an orderly manner. Because of your stupid mistake this man will probably die. Since this medicine is absolutely irreversible, the effect will take place, so there is no need even to pray or to expect God to break into his orderly universe just for you and your stupidity."

Gently the Holy Spirit flooded into her entire being the sure knowledge that she was different! She was a child of the King! And, in so being, had a special privilege that the other doctor had not had. She had the right to ask God the Father, in Jesus' name, to correct her mistake. That was one of the many things for which Jesus had died on the cross.

She abruptly turned and ran to the chapel and fell on her knees before the Lord and prayed earnestly asking the Lord to correct her mistake, laying claim to the fact that she was a child of the King and standing on Hebrews 4:16:

> "Let us therefore come boldly unto the throne of grace, that we may obtain mercy, and find grace to help in time of need."

She arose from her knees and went back down to the CCU. When she arrived she found that the patient's blood pressure had returned to normal and he was pain free! A new Electrocardiogram showed his heart had returned to normal. He was discharged two days later without any heart damage at all.

Rebecca also learned to hear the Lord's guidance more acutely on an hour-to-hour basis. Time after time He would speak in that soft voice in her spirit, bringing a mistake to her attention before it could be carried out, or bringing to her attention something she had forgotten or overlooked, or something that she had read or learned about in the past. She learned to fast and pray, asking the Lord to reveal to her the key to the diagnosis of particularly obscure cases. She also learned to rely on the Lord to give her skill in her hands, and never performed any procedure on any patient without first praying and asking the Lord Jesus, the Great Physician, to put His hands within hers and guide them with His skill. In all of her years so far, the Lord has continuously been faithful and she has never had a serious complication resulting from any procedure she has done.

About six months into her internship, just as Rebecca was again assigned to the Intensive Care Unit (ICU), the young pastor she saw in the emergency room finally recovered enough to talk. Rebecca had followed his progress closely, constantly praying for him and was drawn by the Lord to frequently stop by his room to talk with him. One day he told her what had really happened just prior to his admission to the hospital.

Bob was the pastor of a small Christian church in that city. He had become involved in ministering to some people who worshiped Satan. He told Rebecca that there was a very large satanic community in a town close by, and that Satanism was rampant in that state. He had, at the Lord's leading, been steadily bringing a number of these people to Jesus. They had turned from serving Satan and made Jesus Christ their Lord and Savior. He also helped them cast out the demons that they had asked to dwell in them to gain powers of witchcraft. The night Rebecca first saw him, he had been kidnapped by the satanists and taken to one of their meetings. He was taken up on stage in front of the group and tortured. They were in the process of nailing him to a cross when one of the members shouted out that someone had seen something suspicious and called the police. (The satanists had a police scanner radio and monitored all the calls.) Bob had passed out while being crucified and knew nothing more until he awoke in the hospital bed.

Rebecca was astounded, she had never heard of such a thing. Perhaps this was the explanation of the brooding darkness she could feel in that hospital? The next revelations were quick to follow.

As she started into her second rotation in the Intensive Care Unit, her uneasiness continued to grow. Each night she was on call, she had the responsibility for all of the patients in the critical care units. She began noticing as she was prayerfully working with the patients that there were many deaths which, to her, were unexplainable.

There is normally an orderly traceable sequence of events in the illness and/or death of any patient. For example, if someone went into shock (low blood pressure) because he was bleeding somewhere, once the bleeding was stopped by surgery or whatever and the blood volume he had lost replaced by blood transfusions, the patient's blood pressure should not suddenly drop unless he started bleeding again, or developed some other complication such as an overwhelming infection.

However, many of the patients Rebecca worked with would just reach a stabilized condition and then suddenly, for no traceable reason, take a turn for the worse. Their heart would suddenly stop beating, or they would stop breathing, or their blood pressure would drop to zero. Many of these died shortly despite all measures taken medically to save them. Rebecca followed up on the autopsies of many of these patients, and was even more puzzled when no cause for their death was found other than the original problem which had brought them into the hospital.

The other problem which greatly concerned her was the frequency and content of what is called, in the medical field, an "acute ICU psychosis." When patients undergo the great stress of a critical illness, they are placed in an ICU (Intensive Care Unit) for a number of days, usually with the lights on 24 hours a day, monitors going, and no window to look out of. Because of this a certain percent will become disoriented and start to have hallucinations. (That is, see things that are not real.) However, in this hospital, the incidence of ICU psychoses was many times more than anything Rebecca had experienced in any of the several other hospitals she had worked in, both as a R.N. and a medical student.

Rebecca felt led by the Lord to take the time to talk to

14

many of the patients about just what they were "seeing." Much to her surprise, almost all of them told her that they had seen demons in their rooms!

Greatly concerned about all of this, Rebecca started mentioning the incidence of deaths and ICU psychoses in the medical conferences held with all the interns and residents each morning. Nobody else seemed concerned, or even to believe her. After her third attempt to discuss the problem she was called down to the office of the director of the training program and told to shut her mouth on the subject, that she was not experienced enough to know what she was talking about. When Rebecca pointed out that she also had ten years experience as a R.N. in addition to medical school, she was told that if she continued to create trouble she would be kicked out of the training program.

Her morning prayer sessions took on a new intensity as she earnestly sought a revelation from the Lord as to what was going on. The first break-through came through one of her own patients.

Pearl was an elderly black lady from the Southern United States who had been under Rebecca's care for about six months. Pearl was a very strong Christian and Rebecca had come to know her well and love her very much. One evening Pearl came to the hospital very ill and Rebecca admitted her to the Intensive Care Unit. The next morning as Rebecca went to the ICU to start making rounds the nurses told her that Pearl was having an ICU psychosis. Rebecca was somewhat startled, because she knew Pearl was a very strong Christian, a lady who had suffered much and didn't panic easily.

As she went into Pearl's room she found her crying. When she asked her why, Pearl told her that if she did not transfer her out of the ICU that day that "that night nurse would kill her." Then Pearl told Rebecca about how the night shift nurse caring for her had come in and talked to her and told her that there was no need for her to fight to stay alive, that she could so easily be reincarnated into her next life. The nurse also told Pearl that she would call on "the higher powers" to come and escort Pearl into her next "beautiful life." When the nurse laid her hands on Pearl and spoke words of a foreign sounding language, Pearl recognized it to be an incantation. Pearl knew from her own heritage about voodoo and black magic and demons, and she declared that she had seen demons in the room. She told Rebecca that she was too weak to fight anymore and if the same thing would happen tonight she knew she would die.

Rebecca was astounded! She knew Pearl well enough that she didn't think she was lying and she was sure that she wasn't disoriented in any way. The nurse Pearl was referring to happened to be the nurse in charge of the ICU on the night shift. She was an older lady, pleasant, attractive and an excellent nurse. She was well organized, knowledgeable and saw to it that the patients got good care. She was highly respected by the medical staff and the rest of the nursing staff. Rebecca had always found her a bit cold and withdrawn, but had thought it was the pressures of her work load. She could not find fault with her work in any way.

Rebecca knew she could not talk to any of her colleagues about the problem because they would all say that she was crazy. Neither could she accuse the nurse of anything because she had no proof. At that time Rebecca had very little knowledge of witches and almost no knowledge about demons. There was only one thing she could do. She took the problem to the Lord in prayer. Every spare moment she had that day was spent on her knees in prayer down in the chapel. (She always had the chapel to herself because no one else ever used it.) Late in the day, the Lord confirmed to her heart that Pearl was telling the truth. The Lord also commanded Rebecca to go and sit at Pearl's bedside all night that night as Pearl was too ill to be safely transferred out of the ICU. This was possible as Rebecca was not on call that particular night.

What happened that night was to change Rebecca's life forever. As she sat at Pearl's bedside, not really expecting anything to happen, she felt direct demonic oppression as she had never felt it before. Helen, the nurse in charge of the ICU, did not come into Pearl's room at all that night. Rebecca felt an incredible unseen power coming against her. She felt as if there was a giant unseen hand trying to squash her into a little grease spot on the floor and as if some unseen force was trying to suck the very life out of her. She tried to scientifically reason the feeling away, tried to convince herself that it was just her own imagination, but none of this helped. She felt her body beginning to weaken to the point where she could hardly sit up. Pearl felt it too. So, she and Pearl joined hands, and Rebecca prayed quietly asking the Lord to cover them with a shield of the precious blood of Jesus.

> "And they overcame him [Satan] by the blood of the
> Lamb, and by the word of their testimony . . ."
>
> Revelation 12:11

That night was a tremendous struggle, but Pearl came through the night safely and Rebecca transferred her out of the ICU that morning.

The next revelations came quickly. Rebecca was teaching a weekly bible study to some of the nurses whom she had led to the Lord. One of these nurses, Jean, finally started talking to her one day about the Satanism that she had become involved with prior to her conversion. She told Rebecca that Helen had been training her to become a medium and that she had been ready to be initiated into the group of satanists just when Rebecca came to the hospital and had started talking to her about the Lord. As a result, she had made Jesus her Lord and savior and had refused to have anything more to do with Helen or the other witches.

17

However, Jean was obviously very afraid of Helen and her friends.

Jean told Rebecca that she knew that Helen considered it her "ministry" to assign herself to care for the most critically ill patients in the ICU. Then while she was caring for them, she would talk to them and tell them that there was no need for them to struggle to live as they could be so easily reincarnated into their next life and have no more suffering. Then, with or without their consent, she would lay her hands on them and call up demon spirits which she called the "higher powers" to come and usher these patients on into their next life. Often, these patients would soon take a turn for the worse and die. Jean was afraid to tell anyone else about the problem because Helen was held in high regard by the head nurse and other authorities, and knew that they would not believe her. In fact, after Jean had turned to Christ, she had arranged a transfer to another shift so that she would not be working with Helen.

Jean also told Rebecca about the occult community close to that city which had one of the largest distribution centers of occult literature in the U.S., a very large training camp for witches and also had a satanist church. She confirmed to Rebecca all that the young pastor had told her and was very afraid that the same thing might happen to her. No one around seemed to take the community very seriously, but that, of course, was precisely what Satan wanted.

Then Rebecca learned from several other sources about other nurses and doctors at the hospital that were involved in the occult, and about the satanist cult and community. Again she took the situation to the Lord and received confirmation. She began studying her Bible earnestly to learn more about Satan and his demons. She learned that people could be inhabited by demons and could use demonic powers to do all sorts of things. It was at that point that she began to enter into active warfare against Helen and the other satanists who worked at the hospital.

In her morning prayer sessions she began to ask the Lord to bind the demonic powers within that place and in the specific people she knew were involved. Daily, in the evenings before Rebecca left the hospital, she would walk through the ICU and other wards, and very quietly but out loud, take authority over every demon spirit in those places that either were there already, or that would come there the rest of the day and night, and bind them with the power of the name of Jesus Christ. She also asked the Lord to place a special shield around the patients to protect them from the demonic forces.

Many nights when she was on call, she would be called up to the ICU, or one of the wards to see a patient who had taken a turn for the worse. As God gave Rebecca discernment as to which problems were the result of demonic interference she learned to stand on Luke 10:19:

> "Behold I give unto you power to tread on serpents and scorpions, and over all the power of the enemy: and nothing shall by any means hurt you."

and Mark 16:17:

> "And these signs shall follow them that believe; in my name shall they cast out devils . . . "

Many times she would stand on one side of a patient's bed silently battling in prayer, binding the demons and commanding them to leave, and claiming a shield of faith in Jesus Christ over the patient, while Helen (or one of the other nurses who was a witch) stood on the other side of the bed directing all the demon power available to her, both at Rebecca and against the patient. Rebecca would also, or course, use all of her medical knowledge to try to reverse the downward course of the patient, but she quickly learned that all of her medical knowledge was of little help if it was not combined with the spiritual battling in prayer.

Of course, Helen, Satan, and the other witches did not take kindly to Rebecca's activities, and the battle mounted. Rebecca tried to share with a couple of her Christian co-workers what was going on, but they refused to believe her and told her that she was just ill, and overtired, and imagining things.

As the battle increased in intensity, Rebecca's neuromuscular disease worsened. She came under the care of one of the top doctors on the staff of that hospital. Despite all her prayers and the medical efforts made on her behalf, she was dying, and knew it. Finally, on the last day of her internship year, she became too ill to work any more. A consultation was held with several of the specialists involved in her case and she was told that they did not think she had long to live. There was nothing more they could do. They asked her if she wanted to be admitted to the hospital there, or to go home. She decided to go home. So Rebecca left that city and hospital thinking that she would never see it again, but her heart was so heavy and grieved for the many, many people in that place so lost and held captive by the powers of darkness.

Then followed an agonizing month in which her illness progressed to the place where she was so weak that she could not walk, or even get out of bed by herself. But through it all she had a complete and beautiful peace. Jesus was in control, that was all that mattered. Night after night as she lay awake, in too much pain to sleep, she had sweet communion with her Lord and fervently hoped that it would be His will to call her home soon.

One day towards the end of that long month, the pastor of her home church, Pastor Pat, came to visit her. Being the man of God that he was, Pastor Pat had not just accepted the fact that Rebecca was to die, but had taken the matter to the Lord in prayer. He came and talked with her and told her that the Lord had revealed to him that it was not His will for Rebecca to die.

Then he said, "I know this sounds crazy, but I believe the Lord has revealed to me that what is happening to you is that you are being attacked by a group of very powerful witches. Your illness has worsened to this point because of the demonic powers they are sending to you. Is this possible? Have you been in contact with any witches that you know of?"

Suddenly Rebecca understood! Why hadn't she associated the worsening of her own condition with the battle she had been fighting against the satanists in that hospital? She had never talked to Pastor Pat about any of her experiences, so she told him about all that had been happening the past year.

He paced the floor in deep concern, then turned to her and said, "I *know* it is not the Lord's will for you to die. I have no doubts at all now that your illness is a direct result of witchcraft. We must pray and block the power of those witches."

And pray he did! Not only the pastor, but the elders and also about 200 members of that church fasted and prayed around the clock for a whole week, interceding for Rebecca, asking the Lord to shield her and break the power of the witches who were coming against her.

Toward the end of that week, one night as Rebecca lay in bed, drifting on the edge of unconsciousness, the Lord brought to her mind a portion that she had read in Watchman Nee's book:

> "Unless a Christian plainly knows his work is finished and he no longer is required by the Lord to remain, he should by all means resist death. If the symptoms of death have been seen already in his body before his work is done, he positively should resist it and its symptoms.
>
> To concede — by sizing up of our environment, physical condition, and feeling — that our time has come is an error on our part; we instead need to possess definite indications from the Lord. As we live for Him, so must we die for Him. Any call for departure which

does not come from the Lord ought to be opposed.

To overcome death believers must alter their attitude from one of submission to one of resistance towards it. Unless we cast off our passive approach we will not be able to overthrow death but will be mocked by it instead and finally come to an untimely end. Numerous saints today misapprehend passivity for faith. They reason that they have committed everything to God. If they ought not to die, He verily shall save them from it: if they ought to die, then He doubtless shall allow them to die: let the will of God be done. Such a saying sounds right, but is this faith? Not at all. It is simply lazy passivity. When we do not know God's will, it is fitting for us to pray: 'not my will, but thine, be done' (Luke 22:42). This does not mean we need not pray specifically, letting our requests be made known to God. We should not submit passively to death, for God instructs us to work together actively with His will. Except we definitely know God wants us to die, we must not passively permit death to oppress us. Rather we must actively cooperate with God's will to resist it. Why should we adopt such an attitude as this? The Bible treats death as our enemy." (1 Cor 15:26)

From *The Spiritual Man* , by Watchman Nee, pp. 216-219.

As the Lord brought to her memory the above passages, the Holy Spirit quietly spoke to Rebecca and told her that it was not the Father's will for her to die, that she had much work yet to do. She must begin to stand up and resist Satan, and refuse to accept illness or death from him. She struggled for awhile, because in her heart of hearts, she did not want to live. She did not want to struggle any longer, she wanted to go to heaven with her Lord and have all the peace and joy that she knew awaited her there. But the quiet, soft, voice of the Holy Spirit was insistent.

Finally, with many tears, she placed her feet on "The Rock" and began to rebuke Satan and command him in the name of Jesus to leave — that she would not accept any more of the illness he sought to put on her, and that she would not accept death. Later the Lord revealed to Rebecca that the only reason He had been able to break through that night and reveal to her that He wanted her to stand up and fight and resist death, was because of the powerful intercession by Pastor Pat and the church people.

Rebecca had so much muscle damage that she had a three months recovery period, but the Lord raised her up and completely healed her. So she returned to Memorial Hospital to finish her last two years of training, ready at last for the meeting the Lord was arranging with Elaine, the head witch who had led the attempt to kill her.

CHAPTER 2

Enter Elaine

ELAINE TALKS:

My mother and father's marriage was a very shaky one. My father was a drunkard who believed that he was God's gift to women. He mistreated my mother very badly. When I was born he stood at the foot of her bed and told her that he wished I was dead over and over, until she finally threw a vase at him.

My birth was like any other birth, like hundreds born on that same day all over the world, except that I was born deformed. I had no nose, no upper lip, no roof in my mouth. This is what is called a severe hair-lip with a cleft-palate. My mother wanted to see me right away as soon as I was born, and to her I was a beautiful baby, even with the deformities. Her first question was, "Can she be fixed?"

She was in absolute poverty. She had no money and no way of making any. In those days the welfare programs were not available as they are today, but my mother was not the type to give up just because she was poor.

It so happened that in that same hospital there was a nurse called Helen. She had assisted at my birth. Helen knew my mother's circumstances and also of my father's attitude of hatred. Helen wasn't just an ordinary nurse, she was also a powerful witch and a member of what has become one of the most powerful but little known cults in our country today. This cult calls themselves The Brotherhood and is a Satan-worshiping cult. Helen was, at that time, what is known within the cult as a "contact person." Her contact with my mother was to affect the rest of my entire life, as well as the life of Rebecca.

The day following my birth Helen approached my mother with a proposition. If my mother would give Helen permission to take a very small amount of my blood, she and her "friends" would provide a way to get finances and the help she needed to obtain the best surgical and medical care for me that was available. My mother could not understand just why Helen would do all this in return for seemingly so small a thing. She could never seem to grasp the meaning of what Helen explained to her. But, as there seemed to be no other source of the desperately needed help, and as Helen repeatedly reassured her that she would not harm me, my mother finally agreed to the proposition. Helen was an attractive young lady who seemed genuinely concerned and sincere in her desire to help both me and my mother.

What Helen did *not* explain to my mother was that my blood was, for her, a very important "sale." The small container of blood taken from me was given to another woman called Grace. Grace was also in the satanist cult. She was what is known as a high priestess. The selling of my blood was to give Grace more power, more activity and a higher position within the cult. Helen, too, obtained more power through this transaction.

The blood was taken by Helen and given to Grace. Grace then drank my blood during a ceremony which gave both Grace and Satan possession of me, and opened me up as a home for many demons from that moment on. Grace, at Satan's direction, sent many specific spirits into me which would mold and shape my life and personality and future.

My mother was not a Christian, neither did she know that what she did would make me a marked person, carefully watched by the satanists, and would, later in my life, result in my own involvement in the cult. Had she known that, my mother never would have said, "O.K., you can have a little of her blood." Later on in my life as a member of the cult myself, I was to witness a number of such sales and always my heart grieved as I thought about the consequences in the baby's future life.

Satan now had a prized possession. A new born baby where demons and spirits could have a home and could grow and become very powerful and agile in my life. As I became more and more aware of myself, even in my younger days, I knew something different and special was going on within me, but didn't know what it was.

Four days after my birth, my mother was approached and told that she could take me to a children's hospital at a near-by large medical center. There I would have a number of surgeries. Very many. As a matter of fact, it took sixteen years of plastic surgery to build a face for me. I also had to have long hours of speech and hearing therapy, dental work, everything. This was the beginning of many years of pain, loneliness, and rejection. Pain, because plastic surgery burns with agonizing pain during the days of healing after a surgery. Loneliness, because I was not like the other children. Rejection, because of their reaction to my disfigurement. I had very few friends. I became very rough, a fighter. I learned to fight and fight very well in order to be able to stand up for myself. I had so many interruptions of my schooling because of the surgeries that it was difficult for me to maintain the few friendships I did form.

The children at school seemed to enjoy prodding me and poking me and pushing me and making fun of me until I could hardly stand it anymore. We moved from school to school so that I never went to the same school two years in a row. My parents thought it would help if I never had to face the same group of school children a second year. But, I did face the same children again and again. Every school was the same, the reactions were the same. Nothing changed, year after agonizing year.

My mother remarried shortly after my birth. My parents didn't go to church. They didn't deny me the right to go, but they did not go. They were "waiting on each other." And, like most people, if you wait on someone long enough, you've waited too long if you don't take the first step yourself.

I finally did join a youth group at a church. It was quite an active group in a Pentacostal Church. I was sixteen years old by then and was accepted by the church youth group because I could sing, and play the guitar and drums. I had many talents in the musical field as well as the art field. It was a rather happy time for me for a short while.

As I grew up I found that I had unexplainable powers and I didn't know what to do with them, or what they were, or where they came from. Some people told me I had special "gifts." I have an aunt who is deep into witchcraft and spiritism. She used to have all of us kids over to show us occult "games." I always had far superior abilities with the ouiji board, tarot cards, etc. As I reached my teens I realized that I had a fast growing ability to influence others, to make them do as I wanted. I had unusual physical strength as well.

I remember that in my first year of high school I was approached by a lesbian girl who tried to pull some of her tricks on me after gym class one day. I went into an uncontrollable rage and nearly drowned her in a toilet. She was much bigger than I, but I would have killed her had not several adults intervened.

I remained in the same school throughout high school. The kids there made fun of me too. The worst thing in the world at that age is to have your own peers abuse you and make fun of you. I reached the point where I couldn't cope with it anymore. When I was in the 12th grade, I was walking down the hall one day when the leading player of the football team called out, "Look at the ugly hair-lip." I remember dropping my books and running towards him. The next thing I remember is five teachers pulling me off of him. I had nearly beaten him to death. I had broken his nose, jaw and a number of the bones in his face. I had unnatural strength. That boy weighed close to two hundred pounds and I only weighed ninty-eight pounds at the time. I didn't have a single bruise from the fight, not even on my fists.

This power seemed ominous to me and yet I enjoyed it. It was the only way I could get a little peace. No one could push me around. I look back on it with heart break now, but at the time it seemed worth it just to have a little peace. But all peace, I was soon to find out, was going to be obliterated by a lie from Satan that I would regret for a long, long time and still do. I'm thankful that Jesus loved me all that time, although I did not realize it then. I loved the power that I had. I didn't know where it was coming from, but I wanted to find out how to get more of it. That is when I met a friend named Sandy in my youth group at church. She also attended the same high school as I. Sandy was seventeen and so was I. Sandy was a "recruiter" for the satanist cult and led me into the next step in Satan's plan for my life.

CHAPTER 3

Entering The Brotherhood

ELAINE TALKS:

Sandy became a friend of mine, about the only friend I had. I met her at the church in the youth group I mentioned earlier. I didn't go to church to hear about the Lord, I went to get involved with the other kids. Sandy and I worked together on various youth programs in the church and at high school we also chummed around, studied together, and went out for cokes.

Sandy was a pretty girl. She was richer than I was, very well dressed and very popular. She didn't seem to let that bother her too much where I was concerned. I thought she was my friend more out of pity than anything, but that was because I didn't know she was a recruiter for The Brotherhood. Shortly after the incident with the football player, Sandy mentioned to me that she noticed that I had a special power that few others had. She said she knew where I could learn to have more of that same power.

She also said, "Hey listen, I know that you're lonely and down, and I think I have something that can help you. The church we're going to doesn't really care about you, and God doesn't really care about you. If He did, you wouldn't have been born the way you were." She then offered me a chance to go to a "youth camp" with her run by the "group" that she and her family belonged to. She called it a "church camp." It was located in a small town a few miles away. It was held during the summer. School was out at the time and as I had nothing else to do I decided to go.

I told my parents I was going to a church camp — they really didn't care what I did. I was fearful and yet elated. I thought that I had finally found a friend and that maybe this was the answer to both my loneliness and my questions about the strange power inside me. Sandy talked to me about the camp for days before we actually went. She described it as the ideal place where I would be accepted and wanted and needed. My powers were needed, she told me, and they could be perfected. I would be able to become great and famous, or rich, whatever I wanted I could have. As she talked I felt that strange power within me beginning to stir and build.

What Sandy did *not* do was mention the word "cult," or tell me the truth about this group. I will stop here and give you a capsule summary of the group.

. . . .

This group which secretly calls itself The Brotherhood, is made up of people who are directly controlled by, and worship, Satan. It is a rapidly growing and very dangerous cult. It has two major centers in the U.S. — the West coast, mostly in the Los Angeles-San Francisco area, and another in the mid-western U.S. where I lived. They are divided into local groups, or chapters, called covens. The covens range in size from 5-10 people to several thousand. This is the same cult written about in Hal Lindsey's book, *Satan Is Alive And Well On Planet Earth,* and in Mike Warneke's book, *The Satan Seller.* It is also the U.S. counterpart of the group in England written about in the book *Freed From Witchcraft,* by Doreen Irvine.

This cult is extremely secretive. No written records of membership are kept. Even the contracts with Satan signed in blood by the members are burned by the high priests and high priestesses. (This is not common knowledge among the lower ranking members.) These satanists infest every level of society — the poor and the rich. The very well educated, the police force, government officials, business men and women, and even some so-called Christian ministers. Most all of them attend local Christian churches and are considered "good citizens" because of their involvement in local civic activities. This is all done as a cover-up. They lead double lives and are expert at it; masters of deception.

> "And no marvel; for Satan himself is transformed into an angel of light, therefore it is no great thing if his ministers also be transformed as the ministers of righteousness . . . " II Corinthians 11:14-15.

They all go by code names at their meetings so that, should they meet each other on the street, often as not they would not know each other's real name. They are rigidly disciplined by Satan and his demons. They practice human sacrifice several times a year and animal sacrifice on a monthly basis. The human sacrifices are most often babies — born out of wedlock to various cult members, cared for by the doctors and nurses within the cult so that the mother is never seen in a hospital — the baby's birth is never registered, neither it's death. Other sacrifices are kidnapped victims, a cult member who is being disciplined, or who volunteers, I suspect because they can no longer live with themselves. Many of them are cold blooded murderers, extremely skillful.

Each coven is led by a high priest and a high priestess. These people get to their position by obtaining favor with Satan by various means and by obtaining greater and greater powers of witchcraft. There is much in-fighting within the group. There is an elite society of witches within the cult called The Sisters of Light or The Illuminati.

There are several occult groups in the U.S. who call themselves The Illuminati, most are not a part of The

Brotherhood. There is a group called the Illuminati made up mostly of people who are directly descended from the Druids of ancient England. They are extremely powerful and dangerous people and are linked to The Brotherhood. They practice human sacrifice frequently.

The Sisters of Light first came to the U.S. from Europe in the late 1700's. They date back to the dark ages in Europe, but indeed have their roots back to the sorcerers of ancient Egypt and Babylon who were powerful enough to be able to actually reproduce three of the ten plagues sent upon Egypt during Moses' time. (See Exodus chapter 7.) These witches are incredibly powerful. They are able to produce disease and kill without ever physically touching the victim, even over a distance of thousands of miles. This is all accomplished by demons of course, and these people are deluded into thinking that they control the demons when actually Satan and the demons are just using them.

Incredible atrocities are committed within the cult by humans so controlled by the demons within them that they lose all emotions of love and compassion and become cruel beings that hardly seem human. Some of this will be discussed later in the book.

The rapidity of growth of The Brotherhood is a mark of the end-times we are in and a direct fulfillment of Biblical prophecy.

. . . .

I stepped directly into this cult when I went to that summer camp with Sandy. I was very excited by the time we arrived. With excitement you lose a lot of what you see and hear. We were taken first to the dorms where we were to stay and made to feel very welcome. The camp had many facilities: museums, libraries, different houses where you could go to clairvoyants, hypnotists, palm readers, tarot card readers, voodoo experts, etc. Some of these people lived there the year 'round, some didn't. This was the place where the cult officially meets with the unknowing public.

We attended many classes which taught us how to extend and use our "powers." Sandy took me to the first meeting with the Sisters of Light. Much later I found out that they had been watching me carefully throughout my childhood, from the time of the sale of my blood made by Helen and Grace.

Sandy took me into the large Satanic church on the grounds about two hours before the main evening meeting. The sun was setting and the entire church was dark except for 13 candles in a circle on the floor at the front of the church which cast eerie shadows about the 13 figures also seated on the floor, one behind each candle. As we drew closer I could see that the figures were 13 women, all dressed identically in long white robes with attached cowl-like hoods up over their heads. They were each sitting cross legged on the highly polished wooden floor, backs straight, arms folded across their breasts, staring with absolute concentration into the candle in front of them.

The candles were each about two feet tall and three inches in diameter. They were made of black wax and each one sat on top of a long narrow sheet of paper that was covered with fine writing. The wax from the candles dripped down onto the papers. The women did not wear jewelry or ornamentation of any sort. There was no movement by any of them except for their continuous low-voiced chanting and humming as they offered their prayers to Satan. There was a power there that held me both fascinated and awe struck. I could feel a mighty stirring of the unexplainable power within myself as I sat and watched them throughout their two hour ceremony.

I found myself drawn back again the following night to watch the same ceremony. I knew that they were the Sisters of Light only because Sandy told me so. Other cult members referred to them as "Mothers," and few knew that they were actually this elite group. They never told men of their identity as men were strictly excluded from the group. However, they are the power-house and main strength of the cult, and a strictly guarded secret even within the cult itself. They do not tolerate weakness in any of their members, anyone weak is destroyed. There are very few younger women among them.

After the ceremony the second night I was approached by one of the women. She told me that they had noticed my interest and already knew of my unusual power, and that they would very much like for me to enter into their training program. They were casual and kindly and told me that they could train me to greatly increase and extend my power as no other group could. I swallowed the bait hook, line and sinker.

At first they told me of the greatness I could have, of how I could use the power within me to get what I needed, also, whatever I wanted I could have. This power was of Satan, not of God. They were the first to tell me that and they also told me that Satan is the only true God. They taught me how to chant and hum. Told me that if I wanted anything, all I needed to do was to light my candle and put my prayers underneath it. Requests not only for myself, of course, because I must not be selfish. I could pray either for another person's uplifting or for his downfall, it made no difference as long as there was someone else's name on the paper as well as my own.

At last the final day of the camp came and I prepared to go home. Suddenly I was faced with the fact that all the kindliness of the people at the camp was a front and that my involvement was no longer a game, nor was it voluntary. When I met Sandy for the trip home she told me that she had just had word from the Sisters of Light that they were offering special training to myself and some others who were "specially gifted." Sandy said that they and the high priest and high priestess wanted to speak with me briefly over at the church before we left.

I went over to the church and entered with several others. After we got into the church we saw that armed guards immediately stepped in front of the doors and we were told to stand before the small group at the front of the church. The high priest then told us that we had been selected to join The Brotherhood, which meant signing a contract with Satan in our own blood at a meeting the following night. I asked what was in the contract and was told that I would be giving myself body and soul and spirit to "our great Father Satan" in return for many "blessings" from him. We were also told that if we did not want to do so that they would use certain "persuasion" to change our minds. I told them that under no circumstances would I sign such a contract. At this point the high priestess took over and informed me that I had no choice. I looked her square in the eye and said, "Go to Hell! You bitch! I think you are all weird, I will do no such thing."

Immediately a very large guard armed with a sub-machine gun came up behind me and grabbed my arm at the wrist, pulling it behind me and upwards with such force that I felt as if he had broken it. He told me that I was to bow my knee to the high priestess and ask her forgiveness for my disrespect, that if I did not do so he would beat me until I did. Outraged, I shouted, "Then go ahead and start, because I'm not bowing myself to any woman!"

He swung at me, his fist catching me full force in the temple. I don't remember anymore until I awakened in a small 5 X 5 foot cell. It was completely bare with a hard wooden floor. The door had a small window out to a hallway so that I could be observed. It was almost completely dark. I was in that room for 24 hours. It seemed like days. I was not allowed to sleep, speakers blared constantly. I was told over and over again that all glory and honor and homage was due Satan. That I needed to ask Satan's forgiveness. That Satan was the God of the universe. I was also told that my family was being watched, and that if I did not adhere to the rules and regulations and sign the contract, that they would all be tortured and killed. I was not given any food or water during that time.

The following evening I was taken from the room by two guards into another room where I was met by two women from the Sisters of Light. They helped me to bath, then placed a satiny white robe over my nude body. My feet were left bare. The robe reached the floor and was tied at the waist with a white cord. It had a cowl-like hood and long loose sleeves. It did not have ornamentation of any kind. The women told me that I should not fight any more, that I could not avoid my destiny. They told me what wonderful "blessings" I would receive by giving myself to "my father Satan."

I was transported to the meeting in a closed van so that I could not see where we were going. This meeting was *not* held at the Satanic church on the camp grounds. I caught only a glimpse of the outside of the building as I was hurried inside. It had no windows and was back in a woods. It looked like it was some sort of storage building on a farm, though isolated, and there was some straw on the wooden floor inside.

The building was dimmly lit by many large flickering candles around the walls. The candles were in groups of three, a black, red and white candle in each group. There were 200 to 300 people present, seated on plain wooden benches facing the front of the room. At the front was a wooden platform with torches burning around the edge on about 5 foot tall poles. There was a rough-hewn stone altar down in front in the middle of the platform which looked like it was sitting on saw horses. (I was to learn later that this was indeed the case to provide easy movability.) The stone was gray with many brownish stains — these stains were from the blood of the many sacrifices performed on that altar, both animal and human.

In spite of my exhaustion and fear I felt a stirring of excitement as I felt the tremendous invisible power within that room and a responding stirring of the power within me. Incense was burning, filling the room with its odor. I think it had some sort of drug in it because it quickly made me quite dizzy. The room was absolutely silent as the robed and hooded figures looked expectantly at the empty stage. At some unseen signal many small hand-held bells started ringing as the high priest and high priestess stepped noiselessly onto the stage out of the shadows.

The high priest and high priestess wore identical robes. The robes were both of a black satin material, the same style as my own, trimmed with red around the hood, down the front edges and around the edges of the long full sleeves. Each was tied at the waist with a golden cord. Their feet were also bare as were everyone else's. Each carried a scepter about 3 feet long. The high priestess' was gold. At the top was an inverted cross with a serpent curling around the handle and up onto the cross. The high priest's scepter was of the same design but made of silver. The scepters were carried reverently in the crook of their arms. Their presence was commanding and I became aware really for the first time of the tremendous power they had, and I envied them.

There were many heavily armed guards at that meeting both inside and outside of the building. This was my first attendance of a real cult meeting. All the rest had been games and play and show.

After the opening remarks I was taken forward to the front of the altar by the two guards. I and the others were introduced to the congregation as new members "anxious" to join. The high priest first centered his attention on me.

He said, "Brothers and Sisters of Satan, we bring you this child, this one called Sister Courage (that was my new name). We bring her to you for she has asked to become one of us, and now unto our lord and god our master, the master of the universe, and also the destroyer, Satan, we say: this child, Sister Courage, we give unto you to do your bidding to be what you want her to be. We have promised her as you have given us the word to promise, your blessings."

I was then given a knife to cut my finger with, but I refused to do so. Instantly one of the guards brought a whip down hard on my back causing me to writhe in agony, but I was determined not to bow to them. With a flick of her hand the high priestess signaled the guard to stop beating me. She spoke in a voice dripping with distain and said that there were much more effective ways of showing me my error.

I watched in amazement as she and the high priest took up positions on opposite sides of a large pentagram (five pointed star) drawn on the floor in the middle of the stage. The pentagram was drawn inside of a circle and a black candle sat at each point of the star. With merely a wave of her hand the high priestess lit all the candles at once without touching any of them. Then she started an incantation, the high priest joining in with the chant. The audience also chanted at certain points when directed to do so by the ringing of the little bells.

Suddenly the pentagram was engulfed in a whoosh of smoke and blinding light. The room was instantly filled with a foul odor as of burning sulfur. A huge demon appeared in a physical manifestation in the center of the circle, flames surrounding him. He was huge, about 8 feet tall. He glowered menacingly at me, weaving back and forth. The high priestess (Grace) turned to me and told me that if I did not obey and sign the contract that I would be given to that demon to torture until he finally killed me. That was enough for me! Never had I felt such fear, but at the same time I lusted after the power displayed by Grace (the high priestess). I was determined to become as powerful as she so that I could get revenge on those people for all that had been done to me.

When I signaled my willingness to sign the contract, two women came forward and placed a black robe over my white one. The black robe was made of a cotton material and was of the same design as the white one. The black was a sign that I was no longer a novice. I took the knife proffered me and cut my finger deeply. Then I dipped a quill pen in my own blood and signed the contract with my name stating that I was giving myself body, soul and spirit to Satan.

Immediately after signing the contract, I was engulfed in an electronic charge of energy which surged from the top of my head down to my toes. It was so strong that I was knocked to the floor. As I lay on the floor trying to recover I realized that Grace was doing another incantation. I struggled to my feet to find that she had called up another demon. This one came down to where I stood and told me that he was going to live in me. He reached out and roughly grabbed me by the shoulders before I had time to say anything. Immediately I felt agonizing, searing heat go through my body and smelled sulfur strongly again. In the midst of the agony I passed out and knew nothing more until I was roughly loaded into the van for the return trip to the camp. By that time I was so exhausted and dizzy from the lack of sleep, the beatings I had endured, and the lack of food and water, that I did not fully comprehend the significance of what was happening to me.

I stayed at the camp for a week afterwards so that the most noticeable of my cuts and bruises could heal. When I went home I thought and felt that I was now one of the most powerful people on earth. I knew that I had power that was beyond most peoples' imagination. I thought that nothing and no one could destroy me.

How wrong I was!

CHAPTER 4

Rise To Power

ELAINE TALKS:

I was now a member of The Brotherhood, had a new name and was what is known as a witch. About one month after I had signed the contract with Satan I had my first meeting with the local high priestess. The coven in my home town was fairly large, about a thousand people. The high priestess contacted me and told me that she wanted to see me in her home. I was very surprised to be called by such a high authority. Very few girls are ever called to see the high priestess unless they are to be punished, or if she has something specific for them to do. Her home was elaborate and very beautiful and she ruled with an iron hand. She told me, "You have been specially selected by Satan to be trained for his work and to become a high priestess if you can qualify."

Within the satanist cult this is a great honor. You must be highly ranked to be accepted for that type of training. The high priestess was an elderly lady. She had been a high priestess for many many years. She was very pretty even though she was old. Her personality was one of friendliness and yet there was something very cold about her. She knew that I was to replace her. A high priestess is always destroyed when she is replaced by another witch. She is commanded by Satan or one of his high demons to train another witch to take her place. She has no choice but to obey the command.

I thought it strange that she should ask me to be trained for such a position as I was so young and a new member. What I didn't know at the time was that the demons that I already had were far stronger than hers and that Satan had commanded her to teach me exactly what they were, how to use them, and how, in the end, to destroy her.

In my heart of hearts, I was not, and never would be, one for destruction. I enjoyed living and I did not want to hurt this lady, but I knew that if I did not, she would kill me.

I received intensive training in several areas for the next 20 months. I met with the high priestess mostly at her home or at other meeting places where we met off in another room away from the other members of the cult. We met often, at least weekly.

The contents of my training by the high priestess consisted mainly of incantations. I learned how to conjure up spirits to do my bidding. She taught me how to project and use that strange power that I had felt within me for so long. She taught me that those powers came from demons dwelling within me. She also taught me protocol and how to conduct cult meetings as a high priestess.

The Sisters of Light also participated in my training. They were the principal ones responsible for training me to increase in power as rapidly as I did. Through their training I learned many secrets that most other high priestesses never know. They asked me to join their society but I refused. Secretly I always thought they were very strange.

Arrangements were made for training in the martial arts as well. I already knew some Karate and Judo, but knew nothing about Kung-Fu. I was given into the hands of a middle-aged Chinese man who was a master of all three. He was a well known lawyer in my home town. He was kind to me, but a very tough task-master. I learned much from him. He trained many cult people from the whole surrounding area. He thought that I had much potential and wanted me to participate in public competition. I never did and never wanted to.

Learning the martial arts was a rigorous and very tormentive type of training. I asked special demons to come into me to give me the abilities I needed. The mind and the body must be trained to move as one. I could jump many feet in the air, land on my feet, make summersalts and come up and destroy someone with my feet and/or hands. I became expert also in the use of knives, num-chucks, swords, guns, bow and arrows, stars and many types of oriental weapons that are not well known in this country. Not only do high ranking members of the cult receive such training, but a number of the lower ranking members also receive it so that they can serve as guards, assassins, etc.

I was taught much about Satan, almost all of it lies. I was taught about his power, about his love for me. How I had been rejected by God. How Satan loved me and wanted me as his own and about how I had been chosen among all women to be his high priestess. The Sisters of Light also told me much about the opportunity to become a regional Bride of Satan.

There are only 5 to 10 regional Brides of Satan in the U.S. at any one time. It is a position of great honor and power. The Sisters of Light told me they were sure I had the ability to attain this high position. They constantly talked about all the benefits I would gain if I reached it. I became determined to gain that position.

The first demon that I actually saw, manifested to me in a physical form during that first ceremony when I signed the contract. The next demon I actually saw, was the first "conjured-up" demon of my own. As I performed the appropriate incantation he appeared in a cloud of smoke which smelled strongly of sulfur. The whole episode was a very elaborate, very staged type of thing, but he was very real. Again, he was in a physical form.

43

He was huge, about eight feet tall. He had a body much like a man, yet different. He was all black. We have since come to know this class of demons as Black Warriors. He had fiery red eyes, huge hands, and his armor was really his skin. It was made up of thick, black, hard scales, something like a tortoise's shell. Each scale was about six inches square. I knew that this was a powerful demon and I had called him up just to see if I could do it. As he stood silently staring at me, I told him that I was the "chosen one." His response was, "I know who you are, and I know that I am sent here to guard you and that nothing will ever harm you as long as I'm here, *and* as long as you serve the almighty Satan, our lord and our god." His name was Ri-Chan. He fought many battles both for me, and, when I was disobedient to Satan, against me.

I saw and conversed with many demons after that. As my skill grew in being able to see the spirit world, I was able to see and talk with demons without them taking on a physical form. Indeed, I rarely asked them to appear physically except on occasions when I wanted to impress or frighten someone lower in the cult than myself.

The next major demon I summoned was Mann-Chan. This was during one of my training sessions with the high priestess in her home. She told me that I was at a point in my training where I must learn and do a very special incantation. She did not tell me the purpose of the incantation and I did not ask. I knew this day was an important one because of the special preparations made.

First, I drew on the floor with chalk a very large pentagram, then drew a circle around it. (The purpose of the circle around the pentagram is to keep the demon summoned inside the circle unless you gave him permission to move out of it. The circle is supposed to protect the witch from the demon who comes. In reality, of course, the demons do pretty much whatever they want so I quickly learned to be very careful not to summon a demon that was stronger than the demons I had protecting me.) Carefully, I placed a black candle in each corner of the pentagram, then a much larger black candle in the center. All six were lit. A table with a hot plate on it was set up close to the side of the pentagram. The contents of a kettle had been prepared earlier by the high priest. It was filled with desecrated holy water, that is, holy water from a Catholic church which the high priest then urinated into. He had also taken a dog and killed it and drained its blood into a special jar which he had given to me to take to the high priestess' house. She then gave me some powders and herbs. The water in the kettle was brought to the boil on the hot plate just before I started the incantation.

I asked no questions, but obeyed the high priestess' instructions to the letter. I sat on the floor, staring into the black candle in the center of the pentagram, murmuring: "Oh great Satan, the power and builder and creator of the universe, I beg thee, give me a demon to be the guide and light of my life — to give me all wisdom and knowledge. My beloved, Oh master, grant to me my wish!" At that point the high priestess spoke the name Mann-Chan to me.

I then said, "Mann-Chan come, you are welcome into my body, I bid thee arise from your hiding place." I took the powders and herbs and blood and cast them into the boiling kettle. The steam rose and immediately the room was filled with a very foul odor. I then dipped a desecrated golden goblet into the kettle, filling it. I set the goblet carefully down on the table and waited expectantly. Within about five minutes the liquid in the goblet had completely turned to powder. Then I took the goblet and threw the powder from it into the flame of the large candle in the center of the pentagram.

Immediately there was a woosh and a huge flame. The candle disappeared in blinding white light. As the light died down over the next few seconds, I could see the figure of what appeared to be an incredibly handsome young man. He had coal black hair and piercing black eyes that radiated intelligence. I hurried to my knees beside the pentagram. With a rag, I wiped away the chalk to form a clear pathway through the pentagram.

The young man, who was actually the demon Mann-Chan in a physical form, stepped through to the outside of the pentagram on the pathway that I had made. He spoke to me in perfect English in a gentle manner and with what seemed to be great love. He told me that I was to be inhabited by him and he promised that no harm would come to me. He told me that he would give me all wisdom and knowledge, he would be my teacher and guide. He called himself my "redeemer." I agreed, very much awed by his beautiful countenance. He then walked straight into me. But, in the instant before he entered, he changed from the human form to the demon he really was. **HIDEOUS!**

He was naked, his face had changed from beauty to hideous cruelty. The beautiful coal black locks of hair had become dull brown and were coarse and sparse and stubby like pig bristles. His eyes were incredibly dark and evil, his mouth open to show long sharp dirty yellow fangs. He had very long arms, his hands had stubby fingers tipped with long sharply pointed nails. He uttered a horrible hideous loud laugh of triumph as he stepped directly into my body. I screamed out. First at the sight of him, then at the pain of his entrance. Searing, agonizing pain, such as I had never before experienced. I felt as if my body was on fire. I felt as if I was going to die and at that particular moment I wished with all my heart that I could do so. Ri-Chan stepped forward on hearing my cry, thinking that perhaps I was being attacked from without. But Mann-Chan spoke to him and told him that it was he and not to worry. As the pain died down, Mann-Chan told me that that was a small demonstration of what I would get if ever I disobeyed him and also to let me know that he was there to stay, that *nothing,* and *no one* could ever make him leave!

From that point on Mann-Chan was the main demon in my life. He communicated with me by putting thoughts directly into my mind. I communicated with him either by speaking aloud or by speaking with my spirit body. I did not fully realize it then, but Mann-Chan could *not* actually read my mind. He controlled me and kept all my doorways open to Satan and the other demons so that they could come and go as they chose, and also as I willed. My life became centered around him. I gave all of my time and effort trying to gain control of him, but he had more control of me than I did of him. Often he knocked me unconscious and completely controlled my body, using it as he pleased, frequently speaking through my mouth. He controlled when I ate and slept, how well I did my work, how well I got along with people — my very life itself.

I learned through him how to use demons, how to use them in spiritual warfare. How to use them to strengthen my own spirit body, how to use them in ceremonies, against other people, other witches, churches and even ministers of the gospel of Jesus Christ. He gave me the ability to speak many languages and to walk and talk with great authority and power.

But Mann-Chan was not the light that he promised or the thing of love and beauty as I had first seen him. He was something evil and rotten and was eating away at my soul and body, causing me much suffering and much pain many many times because I would not uphold or participate in human sacrifices. Life was a continuous nightmare from that point on. I was living a double existence. That is, I was a member of the satanic cult and also simultaneously a member of a very large Christian church where I taught and sang and participated in all sorts of activities. I was torn constantly, never free for a moment, completely trapped.

I then began to have many battles with many witches. Battling is done in several ways. The most common is for the stronger witch to call the demons out of the weaker witch into herself, thus making her even stronger and often resulting in the destruction of the weaker because she no longer has the power to defend herself. Demons have no loyalties. They will always go to the stronger person. Satan's entire kingdom runs on the principle of competition; just the opposite of God's kingdom where everyone serves each other.

Battling is rarely if ever done on a physical plane, although witches do often use demons to destroy the physical body of a weaker witch. There was one witch in particular who attacked me. Her name is Sarah. I tried to explain to her that if she did not leave me alone I would have to destroy her. She did not believe me and finally we entered into full battle. What I saw was absolutely horrifying. I saw her grow weaker and weaker as I called demon after demon out of her and into myself. At first her demons fought back and I felt my own body being lifted up, thrown against walls, my throat being strangled without the sight of a physical hand. But what she saw was Mann-Chan and Ri-Chan and many other demons coming against her. They were tearing her body apart. She finally realized that I was truly the chosen one, that I was to be the high priestess and that she had lost the battle.

She withdrew in time to live and I thank God for that. She ended up in the hospital for quite some time as a result of the injuries she sustained in the battle. Years later she told me that it was during that time in the hospital that she accepted Jesus as her Lord and Savior, and she is now living fully and whole-heartedly for the Lord. Believe me, the change is beautiful.

My first meeting with Satan came shortly before the ceremony in which I became the high priestess. He came to me in the physical form of a man and we sat down and talked. He told me that I was to be his high priestess, that I was very special to him. He told me also that there had to be a sacrifice; more blood had to be shed for my "purification" so that I could become his high priestess. I hated that, but was relieved to find that at least it was to be an animal sacrifice.

What I saw was a man, exceedingly handsome, very bright and sunny and shining. He seemed to have great love for me and didn't seem to be in any way a danger to me. Mann-Chan gave no indication of danger and neither did Ri-Chan. I was very much awed by this meeting. I wanted him to come back, I felt a need deep down inside for him. For the first time in my life I felt really loved. How wrong I was. Satan hated my guts. He wanted only to use me for his own benefit and then planned to destroy me.

I attended cult meetings very regularly during my 2 years of training. The meetings were held in barns, churches, houses, lodges, all different places. On the occasions when Satan was personally present, I was drawn more and more to him like a moth is attracted to a flame. He knew very well that he had me trapped.

Just before becoming a high priestess I saw a human sacrifice for the first time. We were in an old barn with at least a thousand people present. A small baby was used. She was selected because her mother gave the child to be sacrificed and thought it to be a great honor. The law never hears of these babies because most of them are illegitimate, they are born at home, the mother never sees anyone for prenatal care and no record of the baby's birth, or death, is ever made.

The baby was strapped down on a stone alter which was in the shape of an upside-down cross. I will never forget the awful sound of her screams as the high priest drove a sharp knife into her chest and ripped out her living heart. Her blood was then drained off and drank first by the high priest and high priestess, then by other members who wished to do so. Many did, not only to receive new and stronger demons, but also because it is believed that such sacrifices provide increased fertility and that the children conceived under such circumstances would be strong and intelligent and powerful in Satanism.

I could not get away. I was trapped within the crowd. I was filled with horror. I was filled with emptiness and coldness and despair. I wondered why Satan wanted such a sacrifice. Wasn't Christ's blood enough? We were constantly being told about Christ's defeat on the cross and that He had been the ultimate sacrifice to Satan. But I was to learn that Satan's desire for blood and destruction is insatiable.

My last and final battle with the high priestess was conducted with the direct approval of Satan. It took place at a big meeting in the church where I had first met the Sisters of Light. Satan was there and with a single nod gave me permission to take her on. She and I battled back and forth. She was very old and the battle was short, lasting only about 20 minutes. I did not kill her. I could not do that because I hold life very, very dearly. She quit as soon as she saw that she had become too weak to fight any longer. The following year she committed suicide.

Then came the ceremony of my becoming the high priestess. The blood sacrifice on that occasion was a cocker spaniel. I was taken to the front of the room, or church. There were many, many people present because it was a very high ceremony and Satan himself was present. I was dressed in a robe of white with gold and red trimming. I had a crown put upon my head made of pure gold. I then signed another contract in my own blood declaring myself a high priestess of Satan. No one in the room made a sound as I signed that paper. Then the high priest, at a nod from Satan, rose to declare that I was now the new high priestess. He proclaimed that I was to be untouched by anyone else in the cult, by any demon, high priest, witch, or high priestess of any other coven, for I was "the chosen one." The crowd became ecstatic, shouting, chanting and dancing. Satan himself appeared to be overjoyed. Again, he was in a physical form of a very handsome man. A man of great brilliance and great authority. He was dressed all in shining white.

The congregation bowed down before me and praised me as the great queen, as the queen of Satan, "lord god almighty," that I was and would forever be by his side and be able to convey to them his every wish and command. I felt as if, for the first time in my life, I had been truly accepted. I felt very proud, very much uplifted, and very, very powerful to the point that I thought that no one, including Satan himself, could destroy me.

I was then put upon the altar of stone, my clothes were all taken off and Satan had sex with me to prove that I was his high priestess. The congregation went wild. Many of them were high on drugs and alcohol and the meeting turned into a sex orgy. Then Satan gave the most hideous laugh of triumph I have ever heard in my entire life. My body became cold and rigid. I remember feeling such guilt, such pain, such hurt. The cold and emptiness that I felt that night I will never forget.

> "And it came to pass, when men began to multiply on the face of the earth, and daughters were born unto them, that the sons of God saw the daughters of men that they were fair; and they took them wives of all which they chose . . . There were giants in the earth in those days; and also after that, when the sons of God came in unto the daughters of men, and they bare children to them . . . "   Genesis 6:1, 2, & 4.

CHAPTER 5

Life As A High Priestess

ELAINE TALKS:

As I assumed my duties as the high priestess of a large and influential coven, I had many privileges **and** many conflicts. I came into conflict with Satan and many of the other cult members because there were many things I flatly refused to do or get involved with.

My major responsibility was to work with the high priest of the organization to plan the monthly cult meetings. Our organizational meetings were held in utmost secrecy and usually occurred a couple of times a month. The high priest and myself met together with the top 13 witches and 13 warlocks of the coven. We sat in a council. The meetings were usually held in a large and rich home with facilities for a very large table to seat all of us. The high priest and myself sat at the head of the table with the 13 witches on one side and the 13 warlocks on the other side in the order of their rank. Satan usually saw to it that there were also a few of what we viewed as undesirables there as well. These people were known werwolves and were always withdrawn, always watchful and always menacing. They were there as humans and did not turn into their other forms unless Satan so ordered and then usually only for disciplinary purposes. We did not touch them or talk to them. They belonged to Satan exclusively, they were totally sold out to him and were feared and disliked by everyone else in the cult. They were primarily guards and disciplinarians, used by Satan and his demons to ensure that the rest of us obeyed all orders.

The council planned the meetings and took care of the business of the coven. Orders from Satan were given to the high priest and/or high priestess either directly, or through their demons. We always tried to plan dramatic, exciting meetings — always making sure that there would be plenty of drugs and alcohol available. I did not purchase the drugs or alcohol, I had nothing to do with that kind of traffic. That was left up to the cult members who were already into that sort of thing. There was never a shortage of such people. I did not, and would not, get involved with it. The higher members of the cult are always very careful not to get mixed up in anything that could involve them with the law, *neither* does any high member ever take drugs or drink alcohol to excess. They don't dare cloud their minds because there are just too many other people who want their positions.

We also met with the higher representatives of other occult groups in the area. Many satanic groups exist which are not part of The Brotherhood and do not even know about The Brotherhood. These groups are carefully watched by and controlled by The Brotherhood, however.

One of the duties I absolutely refused to have anything to do with was sacrifices, either animal or human. Because of that I was severely punished by Satan and the demons on many occasions. The other cult members could not get to me as I had too much power by then, so Satan and his demons did the punishing. Usually it was through physical punishment. I have been tortured beyond description by demons many times. I have had many illnesses, including cancer four times with all the horrors of chemotherapy. But I refused to give in on this issue. I simply could not take another person's life.

Young people please listen to me — *ANY* involvement in

the occult is a trap! There is *no* easy way out. Satan can do to you the same things he did to me and worse. I pray daily that God will somehow show those of you who are so trapped that you *can* get out. Satan doesn't have you even though you have signed the contract. That contract *can* be covered by the blood of Jesus Christ. You can be freed from that contract if you ask Jesus into your life to forgive you, wash you clean from all your sins, to become your Lord and Savior and Master. Satan is *always* working for your destruction, Jesus wants to give you life.

There were some meetings that I did enjoy. Sometimes we got together just to talk and play games, competing with our powers to do things such as lighting a candle from across the room without ever touching it, etc. I also made numerous trips out to California for competitions and conventions. These I usually enjoyed very much.

I flew in a private jet from a private airstrip near to the town where I first entered the cult. No one outside the cult, and few inside, know its location. It is well hidden and heavily guarded. I was usually picked up by the high priest and a few of the higher witches and warlocks. It was always a big occasion. The purpose was to exchange ideas and to compete to see who was most powerful. It was through these competitions that I rose in power to sit on the national council, to the position of regional Bride of Satan, and, finally, to the position of top Bride of Satan within the United States.

The average stay was a week and the conferences were usually held just before a Black Sabbath when the Black Mass was celebrated (Easter weekend). I always found an excuse to return home before the Black Mass. We went to a special place in the hills of California just outside Los Angeles. There is a huge mansion there which was built especially for the cult. I suppose it has thirty or more bedrooms. It has many beautiful stained glass windows specially made with patterns of occult and demonic symbols. The inside is lavishly and beautifully furnished. It contains a huge banquet room with an attached ballroom. And, of course, swimming pools, tennis courts, golf course, etc. It looks like a millionaires' country club. It has 3 sub-basements with huge vaults containing libraries of ancient occultic writings and histories. Vaults also containing gold and silver and currency from all the countries of the world. The entire area is hidden by a forest of trees and heavily guarded both on the ground and in the air.

My last trip there involved the most intense competition I ever experienced. I was by then the top Bride in the country. It was an international competition. The leading man there was a high priest who was different from the others who had been there. He was a tall, darkly handsome young man, but there was a foreboding power about him that made him feared and disliked by everyone. He ran the competition and obviously did not care if anyone got killed if he or she failed to do what was asked. He had snapping black eyes that could chill you to the bone. He ruled with an iron hand and even I did my best to steer clear of him.

The competition consisted of increasingly difficult tasks designed to display the contestant's power. I remember that, at one point, I had to, with no more than a snap of my fingers, change a cat into a rabbit and then back again. The actual physical changes in the animal were accomplished by demons and resulted in the animal's immediate death. By the last day I was the only competitor left, but still the high priest kept pushing me. I had no choice but to comply with his wishes. The last incident would have killed me had my demons not been powerful enough.

I was made to stand no more than 20 feet in front of a man with a .357 magnum. I passed my hand downward in front of my body, calling up the demons and placing them as a shield. Immediately the gunman fired the six shots of the gun chamber at me. There was no way he could miss. The demons were a successful shield, needless to say, and the bullets fell to the ground at my feet spinning around and around. I received much acclaim and honor for winning the competition.

A crown of gold was placed upon my head and my fellow cult members bowed down and gave homage to me. I was treated like a queen throughout the rest of my stay. I was given all the beautiful clothes to wear that I could possibly want, I was bathed, my hair fixed and waited on hand and foot by servants. There were parties and I always had a handsome escort who was also my bodyguard. We went to the most exclusive restaurants in Los Angeles. My escort always tasted all of my food before I ate to make sure that it wasn't poisoned. We went surfing and horseback riding. The members were not permitted to fight among themselves during that time because it was considered a great and high time of praising Satan. I had great pride at that time, but the Lord soon humbled me.

It was during that last visit to California that one of the incidents happened that started me on the road to accepting Christ, started me questioning Satan's claim to being more powerful than God. The high priest gathered a number of us together and told us that there was a family nearby who had been interfering with Satan. They had been converting a number of the cult members to the enemy, Jesus Christ, and were making a nuisance of themselves. Satan had given the order for them all to be killed. The high priest told us that we were all to go together in our spirit bodies (astral project), and kill them. So, we sat down in a circle with our candles in front of us and consciously left our bodies going in our spirits to the house to destroy these people. I was not at all enthusiastic about the project, but had no choice. If I had disobeyed I would have been killed.

Much to our surprise, as we arrived at the edge of this family's property, we could go no further. The whole area was surrounded by huge angels. The angels stood side by side holding hands. They were dressed in long white robes and stood so close together that their shoulders touched. They had no armor or weapons. Nobody could get through them, no matter how we tried. Any kind of weapon used merely bounced off of them doing them no harm. They laughed at us at first, daring us to come ahead and try to get through them. The other cult members got more and more furious with each passing moment. Suddenly their countenances changed and the fierce look from their eyes made all of us fall backwards onto the ground. A very humbling experience, I might add!

I will never forget — as I sat on the ground looking up at them, one of the angels looked directly into my eyes and said to me in the most loving voice I had ever heard, "Won't you please accept Jesus as your Lord? If you pursue the course you are taking you will be destroyed. Satan really hates you, but Jesus loves you so much that He died for you. Please consider turning your life over to Jesus." That was the end of the battle for me. I refused to try any longer to get through. I was very shaken. The others tried for awhile longer, but none succeeded. I doubt the family ever knew of the battle going on outside their house. They were completely protected! We called this particular type of special angels "link angels." Absolutely nothing can get through them. I was secretly thankful that we did not get through and the link angels had given me much to think about.

Inspite of that experience with the angels it was a couple of years before I turned to the Lord Jesus. I still was lusting after more and more power, refusing to face the fact that that power was destroying me and condemning my soul to an eternity in Hell.

CHAPTER 6

The Wedding

ELAINE TALKS:

I had many privileges as a high priestess and I greatly benefited from these in my day-to-day life, but I continued to thirst for ever greater power. A few years after becoming a high priestess I reached my goal of becoming a regional bride of Satan. Many high priestesses call themselves brides of Satan, and in a sense they are, but Satan also has a very few chosen women that become his brides in a much more exclusive manner. Only five to ten, and usually only five, exist in the United States at one time. This position is the highest and most "honorable" position to which a woman can attain within Satanism. One woman is picked by Satan from a large region of the country. That woman is considered the most powerful and respected and loved in the whole area. These women also sit on the national council which runs all the satanists in this country and has also much power internationally because of the great wealth in the U.S.

Satan himself came to me to tell me that he had selected me for this great honor. He presented himself to me in the physical form of a man, very handsome, in fact, the exact image of what I held in my mind as being the "perfect" man. He told me that he had selected me because he loved me above all the others, and that he both liked and respected my courage and abilities. He behaved in a very loving and romantic manner, telling me of his love and of the wonderful times we would have together. He also promised to give me much greater power and many special privileges.

I was honored and excited, mostly excited because I hoped that at last I was truly loved. I thought that I was the most powerful and honored of all women. I thought that Satan had picked me because of my abilities and my love for him which had grown stronger and stronger year after year. I did not, at that time, see that Satan was merely using my love for him to benefit himself. He used me to get other people to do what he wanted and used my love for him for my own destruction. All his declarations of his love for me were lies!

The ceremony was held in a large city nearby. One of the city's largest and most beautiful Presbyterian churches was rented by the cult for the occasion. I am sure that the owners of the church had no idea what their church was being rented for. I had arranged to have a 3-day weekend off from work. The ceremony took place on a Friday night, the first night of the full moon. I was carefully guarded and my every wish attended to. I was so very excited and elated!

As my companions and I approached the church I was briefly impressed with a feeling of a heavy darkness hanging over the church, but I shrugged the feeling aside, turning my thoughts to the love and admiration I held for Satan.

I was taken to a room away from the sanctuary at the church and carefully prepared and dressed for the occasion. At the time my hair was long, blond and curly. The women fixed my hair with live flowers which they wove into it. I was dressed in a white, long-flowing robe-type gown with gold braid criss-crossing my chest. There was a splotch of red over my heart and pubic area. I had a crown of pure gold placed on my head. I carried a bouquet made up of grasses, thistles and poisonous berries, all tied with a black ribbon.

As I stood just outside the sanctuary peeping in, I was surprised and greatly honored to see that not only were there many people there from the surrounding states and California, but also a number of older members of the cult from the Eastern world. This was indeed a great honor. The sanctuary was filled with eerie music from the large pipe organ. Satan's golden throne had been transported to the church and set up on the platform at the front. The signal to start the ceremony was Satan's sudden appearance in physical form on the throne.

Again he appeared as a man, dressed completely in white, wearing a crown of gold with many jewels in it. The whole congregation stood with a shout and much worship was given to Satan. Then, at a sign from Satan, all heads turned to the back and I started forward down the aisle. I was escorted by the high priest, followed by the Sisters of Light. When I reached the end of the aisle I stopped before Satan's throne and bowed down before him and did him homage. Then he gave me the command to rise. As I did so, he arose from his throne and came down to stand beside me. The high priest performed the wedding ceremony. Most of the ceremony was singing, chanting and proclaiming the praises of Satan. The Sisters of Light stood in a semicircle behind us and chanted and hummed quietly throughout the ceremony.

The ceremony took almost two hours, I stood the whole time. I again signed a contract with my own blood. Then I was given a liquid to drink from a golden goblet. I do not know what was in the liquid, but I suppose there were some drugs in it, as I felt rather light-headed after drinking it. It certainly destroyed the clarity of my mind. I was told that the contract was binding. There was absolutely no way to get out of it. Satan doesn't believe in divorce!

Satan himself did not give any of *his* blood, neither did he drink any of the potion. He told me that he could not as he "must keep himself pure" for me. But that I must drink in order to purify myself for him. He was the most beautiful I had ever seen him. He wore what looked like a pure white tuxedo, decorated with gold. His hair was, on this occasion, shining gold and his skin bronzed as with a beautiful tan. His eyes were dark and the love he professed for me and the smiles he gave to me never seemed to reach his eyes. But, I wanted to believe that he really did love me, and that he was really my husband. He treated me with the greatest of respect. He caressed my cheek, my hair, my arms. He told me how I looked to him: great beauty, great power and that I could become what he had really always hoped for — the mother of his son, "The Christ" the redeemer of the world. I was completely taken in by his deception.

Satan gave me a beautiful broad gold wedding band with an inscription inside it which said: *"Behold the bride of the Prince of the world."*

Although Satan showed no hostility towards me, he did towards others. Anyone moving towards him to touch him or to bow down to him was kicked, or beaten and driven away.

Immediately after the ceremony I was taken by the Sisters of Light and changed into an exquisite gown and given a cape of velvet trimmed with pure gold. We were then taken by limousine to the airport where we boarded a luxurious private jet along with several high priests and high priestesses and flown out to California. The wedding supper was served aboard the jet on the way.

Satan did not eat any food, but he did sip at several of the very expensive wines and champagnes available. He had very little to say. By the time we arrived at the mansion in the hills of California, I was pretty hazy from the drugs I had been given. We were escorted with much pomp and ceremony to a large suite of rooms. The bedchamber had a large golden bed in it. Afterwards I was thankful for the drugs I had been given, because once we were alone Satan's beautiful appearance disappeared and the sexual intercourse we had was brutal.

Satan was gone by the time I awoke the next day. I was in agony with many wounds from the night. I was thankful that he did not reappear again that weekend. I was flown home on Sunday. While I was there, I was treated like royalty. I was waited on hand and foot and given anything I wanted.

I received many advantages with my new position. I held absolute power over all the witches and warlocks and even the high priest. I was untouchable. I gained more power and new demons. Only one witch was foolish enough to try to take me on. With merely one look, I pushed her into the wall. Literally into the wall itself so that she had to be cut out. She sustained many broken bones and other injuries as a result. She never again tried to harm me and neither did any other human.

I rapidly rose to the position of top bride and my responsibilities grew also. I became one of Satan's representatives on an international level. I made many trips out to California to meet with government officials from the U.S. as well as foreign dignitaries. Representatives of foreign governments came to the mansion in California to petition for money for arms, etc. Most knew they were dealing with Satan, a few did not. Very large sums of money changed hands. Mann-Chan spoke through me on most occasions, speaking each one's own native language perfectly. Mann-Chan also gave me the interpretation of what those people were saying. I could not begin to speak the many different languages myself, but Mann-Chan knew them all.

I also made a number of trips to other countries. I have been to Mecca, Israel, Egypt, also the Vatican in Rome to meet with the Pope. All of my trips were for the purpose of coordinating Satan's programs with satanists in other lands, as well as meeting with various government officials to discuss aid to their countries in the form of money. A few did not know that I was a satanist, but thought I was associated with a powerful wealthy organization of some kind. People asking for money don't ask too many questions. The Pope knew very well who I was. We worked closely both with the Catholics (especially the Jesuits) and the high-ranking Masons.

It was during this time that I met many of the well known Rock music stars. They all signed contracts with Satan in return for fame and fortune. The evolution of Rock music in the U.S. was carefully planned by Satan and carried out by his servants step by step.

Despite my high position and great power, I lived in constant fear. I had no peace and I felt very trapped. My greatest problem was with the incredible evil perpetuated within the cult. The brutal discipline and above all human sacrifice!

CHAPTER 7

Discipline Within The Brotherhood

ELAINE TALKS:

Sex for the others in the cult was free and easy and just about all the time. Also sex with children. A very high percentage of all children within the cult are regularly sexually molested from a very young age. The cult members mostly pair off with others of the same power level. Almost every ceremony or meeting ends with a sex orgy. Individual members usually have the right to participate in sex if they want to.

There was sexual intercourse with demons also. Demons that could be seen and heard and felt in a physical manifestation. This would occur usually at meetings and sabbaths where a lot of drugs were used. Demons also had sex with unwilling people. People who were being punished for not doing what Satan and/or the demons wanted done. Often a man was forced to watch while more than one demon had brutal sexual intercourse with his wife. That was a very effective way of discipline.

Fear is a tactic that is used more often than anything else. Fear of death, fear of having your family tortured in front of your eyes. Both humans and demons were tortured. Many times demons were forced to physically manifest, then they were tortured and torn into pieces by other stronger demons because of some minor disobedience. The sights and sounds of these hideous episodes were burned into the minds of everyone present. The group was then told that this was an example of what would happen to them if they dared to disobey Satan or the demons.

During many ceremonies, especially the "high" ceremonies in which human sacrifices were performed, demons often took on physical human forms. At times it was difficult to tell who was a demon and who was a human. However demon eyes are cold and lifeless, their touch is like burning coals and yet there seems to be no life in them.

Torture of loved ones, especially children, is also a favorite tactic to ensure absolute obedience. Parents are forced to stand and watch as their children are beaten to death, brutally sexually molested, or stripped of their skin. *If* the child survives, the parents cannot take him/her to a hospital because they would be thrown into jail for child abuse. They could never prove they had not done the torture to the child — there would always be other satanists who would step forward to testify that they had seen the parents abusing the child. The doctors within the cult will not care for them either unless the parents can afford to pay exorbitant sums of money.

Another favorite method of discipline is sacrifice. Always there is a time of breathless horror and fear just before each human sacrifice as every member of the congregation waits to see just who will be sacrificed. Many of the sacrifices are people who have been disobedient, or who have tried to pull out of the cult.

Werwolves, zombies, vampires and other wer animals do exist. I have seen many of them. This is a very closely guarded secret by Satan. No one controls these beings except Satan or his high-ranking demons. He uses them mostly for discipline. I will never forget one incident during a meeting when Satan sent a werwolf after a man. The man jumped up and ran with the snarling werwolf after him. He could not hope to outrun the animal-human. He realized this and turned and pulled a .357 magnum, firing the contents of the chamber directly into the werwolf. The werwolf never even faltered. He tore the man to shreds. No one in the congregation dared move or make a sound, fearing that the werwolf would be turned on them next.

These creatures are human beings possessed by certain types of powerful demons capable of bringing about the necessary physical changes within the human body. Some of the ancient Christian writings from the dark ages about these wer animals in Europe are very accurate. I have never found anything in writing that is accurate about them except in the ancient Satanic writings kept in the vaults of the main Satanic mansion in the hills of California. The wer animals are greatly feared and hated by everyone within the cult. They are loners, 100% sold out to Satan. I suspect that during the Tribulation period they will greatly increase in number and be openly used by Satan for discipline.

Another frequent method of discipline is demonically inflicted illness. Also accidents, loss of job, etc. Demonic illnesses usually are a favorite because few doctors can diagnose what is wrong and the person so afflicted dies a very painful and slow death while doctors think he is imagining the symptoms.

Most of the children born to parents in the cult are dedicated to Satan, much like the baby dedications in the Christian churches. The ceremony involves a "baptism" of the infant in the blood of a sacrificed animal. These children are demon possessed from before birth. This goes on for generation after generation unless some parents are willing to let Jesus Christ become the Lord and Master of their life, and let His blood wash away all that sin.

The blood of Jesus is so powerful, and His work on the cross so complete, that even the werwolves can be saved if

66

they want to be. Jesus can raise the dead today just as he did when he walked the earth in a human body. These people under Satan's control are dead. I praise God that today I am completely delivered, I belong to Jesus, to Him alone, and there is no way that Satan or any of his people, no matter what they do to me, can stop me from telling what is going on in Satan's kingdom.

You, reader, if you are a member of The Brotherhood, *you,* too can be delivered from this bondage. You don't have to stay in Satan's kingdom of evil and darkness and fear. Jesus can and will set you free. All you need to do is ask Him to wash away your sins with His blood, and become your Lord and Master. Don't wait, time is very short. Jesus is coming back soon. There are not many days left. Make haste while there is yet time. Will you be left behind when Jesus comes and takes home all of His own? Please turn to Him now !

CHAPTER 8

The Black Mass and Human Sacrifice

ELAINE TALKS:

Human sacrifice is a subject that few, if any, ex-cult members are willing to talk about because of the legal implications. I am doing so only at the Lord's command. It is a fact and a practice of The Brotherhood. I have spent most of my life in hospitals and operating rooms because of my persistent refusal to bow to Satan in this area. I flatly refused to participate in human sacrifice.

Because of my extremely rapid rise in power I quickly attained a position in which I could determine what I would and would not do. That is, as far as other humans were concerned. I was more powerful than the other satanists so they could not touch me. Satan and his demons could, however. I have been brutally disciplined and tortured by demons on many many occasions because of my refusal to obey Satan in this area. I have had cancer 4 times with many surgeries and all the horrors of chemotherapy. The cancer was directly given to me by Satan as punishment for my refusal to participate in human sacrifice. I have no doubt that I would probably have been killed shortly if the Lord had not had mercy on me and saved me out of Satan's captivity when He did.

The customs and ceremonies involved in human and

animal sacrifice differ somewhat in different areas. Also, in recent years, especially on the West Coast, large numbers of young people are becoming involved in Satanism through Rock music, occultic role-playing fantasy games and, of course, by much individual recruitment. These independent groups are usually heavily involved in drugs, are very open, careless and blatant in what they do, and are not directly involved with The Brotherhood. Many of them do not even know the group exists. These are the groups careless enough to get caught in their various crimes of ritulistic child abuse, human sacrifice, etc. At the time I left Satanism, there was a growing concern among the leaders of The Brotherhood about the carelessness of these people. However, Satan is rapidly becoming so bold that he really doesn't care and he certainly doesn't care how many of these people end up in jail for the crimes they commit. Satan *knows* he doesn't have many years left and he is rapidly moving to perpetuate as much destruction upon this earth as possible.

In the United States there are eight "holy days" out of each year when human sacrifice is usually performed. (Human sacrifices may also be performed on other days for other reasons such as discipline, fertility rites, etc.) Smaller covens who do not have the necessary facilities, usually join with the larger covens nearby on these occasions. The "holy days" are Christmas, Easter, Halloween, Thanksgiving, and as close as possible to the first day of spring, summer, fall and winter. (Satan wishes to desecrate each of God's mercifully ordained seasons.)

Halloween has, since its inception by the Druids in England, been a special holiday for human sacrifices to Satan. It continues the same in our day. The sudden epidemic of harmful substances and objects being placed in the various Halloween treats for "trick-or-treaters" is no accident. It was a carefully planned effort by Satanists. The children injured and killed by these treats are *sacrifices to Satan.*

The purpose of the sacrifices as taught to cult members, is to "purify" them so that they can receive Satan's "blessings." Also, anyone who drinks the victim's blood or eats their flesh gains new demons and therefore greatly increased power. The drinking of blood is an important part of all Satanic activities. This is no accident, Satan constantly strives to defile all of God's principles.

> "And whatsoever man there be of the house of Israel, or of the strangers that sojourn among you, that eateth any manner of blood; I [God is speaking] will even set my face against that soul that eateth blood, and will cut him off from among his people. For the life of the flesh is in the blood . . . "   Leviticus 17:10-11.

Human sacrifices, as with all cult meetings, are never held the same place twice. Most members do not find out the location of the meeting until a few hours prior to its start. Sacrifices are always held in the most hidden and isolated areas possible. In large cities this sometimes becomes a problem, but there are usually enough vacant or abandoned warehouses and buildings available. Rarely does The Brotherhood hold a human sacrifice outside except when very secluded and isolated country or swampy areas are available. This is not true with the younger bolder people tripped out on drugs. They are not overly concerned with security and because of this The Brotherhood sees to it that many of them are discovered by the police and arrested, or are simply exterminated to prevent trouble. They are always declared to be insane, The Brotherhood sees to this so that a serious connection with Satanism is not made.

Specific committees are appointed and maintained within The Brotherhood to set up the necessary equipment and to provide clean-up afterwards. Satanists who are also policemen are almost always on these committees. Their function is to prevent any interference from law enforcement agencies. The equipment, such as the altar, in large cities Satan's golden throne, etc. is transported in plain vans. It can be quickly set up and taken down. The bodies are almost always disposed of by cremation. Babies are rather easily ground up — even in a garbage disposal, and are often disposed of in this manner. Occasionally the body is cremated at the site of the sacrifice, when this is not practicable there usually is no difficulty in using the facilities of a nearby mortuary. Also crematory facilities at veterinary hospitals or animal shelters are frequently used. The highly disciplined and carefully planned work of both the set-up and clean-up committees has been responsible for keeping the practice of human sacrifice out of the public eye for many many years.

Security at such ceremonies is always tight and police radio frequencies are continuously monitored throughout the ceremony. *Anyone* who has witnessed such a ceremony of human sacrifice and then tries to pull out of the cult does so at the cost of his or her own life. The *only* way to get out is through the power of Jesus Christ and even then it is not easy. The demons closely monitor everyone who has ever been even slightly involved with such a practice.

I will describe here a Black Sabbath (also called the Black Mass) that I was forced to attend. I was, at the time, a minor, not yet a high priestess and was literally a captive. Black Sabbaths take place once per year. Always at the time of the full moon and on the Easter weekend. Most of the competitions that I attended in California were just before Easter and culminated in the Easter Black Sabbath. Regardless of the cost I always managed to get away just before the ceremony. Satan saw to it that I paid dearly for that rebellion, but I didn't care.

I was very young at the time of that horrible weekend, still a child actually, but the memories of it torment me still and always will. I had been a member of the cult for less than a year. I was informed by the high priestess that a very important ceremony was coming up, that I was "privileged" to be "invited," but she also made it very clear at the same time that I had no choice, I *would* attend. Only those who are

71

invited attend and those invited have no choice but to attend. Few are willing to incur Satan's wrath by not attending because they are afraid that if they did so they would be likely to end up the sacrificee at the next Black Mass. I was not permitted to go alone but was taken by my "master" (the high priestess) and several other witches.

The meeting was held in a very large isolated barn which had been roughly remodeled for the purpose. I suppose that there were a couple thousand people there from the whole surrounding area. Most had already been taking drugs prior to coming and all were given potions to drink containing drugs and alcohol at the beginning of the meeting. I always avoided taking any of these drugged drinks because I knew the danger of clouding my mind. There were too many who coveted my position of being trained to be a high priestess. The higher members of the cult never partook of these drugged drinks and despised those who did so.

I didn't know what was going to happen as I entered the barn with my companions that night. It was a Friday night, Good Friday. The meeting was to run through that Sunday. I saw that the barn had a platform across one end. Above the platform sat a throne made of pure gold. That throne was for Satan. This was obviously an important occasion if Satan was to put in a personal appearance. I was to learn later that split second timing of such sacrifices is required by Satan and absolute coordination between covens across the country because Satan can only be in one place at a time. The timing must be accurate so that he could attend every meeting. He is *not* omnipresent like God.

As the high priest and high priestess came out onto the platform an absolute silence fell over the crowd. A silence so intense that you could hear a pin drop. The silence was one of fear. Each one was afraid that he or she might be chosen to be the sacrifice. At that moment Satan was no longer a glory to anyone, no longer an honor. A ripple of relief went through the crowd when the victim was dragged kicking and screaming through a side door and up onto the stage. The main Easter sacrifice is always a man. Occasionally additional sacrifices of women, children, or animals are made, but the ceremony centers around the sacrifice of a man. Often a hitch hiker is picked up some days before the ceremony and carefully guarded until the time of the meeting. In the eyes of Satan and the crowd, that man becomes Jesus and Satan's supposed victory over Jesus at the cross is celebrated.

I watched in utter horror as a crown of huge long thorns was driven into the young man's head. The thorns going in so deep as to pierce into his skull. Then he was stripped and beaten with whips tipped with metal studds, and tortured with spikes, and red-hot pokers. Finally he was nailed to a wooden cross which was then picked up and placed in a hole in the ground just in front of the middle of the platform. I will never forget the stench of the burned and tormented flesh, the screams of the victim, his writhing agony, his pleas for mercy. The crowd roared like a pack of wild animals, the inhuman voices of many demons from within the crowd joining in. They jeered and cheered as the cross was raised into place and dropped down into the hole. Satan had appeared by that time and sat on his throne nodding in approval. The high priest urinated on the victim and members of the congregation threw feces at him while everybody cheered Satan's supposed victory and then bowed down and worshiped Satan.

Satan appeared in human form as usual, dressed completely in shining white. But his eyes glowed red as a flame and he threw his head back and gave a howl and a scream and a hideous laugh of victory as the high priest drove a long spike through the man's head, pinning it to the cross, killing him. The crowd went crazy, screaming and shouting and dancing in crazed ecstasy at the "victory." They loudly proclaimed all victory and power and honor to their father

Satan. Satan vanished shortly after that to go on to the next Black Sabbath sacrifice.

At his departure the meeting turned into a sex orgy. Human with human, and demon with human. Every type of sexual perversion imaginable was practiced. The victim's blood was drained off and mixed with drugs and alcohol and drank by the high priest and high priestess and passed through the crowd. Many of the crowd went up to desecrate the body. The night hours passed by while the drugged demonic drunken frenzy of the crowd continued. Eventually the body was severed from the head and ground up, and portions mixed with drugs and other substances. Those who wanted more power ate some of the mixture. The third day, as people began to come down from their drugged state, they left for home in two's and three's. All proclaiming that their great and glorious father Satan had won yet another victory over the enemy Jesus Christ.

What a mockery the Black Sabbaths are! Satan *knows* that they are a mockery! The ceremony itself is supposed to be symbolic of the death of Christ. Satan proclaims that Jesus Christ was the ultimate sacrifice to him, that he won over Christ by killing him on the cross. Satan is lying! He knows that *he* was defeated at the cross, not Jesus, and so do all of the demons. But the people don't. I am one of the fortunate ones, I found out that it is all a lie. It is all an indescribably horrible lie. I declare to *you* the reader, *you* who are yet satanists, *you* who have not yet made Jesus your Lord and Master, *SATAN WAS NOT VICTORIOUS AT THE CROSS!* God's word sums it up the best:

> "And having spoiled principalities and powers, he made a shew of them openly, triumphing over them in it [referring to Jesus' death on the cross]."
>
> Colossians 2:15

JESUS IS ALIVE! Satan has no right to any of us. We can be free from bondage to Satan. All we need do is ask Jesus to set us free. He already paid the price. Won't you ask Jesus today? Tomorrow may be too late.

CHAPTER 9

Turning Points

ELAINE TALKS:

The first real turning point in my life came about a year after I became the regional bride of Satan. My dream world of believing that I was actually loved by someone — Satan himself — was cruelly shattered.

Apparently I had committed some minor offense against Satan, so minor in fact, that I had not even realized that I had done anything. I was home alone one day when suddenly four huge demons appeared in a physical manifestation. They were all four identical, they were dark, about seven feet tall and covered with black scales similar to Ri-Chan. They had vicious faces, long fangs and even longer fingernails that were like razor sharp steel.

Without any warning they came and attacked me. They clawed me with their long nails, shredding my flesh. They beat me and tossed me back and forth from one to another like a rubber ball. I screamed and cried and begged them to stop hurting me, begged them to tell me why they were doing this but they never answered a word. They just snarled and laughed hideous laughs. Mann-Chan and Ri-Chan, my guardians, simply stood by and made no move either to help me or to make any explanation as to why they were doing this to me. After about a half an hour they left as suddenly as they had come.

I was left lying on the floor, exhausted and in agony. My

back was torn in shreds, I had huge bruises from head to toe. The furniture was all tossed about and my blood was everywhere. As I lay there sobbing and panting and trying to recover a bit, Satan walked through the closed door. As usual he was in his favorite guise of an extremely handsome young man. He stood looking down at me and then threw back his head and laughed! He continued to laugh as I lay there sobbing, asking him why the demons had so cruelly tormented me. He never gave me any answer except to tell me that I was being disciplined. He went on to add that he thought that the demons had done a rather good job of it. Then, without making any move to help me, he disappeared.

I didn't have any answers except one, Satan hated me and was a liar. That knowledge was a wound deeper to my heart than any wound on my body. I was left to clean up myself and the apartment as best I could. By that time, I was a nurse, and I had to use every bit of my nursing skill and knowledge just to survive. I could not go to anyone for help as I could not explain what had happened to me. No one cared enough about me to come and find out what was wrong with me or to help me. When finally my wounds healed there was no scarring. Satan saw to that. He left no evidence that I could possibly use against him in the future.

It was then that I knew beyond a shadow of a doubt that Satan hated and despised me and did not love me as he said he did. I also realized that the demons, too, were using me for their own ends. It was Mann-Chan and the other demons that had told on me for whatever small thing I had done. Many times I had covered for them about something they had done in order to protect them from Satan's wrath. They had betrayed me!

It was then that I decided to get out of the cult if possible, although it was a couple of years before God showed me the way. I felt overwhelmingly trapped. Demons were all around me and within me. At that time I also thought that

76

they could read my mind. I dared hardly think about wanting out and certainly could never speak about it or the demons would know. I did not know where to turn for help. Where in the world could I ever find the power to overcome Satan and his demons, supposing I even survived long enough to try? I had to pretend continually that I was still willing to be within the cult. I knew that ultimately Satan and the demons planned my destruction. If Mann-Chan or any of the other demons found out what I was thinking it would have meant death and an agonizing death at that.

Two years after that episode of discipline, a lady I worked with started inviting me to go with her to her church. I continuously refused. I had troubles enough without going with that "fanatic." Then Satan came to me again as the handsome young man. He put his arms around me, acted very loving and told me that he, my husband, had been terribly insulted, and that only I could get revenge for him.

He knew of Esther's (the lady at work) invitations to go with her to her church. He wanted me to go and destroy that church because the people there were daring to proclaim that he, Satan, not only was alive and well but that he was evil and should and *could* be fought against. I was to go and join the church and then split it and destroy it. He wanted me to use the eight-part plan that his servants (including myself) had used and are using so successfully all over the world to destroy Christian churches. (These 8 points will be discussed in detail in Chapter 17.)

I tried twice to go. The first time I couldn't even get out of the car because the power of God was there so strongly. I had never experienced such a thing before. The second time I made it to the door, but literally could not take hold of the door knob. Again, the power and presence of the Lord was too strong. The demons within me felt it as well and flatly refused to go in. I don't know if I would ever have gone in if Esther hadn't approached me again at work. She dared me to go! Esther knew me well enough by then to know that I would never turn down a dare.

So finally I went, slipping in on the back row. Esther was watching for me and when she saw me come in she motioned for me to go up to the front and join her but I refused. So she came back and sat with me, telling me that "It's O.K., God is here on the back row just as much as on the front row!" I did not appreciate that at all!

It so happened that the young man preaching there that night was applying for the position of pastor. It was all I and the demons could do to sit through his sermon and I was a hardened church goer. Then, to make matters worse, immediately after church he made a bee-line to the back row where Esther and I sat and talked to me and tried to get me to give my life to Jesus. I told him in no uncertain terms that I did not want or need Jesus. He just smiled then and said, "Well I'm sure that you won't mind if I pray for you." Remembering in the nick of time that I was supposed to join the church, I managed to stifle my initial response and muttered "No, I don't mind."

Then, much to my horror, he put his hand on my shoulder and proceeded to pray for me right there out loud! I couldn't stand to be touched by anyone, especially him, neither could the demons! I squirmed, but that didn't seem to register with him, he just went on praying. I scrambled out of the church as quickly as I could after he finished. But something had touched me. On the way home, I told the Lord that if He did exist and wanted me to be His, that He must let that young man become the pastor of that church. The following Sunday the church voted to make him the pastor. It was almost a year before I kept my side of the bargain.

During that year another incident happened that also was very *key* in making me realize that Satan was lying, that there *is* a power greater than his and that Jesus must be the answer. Shortly after I had started going to the little church,

Satan came to me, obviously very angry. He told me that there was a "young smart-alec doctor" at his "special" hospital in a nearby city. This doctor was not only greatly interfering by "preaching and praying everywhere," but had also actually dared to interfere with a number of his top witches and their work at that institution.

Satan ordered me to organize a nationwide effort among all the top witches for that doctor's destruction. He didn't care how we did it, but that doctor *must* be killed, and quickly. I did not know until almost two years later that Rebecca was the doctor who was on the receiving end of that massive effort to destroy her by witchcraft. I shudder to think what might have happened if we had succeeded. Praise God that we did not!

Dutifully, I picked up the phone and called Helen, who was by that time the head witch at that particular hospital. I told her of Satan's order and delegated her to organize the rest. I thought little about the matter again for several months except to do the necessary incantations periodically. Then, suddenly, after about six months, I began to realize that every time I did an incantation in the direction of that doctor the demons came back to me unable to get through. They were not pleased! This was a complication that I didn't need just then! I was puzzled as I had never experienced such a thing before. I did not talk to anyone else about the problem because to admit that my power was failing would have been fatal for me.

Then about three weeks before I turned to Jesus, I received a phone call from Helen. That doctor who had left the hospital dying four months earlier had just that day returned to work. Not only had she returned, but she was completely healed! I was shocked. How could that be? I realized then that a power much greater than anything I had ever seen had blocked us and again I remembered the link angels in California. This doctor must possess the same power that that family had. I realized that that power was Jesus Christ.

Later that day Satan showed up again, most unhappy, to ask me why we had failed. "Don't *you* know?!" I asked. "Yes," he replied, "but I want to know if you know."

"Well I assume somebody must have blocked us by prayer."

"That is right," was his curt answer, then he vanished.

During that period of time I had gone to the little church regularly. It wasn't long before I realized that I was powerless to destroy it. Those people were on to every trick I tried, but they just kept on loving me and praying for me. I fell in love with them. Those people were genuine. They loved the Lord so much that they didn't care who I was, where I came from, how I dressed or talked. All they cared about was my soul. They cared enough to keep on praying and praying.

They prayed me right up to the altar one Sunday night where I finally said, "Jesus, I want and need you, please forgive me and come into my heart and life." What a struggle that was. Mann-Chan and the other demons tried to hold my mouth shut. They kept screaming in my mind that I had been lied to, God didn't exist and Jesus was really dead. But I knew that they were liars and would not listen to them.

At that time Mann-Chan and the other demons had a lot to say and do. The first thing that they did was fly right off and tell Satan what I had done. Then the fur started to fly!

That night after I had returned home Satan came to talk to me, but things were strangely different. Usually Satan would come up to me and put his hands on my shoulders, or hold me in his arms. This time he stood back away from me. I could see that he had many very powerful demons with him, but they, too, stood back away from me. Satan was steaming mad! He shouted at me,

"What in the Hell do you think you are doing?!!"

"I'm leaving you," I replied.

"*You* can't do that!"

"The Hell I can't, I just did!"

"You're my bride, I won you, if you don't do as I say I'll kill you. You can't get out of that contract!"

"I'd a lot rather die for God than I would stay your bride. That contract is no longer valid because it is covered by Jesus' blood. You have nothing to offer me but lies and destruction."

"You've made the wrong decision, I'll prove that to you shortly."

"You !*@#?* get out of my house!"

"See, you're not really a Christian!"

"What do you mean?"

"Christians don't swear."

I had not thought about that, but then I had only been a Christian for a couple of hours and was used to using any language I pleased when away from the church.

"So what, I know I am, because I know that I asked Jesus to forgive my sins and to come into my heart, *and* I know that he has!"

"You just think that, it didn't really happen."

I was by then so angry that I tried to take a step toward Satan to punch him in his nose, but for some reason I couldn't get my feet to move. By that time Satan was so angry he was screaming threats at me. I suddenly had a warm feeling of peace sweep over me and I unmistakably heard the Lord speak to my heart and spirit for the first time. He said,

"Do not be afraid, my child, *I AM* here, he cannot harm you." Again I told Satan to leave, but this time I used the name of Jesus and in an instant he disappeared.

I suppose Satan came to me nearly twenty times over the

next two weeks. Sometimes in a very charming mood, attempting to be a lover, but usually in a rage. He tried to persuade me to change my mind. He told me that Jesus was dead. He threatened many things, but not once did he come near to me. He always stood at a distance and so did the demons.

Many times many demons came obviously planning to torture me as the four had done in the past, but always they stopped short of me and looked confused and horrified and then turned and left without saying a thing. Gradually I realized that I must have some kind of special protection from the Lord. Even Mann-Chan, though he badgered me all the time, did not seem able to tear me as he had done in the past and now I had more control over him than he had over me.

Despite the special protection I had Mann-Chan did succeed in making me very, very ill and within two weeks I ended up in a hospital in another city away from my home town. I did not at the time realize that the Lord had permitted this. The long road to my complete freedom from the demons and arrival at a full and complete commitment to Jesus as Lord and Master as well as Savior was to start in that place. So I ended up a patient in a strange hospital, in a strange city. I lost almost everything I had gained through Satanism within two weeks of accepting Jesus. But Praise the Lord, He was in control of all of that, and I began my new life with Jesus, *and* at last met the very person I had tried so hard to kill — Rebecca.

CHAPTER 10

The Meeting

ELAINE TALKS:

Within two weeks of the day I made Jesus my Lord and Master instead of Satan I became extremely ill. I had fled to another city which happened to be the city in which Memorial Hospital was located. I collapsed at work and was taken to the emergency room by ambulance. I did not know a physician in that city so became what is known as a "clinic patient" which meant that I was assigned to the intern and resident physician on call for that night. I was desperately ill, in severe pain and so very lonely and frightened. It was in this state as I lay there on the uncomfortable cart in the Emergency Room that Rebecca walked into my life.

I was shocked. In the first place, I had never had a woman doctor. Secondly, she was both young and very pretty. But more than that, she radiated something that I couldn't put my finger on but felt strongly. The demons in me felt it too and they didn't like it at all. I could feel them begin to twist and squirm and grumble, telling me not to have anything to do with this person.

Miserable as I was, while she stood talking to me, my eyes seemed to be riveted to the collar of her white coat where she wore a golden pin which said, "Jesus Is Life." Finally, my curiosity overcame my shyness, and, reaching up to touch it, I asked,

"Are you a Christian?"

"Yes," she answered smiling, "are you?"

I nodded. "I became a Christian two weeks ago."

"Good for you!" she said warmly, "That's the most important decision anyone can ever make."

Then, for the second time, that warm quiet voice within me spoke saying, "Listen well to this young woman, she is my servant and will teach you much that you need to know." I knew by then that that was the voice of the Lord, but I was still too scared and uncertain to trust it fully. It was many months before I was to reach the point of trusting either the Lord or Rebecca.

Rebecca admitted me to the hospital that night. The next morning, much to my disappointment, I found that she was not going to be my primary physician. I was assigned to a young man under her whom I disliked intensely. He reciprocated the dislike, I might add. He did not believe that I was having pain or even that I was ill. I spent many days and nights in pain and tears because of the uncaring attitude of that young man.

The second day after I was admitted, Rebecca came back to talk with me. She brought along a Bible which she gave to me. I was shocked again. Doctors just don't go around giving their patients Bibles! At least not in my experience. No only did she give me a Bible, she also gave me reading assignments and prayed with me!

The first assignment she gave me was to read the book of James. As I read that book I became more and more angry as it pricked my conscience again and again. The demons didn't like it either. We were all in a thoroughly foul mood by the time she came around the next day. So angry in fact, that I threw the Bible at her. She just dodged, picked it up, laughed, and said:

"What's the matter? Did God's word strike some sore spots? Now here's your next assignment . . . "

Both the demons and I were absolutely furious that our anger didn't seem to affect her at all! That was the first of many sessions with Rebecca looking into the scriptures.

Slowly I began to grow spiritually. The demons were most upset about that. After that the demons would almost always block me and talk to Rebecca instead of me. They were anything but polite as they tried to drive her away from me. Each day I thought that I surely would not see her again, but she always kept coming back for more.

REBECCA TALKS:

When I first met Elaine, I had no idea of who she was, or of her involvement in Satanism. I bought the Bible for her at the Lord's command. I did not realize at the time that I was speaking mostly with the demons within Elaine instead of Elaine herself. She was obnoxious! Or, rather, the demons were. She made me angry, that is why I assigned James to her first because James has to much to say about taming the tongue.

Elaine's first stay in the hospital lasted six weeks. We put her through every test possible and still could not find out what was wrong. I had not learned about demonic illnesses yet and all my prayers seeking for guidance in her case seemed to be deliberately unanswered. The other physicians all concluded that nothing was really wrong but I had no peace with that conclusion. Nevertheless she was finally discharged.

Two days later, on my weekend on call, Elaine came to the Emergency Room. She was again my responsibility until my intern came back on the Monday. She had the same complaints of pain and illness. It was a difficult situation. I really thought that she was ill but had no idea what was wrong. Her question to me was a challenging one:

"Dr. Brown, why am I still sick? I even went and asked the elders to anoint me with oil and pray and ask God for healing. Why doesn't He answer? Have I done something wrong?"

This was a real challenge. Not only did I not know what was going on in her body, but the Lord had chosen to remain strangely silent about her despite my many prayers seeking His guidance. I told Elaine that I did not know why the Lord had chosen not to heal her but that I was sure that the Lord had a purpose for it all. I wrote the admitting orders, thinking that I would simply turn her case over to my intern and one of the specialists and would not have to worry about her anymore. However, the Lord *and* Elaine had different plans!

ELAINE TALKS:

Until this second admission under Rebecca's care, I had been relatively safe at the hospital. Satan and his demons are not omnipresent like the Lord and news often does not travel very fast in his kingdom. No one at the hospital had known about my desertion of Satan and conversion to Christ. But this time things were different. Many of the doctors and nurses were satanists and the word was out. I was to be killed for becoming a traitor to Satan. I spent my whole time fighting for my life. I was much stronger than any of the satanists there and won fairly easily.

I did not know that I was not supposed to use my powers and Satan and the demons continued to let me use them because they knew that so long as I did so I could not really grow as I should spiritually. I did not, of course, tell Rebecca about any of this. I did not trust her yet, but she was so different than any other doctor that I had ever run into that I was determined to keep her as my own physician.

The next day when the specialist came to see me I recognized him immediately. He was one of the higher satanists locally. I had never liked him. I deliberately picked a fight with him and my demons thoroughly beat him up. In fact, after that first battle he was so wounded physically that he could not come into the hospital to work for three days. It only took one week to make him hate and fear me so much that he refused to see me anymore, which was precisely what I wanted. The intern was a different matter. He was not a satanist, but not a Christian either. He already disliked me, but was bound by the rules of his training program to care for me.

I made his life miserable even as he made mine miserable. I astral-projected into his apartment and wrote all over his walls *very* impolite messages with a black marking pen, then signed my name to it. I threw dishes at him when he was home and several times unplugged his refrigerator so that all the food in it spoiled. Everytime he tried to bring anyone to see the messages on the walls one of my demons would tell me ahead of time and I would have the demon completely clean the wall before anyone else could see the writing. He quickly learned that he couldn't say anything to anyone else about what was going on because they all thought he was going crazy. He grew to hate and fear me so much that within two weeks he, too, refused to remain on my case. That left Rebecca. There was a love which radiated from her that I could not understand but was drawn to. I was fast growing to love her and deep down knew that she was the only one who had the answers to set me free.

REBECCA TALKS:

My relief concerning Elaine's case was short lived. Less than two weeks after her admission the intern came to me and told me that he did not care what the consequences were, he would not have anything more to do with Elaine, *and* by the end of that first week, the specialist came and told me that he did not care what I did with Elaine, he was washing his hands of her case. He would not be seeing her again. I was stuck! I didn't know what to do with her either!

As I saw Elaine from day to day we seemed to consistently reach only a certain point in her spiritual growth and then were blocked by something. Mostly she was completely obnoxious. I did not know that the demons in her were trying to drive me away. I did not even know she had demons! Time after time, in total frustration I wanted to simply discharge her and tell her there was nothing more I could do to help her. Always when I reached that point, the Lord would allow Satan to tempt me so that I would fall flat on my face and fail, and would have to humbly ask the Lord's forgiveness. When I did, He always said to me, "Now see the patience I have to have with you, can't you extend that same patience to my child Elaine?" Of course, the Lord always won! So, again I would ask the Lord to put His love in my heart for Elaine, and go back to see her the next day.

Finally, after about three weeks I got serious and spent a whole weekend in prayer and fasting asking the Lord to give me the key to Elaine's case. Late that Sunday evening Father spoke to me and said, "You have not talked to Elaine about her deep involvement in the occult." It all seemed so simple then. I should have recognized the symptoms, but Satan had blocked my mind.

That Monday morning, I went in and told Elaine that there was one area that we had not yet discussed.

"What is that?"

"Your deep involvement in the occult."

She was obviously shocked. She sat staring at me in silence for a full minute.

"How did you know about that?!"

"I spent this past weekend in fasting and prayer asking Father to reveal to me the key to your case. He told me."

I told her that as a Christian she must confess any and all involvements in the occult to the Lord as wrong and ask His forgiveness and then ask Him to take it all away and to close the doorways with His precious blood. She was completely resistant to this. Finally, in desperation, I said:

"Elaine, I can't handle you. But I know who can and that is the Lord. So I'm going to pray now and commit you into His hands and ask Him to deal with you." I did so, and left.

ELAINE TALKS:

I have never been so shocked in my life as I was when Rebecca coolly walked in that day and asked me about my involvement in the occult. I knew that there were only two places she could have gotten that information. One was from Satan and the other was from God. That was a real turning point in my life, however. When Rebecca prayed asking the Lord to "handle" me, He certainly did! In fact, Rebecca prayed that prayer daily from that point on. How I hated for her to do that, but the Lord broke through all the demonic interference and over the following days and weeks I slowly began to understand that as a Christian I must make Jesus the total *Master* in my life as well as Savior.

I came to trust Rebecca more and more and my love for her grew as well. I came to realize her deep commitment to the Lord and began to try to pattern my life after hers. I learned through her that the contract I had first signed in my own blood years ago was indeed completely cancelled out by the blood of Jesus. The struggle was not easy for me, or for Rebecca. But each day, through God's grace, I grew a bit more spiritually and my physical problems began to clear up. At last the day came when Rebecca told me that she had received guidance from the Lord that the time had come for me to learn to stand on my own feet against Satan outside of the hospital. So, I was discharged for the last time.

CHAPTER 11

Entering Spiritual Warfare

REBECCA TALKS:

I continued to see Elaine as an outpatient for a month after she was finally discharged from the hospital. Then Satan "lowered the boom." Elaine called me at home one night and I immediately recognized that she was deeply upset. She had received a letter from The Brotherhood that day and so had I.

The letter to me detailed my activities of the past two weeks perfectly, right down to what I had bought at the grocery store. They knew my address and phone number. They told me that if I ever spoke to or saw Elaine again that they would come and get me and sacrifice me. Elaine's letter told her that if she ever saw or spoke to me, and that if she did not return and repent and serve Satan again, that they would get her and sacrifice her at the upcoming Black Sabbath. One line in each of our letters was very similar to the letter from the field commander of the king of Assyria to King Hezekiah. They said, "You two are fools if you think your God can protect you from our Prince of Darkness!" (See Isaiah chapters 36 & 37.)

"What should we do?" Elaine asked. She wanted to sever all contact with me in hopes of preventing the cult from harming me, but I was sure that that was not the Lord's will. Shaken, I told her that I must take the situation to the Lord in prayer and ask Him what He wanted us to do. I knew that we could not run away. You cannot hide anywhere from Satan. I knew too, as did Elaine, just how capable these people were of carrying out their threats. I remembered the young pastor who had fallen into their hands and was almost tortured to death. I also knew what was awaiting me if the cult got their hands on me. The Lord had, not long before, given me a vision of how a virgin is sacrificed in that group — death is a pleasant release for the victim!

I took the problem to the Lord in prayer. He told me that He wanted me to have Elaine move in with me immediately as she did not yet have faith enough to stand on her own. Her husband had left her and remained with the satanists. Her daughter was temporarily staying with her step-sister because of her prolonged illness and hospitalization, so she was alone. Father told me that she would commit suicide rather than fall into the hands of the cult. She knew only too well what fate awaited her. Moving Elaine in with me would bring the attack directly to my own home.

I was literally ill with fear for two days as I struggled with the decision. Basically, I am *not* martyr material! I could not face the physical torture that surely awaited me if The Brotherhood got their hands on me and, by that time, I had grown to love Elaine and could not face seeing her so tortured either. I also realized that I had been daily asking the Lord to allow me to stand in the gap for that area for almost two years. I knew that since I was in the gap it might be necessary for the Lord to allow Satan to put his hand on me as he has on so many down through the ages from Stephen, the first Christian martyr, on.

I knew that to take the problem to the police would be useless as so many of them were involved in The Brotherhood in that area. Elaine and I were helpless in the face of so large and well trained an army as Satan had. Yet at the same time I also knew that to refuse to do Father's will would be the same as denying Jesus. Finally, the second night, I got honest with the Lord. I threw myself prone on my face before Father and sobbed my eyes out, saying:

"Father, Father, I am so terribly afraid. I just cannot face such physical torture or face the possibility of seeing Elaine so tortured. But also, I simply cannot deny Jesus or You. I just can't! I will do your will, but please help me, I am so afraid!"

At that point the Lord began to minister to me. I really wasn't any less afraid, but somehow I had the strength to go on and do what I knew I had to do. I called Elaine the next morning and told her that I was coming to get her that afternoon after work, that she must come and move in with me. She was shocked and told me that I was absolutely crazy and that she did not want to do so. But I told her that that was Father's command and that she did not have any choice *if* she really meant to follow and serve Jesus. So that day Elaine moved in with me and we have lived and served the Lord together ever since.

We had two weeks to wait before the night of The Brotherhood's Black Sabbath. They were furious about Elaine's move and let us know in no uncertain terms in all kinds of harassment. Phone calls at all hours, banging on the side of the house and at the doors in the middle of the night, rocks thrown through our windows at night, they even shot holes in the walls of the house.

In the meantime, I felt that the battle was really a spiritual one. Only God could fight it. I read and shared with Elaine the story of King Jehoshaphat in II Chronicles 20. A vast army had marched against King Jehoshaphat. He could not hope to stand against that army. So he, and all his people took the problem to the Lord in prayer, and the Lord answered them that the battle was *His* and that *He,* the Lord, would protect them. I told Elaine that our only hope was to stand in faith that the Lord would fight this battle for us. We had to simply trust that if He did not choose to do so that He would give us the strength to endure whatever His will was for us. My prayer was that if He did allow the group to torture us that He would give us the strength not to deny Jesus no matter what they did to us. Whatever the outcome was to be, I knew that I was to stand by Elaine and support her faith to the end.

I did not share any of this with my parents as I did not want to risk bringing the wrath of The Brotherhood upon them. In fact, we had no one to turn to for help except the Lord. I did have to tell my roommate what was going on, and she was so scared that she moved out for those two weeks.

As the two weeks passed by and the harassment grew, over and over Elaine and I sat down and read that passage in Chronicles. The day before The Brotherhood's Black Sabbath, I was sitting in the library of the hospital when one of the Christian medical students came by and dropped a card in my lap. It had some scripture verses on it. She told me that she didn't know why she was giving them to me, but that Father had been steadily putting it on her heart to write them down and give them to me for the past three days. I still have that card. Here is exactly what it said:

> "Fear not and be not dismayed . . . for the battle is not yours but God's. You will not need to fight in this battle; take your position, stand still, and see the victory of the Lord on your behalf."
>
> II Chronicles 20:15 & 17

Those were the very verses that Elaine and I had been standing on! I will never be able to express what I felt in that moment. For the first time, I knew, without doubt, that Father meant to fight the battle for us and that we would be safe. And so we were.

The night that The Brotherhood had specified, Elaine and I sat up until midnight listening to records and singing praises to the Lord. As the clock struck 12 midnight, the record playing was by Bill and Gloria Gaither. The song they were singing was *It Is Finished.* And we stood and praised God that it *was* finished. He had kept His word. He had fought the battle for us. We were unharmed. We went to bed then and slept in peace the rest of the night.

The next day after the Black Sabbath of The Brotherhood, the battle really began in earnest. The demons in Elaine began to openly try to kill her. Up to that point, she had persistently denied that demons were in her, but that evening she was suddenly seized and thrown to the floor with excruciating chest pain as if she were having a heart attack. I didn't know what to do, so I cried out to the Lord to intervene. He did and the pain ended.

"Elaine, that must have been a demon! Why do you continue to refuse to admit it?"

"Yes, it was Mann-Chan. He is trying to give me a heart attack."

"Who is Mann-Chan?"

"Mann-Chan is the demon that has been my guiding spirit for years. He has orders from Satan to kill me."

I knew very little about fighting demons at that point but I thought that they surely must be resisted in the same way the Lord had taught me to resist Satan — that is, out loud and in the name of Jesus. I told Elaine about this and told her that she should, out loud, in the name of Jesus, command him to stop and go away. Elaine found such a suggestion very embarrassing and flatly refused to address Mann-Chan out loud. Time after time over the next two days Mann-Chan threw Elaine to the floor. Always she refused to open her mouth and finally I would command him to stop in the name of Jesus and he would stop.

I knew that Elaine must learn to fight also, that the Lord would not permit me to fight for her indefinitely. I had come up against the stubbornness that had enabled Elaine to survive all these years, only now, it was directed in the wrong way. Finally, the third day, in utter desperation, as

Mann-Chan was attacking Elaine, I marched her to the front door. Opening it I told her:

"If you don't humble yourself and address Mann-Chan out loud as the Lord wants and stand up and fight him, he will kill you. Now go outside where no one can hear you and don't come back until the issue is settled! If you let him kill you, I don't want him doing it in the middle of my living room floor!"

Out she went and immediately I was engulfed in horror. What had I done? Suppose he did kill her? I certainly did not want that to happen. Had I been too harsh on her? I fell to my knees and prayed intensely for her. As I was praying, a couple of minutes later, Elaine sheepishly came back into the house. I was immensely relieved to see that she was all in one piece.

"Well, what happened?"

"I did as you said and commanded him to leave, and he did."

From that time on the battle grew. Ri-Chan began to afflict her and many others. Within a week I knew that if the demons were not cast out that they would kill her. I had never really dealt with casting out a demon and was not sure what to do. So, I called Pastor Pat on a Wednesday morning and told him about the situation. (I did not contact the pastor of the church I attended locally by the hospital because I did not feel he would be able to help me. Later his actions proved that the discernment given to me by the Lord was accurate.) I told him that I felt that if Elaine wasn't delivered that day that she would be killed. He told me to bring her down to the prayer meeting that night and that afterwards we would deal with the demons as the Lord led.

It was a major battle to get Elaine down to the church as the demons in her did everything to keep me from getting her there. I had to practically carry her out to the car and then seat-belted her in. The suffering Elaine was enduring by the time the prayer meeting was over no one but the Lord will ever know. The demons were ripping and tearing at her body from the inside, trying to kill her before they could be cast out. I greatly admire Elaine's courage and determination to be delivered. She did not once complain of the agony she was enduring.

After the prayer meeting Pastor Pat asked Elaine and I to join with him and two elders of the church in his study. I don't think that either of the elders had ever participated in a deliverance session before either. Pastor Pat had. He opened with prayer. He asked the Lord to seal that room with His angels so that nothing could get in and we could not get out until the work we had come to do had been completed. Elaine and I looked at each other. I knew that she was thinking the same thing I was: ***"WOW!! NOW WHAT?"***

After praying, the Pastor addressed Elaine asking her to confirm that she had made Jesus the Savior, Lord, and Master of her life, that she rejected Satan and anything from him and that she desired the demons to leave. She did so. From that point the battle was on. The demons began to surface and speak through Elaine. I had never seen anything like it. Her eyes, voice, and whole face changed. I will never forget the first demon. Suddenly a gutteral male voice said,

"I am Yaagogg, the demon of death, and you are all fools, you cannot win, we ***will kill*** this foul traitor. She belongs to Satan and he will not permit her to live."

Pastor Pat didn't bat an eyelash.

"You lie, you foul spirit! Elaine is now holy ground, she belongs to the Lord and you know it! I command you in the name of Jesus to come out of her!"

The battle raged for eight hours. Many many demons were

brought to the surface, forced to identify themselves and were cast out. It was a beautiful experience. The Holy Spirit was absolutely in control and there was a smooth coordination of all of us as He used first one of us then another. The presence of the Lord in that room was felt by all of us. We commanded the demons to come out of Elaine by the authority of the name of Jesus, read scripture aloud, sang songs of praise to the Lord and prayed and praised Jesus for His complete victory over Satan. The demons were particularly tormented by our praise and they seemed to lose strength rapidly then. Most of them came out by violent coughing.

What a time of joy and rejoicing we had when the deliverance session finally ended. We all stood crying, clapping our hands and praising the Lord in complete and beautiful unity. Exhausted but overjoyed, Elaine and I praised the Lord all the way home.

The weeks following Elaine's first deliverance were intensive weeks of decisions that would affect the rest of both of our lives. The Lord spoke to me at the beginning of that week. He asked me if I would be willing to commit my life to Him in a new way, to be used by Him in any way *He* chose to directly fight Satan, and stand "in the gap" so that many souls could be saved, especially among those of The Brotherhood. The Lord told me that if I chose such a course that I could expect suffering and persecution. Also that I would have to change my career plans. He showed me that I could expect much loneliness and rejection and eventually have to lay down my medical career completely, but that He would always be with me. He also told me that I would lose my entire family, which I have.

It was a big decision. I have always loved the field of oncology and had, just the month before, been accepted into a Fellowship Program to train in oncology at one of the oldest and most prestigious institutions in the U.S. Oncology is the field in medicine which specializes in the treatment of cancer. Being accepted to that particular program was considered a great honor. I wanted very much to specialize in that field. The Lord told me that He does not give His children second rate options and that if I did not choose to commit my life to doing battle with Satan, that He would greatly bless me anyway.

The decision was a hard one. The Lord wanted me to stay in internal medicine and open a private solo practice so that I would have a broader range of patients. This was necessary so that He could bring to me the people I was to minister to, especially cult members. As I thought about it, I realized that I loved the Lord too much to do anything other than His first choice. As I mentioned this to a few of my "Christian" colleagues at the hospital and the fact that I would have to refuse the position in the oncology fellowship, they all told me that I was crazy to even think of refusing such a position.

Also, many of my friends were beginning to pressure me to have Elaine move out. Those that did not know that I had moved Elaine in with me also began to turn against me for no explainable reason. Satan worked in such a manner that by the end of that week I did not have one friend left. My family and my roommate were also pressuring me to have Elaine move out. They did not think I was hearing the Lord correctly. Even the minister of the church I attended locally by the hospital, called me and counseled me to have Elaine move out. He, too, told me that I " . . . got too involved with people, and especially with Elaine." Then he went on to tell me that I was not welcome to return to his church until I had gotten rid of Elaine!

I was shaken and began to wonder if I had really heard the Lord correctly. But during that time, the Holy Spirit forcibly brought to my mind the scripture in I Peter 1:22, " . . . see that ye love one another with a pure heart fervently." That certainly didn't sound like a surface-only involvement to me. Also the Holy Spirit quickened Galatians 6:2 to my heart, "Bear ye one another's burdens, and so fulfill the law of Christ." Once again I had peace in my heart and spirit that I was hearing the Lord correctly.

Nevertheless, by the end of that week, I was both discouraged and depressed. I saw Pastor Pat that next Sunday again, and shared with him what had been happening, and also my depression. I will never forget the experience. Pastor Pat looked me square in the eye and said:

"Rebecca, entering into spiritual warfare in a deep commitment such as you are describing will mean much rejection and suffering. If you can't take it, then you'd better get out now!"

I felt about two inches tall! But it was what I needed to hear. The next day I made my decision. I told the Lord that I gave my life to Him to be used in this new dimension, totally committed to Him to be used in any way He chose to directly battle Satan in order that souls could be saved, and Jesus glorified.

Then I sat down and wrote the director of the fellowship program in oncology and told him that after much prayer I knew that it was not the Lord's will for me to take that direction in my career, that I would not be coming after all. What a furor that decision raised at the hospital!. The directors of my program were angry and could not understand my decision. I tried to explain to them that it was not the Lord's will for me to become an oncologist. They thought I was crazy, after all, "God doesn't speak to people like that."

Most Christians are quite unaware not only of the spirit world, but of the fact that every action we take in our physical world also affects the spirit world. Charles G. Finney describes this cause and effect relationship between the physical and spiritual worlds beautifully:

> "Every Christian makes an impression by his conduct, and witnesses either for one side or the other. His looks, dress, whole demeanor, make a constant im-

pression on one side or the other. He cannot help testifying for or against religion. He is either gathering with Christ, or scattering abroad. At every step you tread on chords that will vibrate to all eternity. Every time you move, you touch keys whose sound will re-echo all over the hills and dales of heaven, and through all the dark caverns and vaults of hell. Every movement of your lives, you are exerting a tremendous influence that will tell on the immortal interests of souls all around you."

The Last Call . . . For Real Revival, by J.T.C., p. 31.

An incident happened which suddenly made this truth a reality to me. I had not realized the significance of the waves of reaction in the spirit world to the events in my own life. First, I had been involved in using the power of Jesus Christ to block much of the witchcraft in one of Satan's special hospitals. Then, the Lord had involved me in the battle in which Satan lost one of his top brides — an event which certainly caused Satan to lose face in his kingdom. Shortly after that Satan and his demons failed in their attempt to use Elaine and myself as human sacrifices because the Lord had intervened and protected us. I guess the last straw, so to speak, was my total committal of my life to the Lord to be used in warfare directly against Satan.

Quite unaware of the "waves" all of this was causing in the spirit world, I calmly went out into my back yard one day to have a quite lunch on my picnic table under the trees. As I was sitting there enjoying the sunshine God permitted the veil between the spirit world and the physical world to be briefly torn assunder.

Suddenly, a shining figure appeared and sat down across the table from me. He was in form as a man. As I sat staring at him in silent amazement the Holy Spirit forcibly revealed to me who he was! This was the *last* being I had ever expected to personally meet. This shining figure presenting himself to me in radiance as an "angel of light" was actually the Prince of Darkness, the Prince of the Power of the Air, ruler over a vast kingdom of evil — Satan, himself! I don't remember details about his appearance because I could not seem to draw my eyes away from his, his eyes were so evil. They were like black coals and had a depth and blackness and evilness that seemed to reach out threatening to engulf me. For an instant I felt as if I was falling forward into the black pit that was in those eyes, but something held me back, stabilizing me. I could tell that Satan was angry, very angry.

"Satan!" I exclaimed. Upon receiving his curt nod acknowledging his identity, I asked, "What do you want?"

"Woman, do you dare to come against me?"

"My life has been so committed."

"I know, but, **DO YOU DARE** to actually come against **ME**?!"

I was very puzzled and surprised at his repeated question. It was obvious that his anger was growing by the moment, but the Holy Spirit filled me with a complete peace such that afterwards I marveled that I had felt no fear.

"Satan, I am not coming against you in my own power, but in the power and authority of Jesus Christ."

"You had better count the cost, this Jesus whom you serve advised His followers." (And he quoted accurately word for word the following:)

> "For which of you, intending to build a tower, sitteth not down first, and counteth the cost, whether he have sufficient to finish it? Lest haply, after he hath laid the foundation, and is not able to finish it, all that behold it begin to mock him, Saying, This man began to build, and was not able to finish.
>
> Or what king, going to make war against another king, sitteth not down first, and consulteth whether he be able with ten thousand to meet him that cometh against him with twenty thousand? Or else, while the other is yet a great way off, he sendeth an ambassage,

and desireth conditions of peace.

So likewise, whosoever he be of you that forsaketh not
all that he hath, he cannot be my disciple."

Luke 14:28-33

"Woman you had better count the cost because I tell you, I
will make your life an agony and an anguish that you never
knew could even exist!"

I knew this powerful creature was deadly serious and that
since I had committed everything to the Lord (all my
possessions, career, family, my very life itself), I had no
doubt that Satan would petition Father for it all just as he
had done many years ago with Job. It was a very sobering
thought. Finally I replied:

"I have counted the cost to the best of my ability and I
know that whatever is to come in the future will be under
the complete control of my God, and I simply trust that His
grace will be sufficient for me. So, **YES,** Satan, **I DO DARE**
to take up the authority and power that Jesus has given me,
and I **DO DARE** to come against you in the name of Jesus
Christ my Lord!"

My eyes locked with Satan's for a long moment of silence.
Again I had that peculiar sensation that if something had
not been holding me, I would have fallen forward into the
awful evil that I saw there. Then Satan nodded curtly and
said, "So be it." With those words, he vanished.

I sat pondering the experience; wondering that the sun had
continued to shine warmly, the breeze gently rustling the
leaves on the trees, and the birds had continued to sing. I
sensed that somehow I had just taken a major irrevocable
step. At the time of this writing the cost has indeed been
great. I have lost my entire family, my career and everything I had in terms of worldly possessions. I have also suffered much in my physical body. **BUT** through it all, the
Lord **HAS** been with me and what Satan means for defeat
the Lord will turn into victory.

103

The road has indeed been very long and rocky since that first meeting with Satan and he has made my life an agony and an anguish that I never knew existed, and I know also that there is more to come. But, also, never could I have come to know the Lord as I do, and though I know I'm just getting started there, too, getting to know Him this much is worth anything! I know at last the meaning of Matthew 6:19-21 where Jesus said:

> "Lay not up for yourselves treasures upon earth, where moth and rust doth corrupt, and where thieves break through and steal: But lay up for yourselves treasure in heaven, where neither moth nor rust doth corrupt, and where thieves do not break through nor steal: For where your treasure is, there will your heart be also."

The most valuable treasure anyone can have is personal knowledge of Jesus, and Father, and the Holy Spirit!

CHAPTER 12

The Battle

REBECCA TALKS:

The next chapter in our lives was a relentless battle which lasted for eight weeks. As I look back, I realize that the Lord was putting us through a period of intensive training, taking us stage by stage into an ever deeper knowledge of Satan's kingdom and how to combat it. I had very little awareness of the spirit world prior to that time and the Lord was also training me in this area. Many times during that eight weeks I asked the Lord how much longer the battle must continue and always His answer was, "Until you have learned enough." Because Elaine had been so very deeply involved in the occult there was much we had to learn before she could be completely cleared of the demons.

During the entire eight week's period neither one of us had more than one to two hours of broken sleep per night. I continued to work full time at the hospital, of course, but fortunately I was on a rotation that did not require night call and was mostly research. Each morning as I prepared for work after yet another sleepless and exhausting night I paused a moment and quoted Isaiah 40:31, laying claim to the promises there:

> "But they that wait upon the Lord shall renew their strength; they shall mount up with wings as eagles; they shall run, and not be weary; and they shall walk, and not faint."

Each day as I laid claim to that promise, somehow, the Lord gave me the strength to keep going during the rest of the day. I dared tell no one what was going on. There was no one who would understand and everyone was hostile to me anyway. My dear parents were not, of course, but I did not want to worry them. So, Elaine and I battled completely alone except for the Lord. Toward the end of that period of time the Lord instructed me to read the book of Nehemiah. There I discovered the passage where Nehemiah's enemies threatened to attack the Jews to stop the rebuilding of the wall of Jerusalem. Chapter 4:21-23 says:

> "So we labored in the work: and half of them held the spears from the rising of the morning till the stars appeared. Likewise all the same time said I unto the people, Let every one with his servant lodge within Jerusalem, that in the night they may be a guard to us, and labor on the day. So neither I, nor my brethren, nor my servants, nor the men of the guard which followed me, none of us put off our clothes, saving that every one put them off for washing."

Nehemiah 6:15 told me that it took 52 days to complete the wall. I figured that if the Lord could keep Nehemiah and all the people going day and night without sleep for 52 days that He could give me the strength to keep going too. That scripture was a great comfort to me, especially as some people were telling me that I looked tired and that it was "My responsibility to the Lord to be sure that I got adequate rest every night. The Lord would not require otherwise."

The battle took place simultaneously on three fronts: against demons, against the human spirits of cult members and against physical people from The Brotherhood who were sent to try to kill us.

The battle began a week after Elaine's first deliverance. I had just talked to Pastor Pat that afternoon as described in the preceding chapter. He had counseled me not to try to deal with any demons by myself as he was afraid that they might be too strong for me. Elaine had started having chest pain again that day but had not told me.

That evening after the pastor left she had another severe episode of chest pain. I will never forget how down and discouraged we were as we sat on the couch in my living room afterwards. I turned to Elaine and said,

"Elaine that pain must have been from a demon. They must be back again. Why didn't you say something earlier when Pastor Pat was here?"

Of course, what I did not know then, was that the demons had blocked Elaine from saying anything when the pastor was there. We both sat in silence for a few minutes. Then Elaine's voice said,

"Well, I'm *not* going to be defeated a second time!"

"But Elaine, when were you defeated the first time?"

No answer. So I reached over to touch her arm to get her attention. She jumped and turned to me, her face contorted into a snarl, hands reaching for my throat. Instantly I realized that I had not been talking to Elaine but to a demon in her. I jumped back out of reach, passing my hand in front of me exclaiming:

"I put a shield of faith in Jesus between you and me, you may not touch me, demon!"

A harsh guttural voice said, "My name is Legion. I am going to kill you! There is only one of you now and not more than four hours ago your own pastor told you not to try to take us on yourself, you're not strong enough. Now that you're alone, I'm going to kill you! You have interfered with Satan's bride long enough."

I don't think I have ever been so frightened in my entire life. I felt overwhelmed with the presence of evil in that room. I knew only too well that the demon had been listening to every word of my conversation with Pastor Pat earlier that day. He knew of my depression and discouragement as well. Instinctively I also knew that I dared not let him see how afraid I was. I had no doubt that if I let him get the upperhand that he would indeed kill me. Elaine's body was much stronger than mine to start with and I had no doubt that under complete demonic control it would be many times stronger. I swallowed hard and answered in what I hoped was a commanding voice.

"Oh no, demon, Elaine is no longer Satan's bride. *You* are the trespasser. I may be alone, but Jesus *IS* with me and it is *His* power that will overcome you, not mine. I don't have to be stronger than you because Jesus already is."

"You don't know what you're talking about. I'm going to enjoy watching you squirm as I strangle you to death. Just watch!"

As he spoke he reached out for me again. Again I passed my hand in front of me and laid claim to the shield of faith in Jesus. Much to my joy the demon had to stop short. There was an invisible barrier between him and me and he could not reach through it, hard as he tried. He became very angry as I praised the Lord for His faithfulness in protecting me.

The battle went on for 45 minutes. I prayed, sang hymns, read and quoted scripture. Over and over again I commanded the demon to come out. Many times he tried to use Elaine's body to harm me physically but always he was stopped as I steadily claimed that protecting shield.

The Holy Spirit brought scripture after scripture to my mind. I quoted Luke 10:19, Job 30:2-8 and Colossians 2:15 to him repeatedly which tormented him. I read from Revelation chapter 18 about the fall of Babylon, telling him that he, too, was falling in that very hour. He shouted at me, cursed me, threatened and finally began to cajole me to leave him alone; but I pushed my advantage. At last, with a scream of rage he came out of Elaine in an episode of violent coughing.

108

I was so relieved and unnerved that I burst into tears. Poor Elaine, she had been unconscious all that time. She could not understand why I was crying so uncontrollably. I was shaking from head to toe, I had been so frightened. But as I sat there telling Elaine what had happened, the realization filled my soul that Jesus *had* been faithful and had indeed given me His own power and authority over those foul things. Scared as I had been, Jesus had stood firm and had delivered me out of the hand of my enemy. Elaine felt much better after Legion was out and we went to bed for our last night of sleep for the following eight weeks.

The following days and nights blurred together as demon after demon came into Elaine to try to kill her, or me, or both of us. The battle was continuous and unrelenting. Fortunately the hospital was only a two minute's drive from my home. Many times during the day the Lord would speak to me urgently instructing me to hurry home, that Elaine was in trouble. Always I would arrive home to find her on the floor unconscious, often with a belt around her throat, blue from lack of oxygen. Her own hands were under the control of a demon pulling the belt so tight that she could not breath. Sometimes she would be bleeding from a cut, knife still in hand. Sometimes in a coma so deep that she was hardly breathing. Sometimes being strangled with her own hands as the demons sought to crush her larynx (voice box). I know that it was a direct provision of the Lord that I was on a rotation which was mostly study so I was free to run back and forth from the hospital.

The next day after my first meeting with Legion, the Lord spoke to me and gave me the scripture in II Timothy 1:14 which says:

> "That good thing which was committed unto thee
> keep by the Holy Ghost which dwelleth in us."

The Lord showed me that Elaine was the good deposit given to me — that I must guard her diligently with my very life.

As the battle grew rapidly I became most concerned as to why the demons that were cast out could come back into Elaine again in a very short time. As I prayerfully considered the situation the Lord brought to my mind a passage from a book I had read some months before. It is called *The Conquest Of Canaan,* by Jessie Penn-Lewis. She wrote:

> "Galatians 5:24 is also a passage which meets the case just here: 'They that are Christ's have crucified the flesh with the affections and lusts.' This is judicially the position of all the children of God, but it must be experimental also. For in this spiritual battle, unless the knife is applied to what the scriptures term the 'flesh,' it will always be ground for the enemy to attack, so as to weaken us in the conflict. The 'flesh' must be kept under the knife of the cross, for if there is any self-indulgence, or anything that is doubtful in your life, and you venture to take the aggressive against the foe, the enemy will come back on you, and — fastening on that uncrucified 'ground' in you — will press you with appalling power. You must have the knife of the cross steadily, persistently, and unbrokenly applied to the flesh; to the appetites of the flesh, to self-indulgence in any form, and to the pride of the flesh." page 9.

As I sat pondering and praying about this passage as to how it might apply to our current situation with the demons in Elaine, the Lord suddenly flashed a clear picture into my mind which the Holy Spirit confirmed to me was a spiritual vision. In the vision, Elaine was standing in the center of a ring of circling animals that looked like huge and vicious cats. They were very ugly. They were circling around and around her, sniffing, sniffing. Suddenly one of them stopped, sniffed and then jumped right into her. Then I understood.

The cat-like animals represented demons. They were circling around Elaine continuously trying to find an opening or doorway to get in. When they did, they jumped into her and almost immediately manifested to me. I told Elaine about the vision, and showed her the passage in the book. I felt led by the Lord that she needed to ask Him to search her and reveal to her any open doorways in her life that needed to be closed by confession, forgiveness and the blood of Jesus. I greatly admire her courage and persistence.

She went through two days and nights of intense searching. I'm sure it was a terribly painful experience for her. The vision was in my conscious awareness continuously during that time. Everytime one of the animals jumped into Elaine immediately a demon would surface and the battle would be on until it was cast out. Then followed a time of waiting prayerfully on the Lord to reveal to Elaine or myself the doorway it had used. Steadily, door after door was closed as Elaine confessed particular involvements or sins, received forgiveness and then asked the Lord to close that door forever with His blood. Finally, about 2 A.M. on a Monday morning, I suddenly realized that the "animals" were circling in the opposite direction. I exclaimed in surprise:

"Elaine, why are they going in the opposite direction now?"

"Why is what going in the opposite direction?"

I petitioned Father to let Elaine see the vision too, which He did immediately. She was thoughtful for awhile. Then,

"I suppose because they can no longer find any doors the way they were going."

Even as she spoke, both of us saw one of the demons stand up on its hind legs and paw against what seemed to be an invisible barrier.

"Elaine!" I cried out, "We must close the top!"

But I was too late. The demon had jumped up and over the invisible barrier into the obviously open top and Elaine was in a deep coma. She was under the control of a pair of demons called Coma and Endless Sleep. These two gave me untold trouble! They were very powerful and they would put Elaine into a coma so deep that her heart rate would slow down to 30 per minute or so and she would sometimes stop breathing. They were also very hard to deal with because they would not speak to me and they could seemingly not hear me because Elaine's body was in such a deep coma.

This time was no different. I feared for her life. Nothing worked. I prayed, sang hymns, shouted at them, slapped Elaine's cheek. Nothing but a deeper coma. Finally in desperation, not knowing what else to do, I picked up my Bible and began to read aloud from the book of Revelation. Demons hate that book. I read and read, my heart sinking within me, but standing in faith that the Lord would save Elaine's life. When I had read about half way through the book the demon suddenly reached out with Elaine's hand and tried to tear the Bible away from me.

"Shut-up!" he snarled. "We can't stand to hear any more of that."

"Too bad, demon, that book tells of your final down-fall and total destruction. If you hang around, I'll read the rest of it to you. I'll read it over and over again, and what's more, I'll ask Father to prevent you from stopping your ears so you can't hear me. You'll have to listen to it, I know He'll make you."

"You can't do that."

"Oh yes I can!" And then I prayed aloud and asked Father to make those demons hear every word I read. I started reading again. The response was prompt.

"Shut-up!!" The demon was so frustrated that he was screaming at me. Of course I refused and finally he had to come out. I had discovered a key in handling these difficult demons. I could ask Father to do things to them, such as make them hear, and He would.

The top doorway was difficult to close as it involved an area that was dear to Elaine's heart. But her courage and commitment to the Lord prevailed and at last it was closed. Almost immediately in the vision I saw one of the "animals" digging at the ground at Elaine's feet.

"Oh NO! The bottom!" Again I was too late. The demon was in. I had another hour's battle before that one was cast out. Elaine and I began asking the Lord to reveal the bottom doorway. The Lord revealed it to both of us at the same time. Pride. Again, I was to run into Elaine's stubbornness as I had in the first incident with Mann-Chan. Up to that point, Elaine had steadfastly refused to get down on her knees to pray. The Lord had dealt with me on this subject some years before. It is humbling to get down on your knees, but I had learned also what a comfort it is. There were other areas under pride as well, but they seemed to focus in that one issue at the moment. I told Elaine that I thought that the Lord was asking her to simply get down on her knees and ask Him to forgive and deal with her pride. She flatly refused. I was so frustrated as with each refusal another demon got in and I had an hour or so battle with each before it finally came out. Finally, I got out the book .*The Conquest Of Canaan* and made Elaine read aloud the passage I mentioned earlier. Then I told her:

"Now, go into the living room and settle the issue with the Lord. Don't come back until you do!"

I do not know, and never asked, what transpired between Elaine and the Lord in the dark living room at about 5 A.M. that morning, but as Elaine returned to me somewhat sheepishly, she had a peace about her that I had not seen before.

Instantly we both "saw" the completed work. An incredibly beautiful shining cylinder of light. It hung in the room, filling it with its brilliant warm, lovely light. I saw the demon-animals fleeing into the shadows. We both sat down and basked in the warmth and light from the cylinder as if it were the noon sun. We did not realize it at the time, but we were seeing and feeling the glory of Jesus as that part of His work in Elaine's life was finished.

We did not actually see the cylinder and its light with our physical eyes, but were seeing it in our minds through our spirits as the vision was given to us by the Holy Spirit. However we also experienced the warmth and love radiating from it in our physical bodies. (See chapter 14.) We both fell asleep for the first time in four days. One hour later, as I got up to go to work, I was delighted to "see" that the light-cylinder was still there. Its warmth and shining love was a tremendous comfort to both of us. I thought that the battle was finished then. How wrong I was, I didn't realize this represented only one part of the work to be done of clearing Elaine's life.

I was dismayed when I came home that afternoon to find Elaine on the couch, blue, not breathing, belt around her neck, her own hands under demonic control pulling it tight so that she could not breath. I was broken hearted as I dealt with the demon that was trying to kill her. How could this be? I still saw the completed shining cylinder in my spirit. How then could yet another demon have gotten in? Again and again that evening demons got in, always catching me unawares. I couldn't accept that they were getting in. I was so exhausted and I had been relying on the cylinder as a sign that they could not get in anymore. Finally, with many tears, I prayed and asked the Lord to remove the vision as I realized that I was depending on it instead of the Lord, and therefore Satan was able to use it to manipulate me. Even as I asked, instantly the lovely light-cylinder vanished. That evening we entered a new area of battle.

I was in the kitchen fixing dinner when Elaine came under the control of what I thought was a demon. I realized she was in the kitchen when I was stabbed in the back with the large knife I had been using to cut up the meat. I grabbed her hand saying:

"No, demon, I bind you in the name of Jesus. You *will* give me the knife."

I was surprised to hear a very feminine voice answer me.

"You can't order me around like some demon! I don't have to obey you and your stupid commands because *I'M NOT* a demon! Now I'm going to teach you both a lesson."

An all-out wrestling match ensued during which I received a number of rather severe cuts. Blood was all over the kitchen. As I struggled for both the knife and our lives I keep saying,

"I don't care who or what you are, I *will* defeat you in the name and power of Jesus." At last I managed to wrest the knife out of her hand. Panting and at the end of my strength, I forced her to sit in a chair.

"Now, I command you in the name of Jesus, to tell me who, and what you are!"

"I am Sally."

I was surprised. I knew that Sally had been a friend of Elaine's and the witch whom Elaine had been tutoring. She became Elaine's successor as high priestess. She was more arrogant that any demon I had run into and just as deadly. I could feel her hatred.

"Well, Sally, human or demon, you *will* bow your knee to Jesus. You have no choice, you know, because God's word says so. In Philippians 2:6-11 God says:

> 'Who, being in the form of God, thought it not robbery to be equal with God: But made himself of no reputation, and took upon him the form of a servant, and was made in the likeness of men: And being found in fashion as a man, he humbled himself, and became obedient unto death, even the death of the cross. Wherefore God also hath highly exalted him, and given him a name which is above every name: That at the name of Jesus every knee should bow, of things in

> heaven, and things in earth, and things under the
> earth; And that every tongue should confess that Jesus
> Christ is Lord, to the glory of God the Father.'"

As I quoted those beautiful verses I felt the Lord strengthening my body.

"So you see, Sally, you have no choice. The fact that you are human and not demon makes no difference. Your knee, too, must bow to Jesus."

She laughed mockingly at me. "You think your so called Jesus is so great. That is all a bunch of lies. I will never bow to Him!"

I was absolutely filled with rage! Without thinking, I reached out and grabbed her by the shoulders, literally lifted her out of the chair, and pushed her down on the floor on her knees. Then I put my hand on the back or her head and pushed her nose to the floor.

"Now what do you think of your fine statements that you'll never bow to Jesus?! That's exactly what you're doing now, because He is standing right here!"

I'm not sure who was more surprised, Sally or me. Elaine is not exactly light and I was already exhausted from our frantic struggle over the knife a few moments before. I let Sally bring poor Elaine's nose up off the floor, but continued to hold her on her knees.

"Sally, you **must see.** Satan is lying to you, just as he lied to Elaine. Jesus is the victor, not Satan. Satan wants only to destroy you. If he were the stronger as he claims, then why are **you** on the floor instead of me? Sally, your only hope is to commit your life to Jesus!"

"I'm not listening to you any longer, but I'll be back and you both will be sorry!" Instantly she was gone and Elaine's unconscious body sagged against me. Then she roused and looked up at me.

"Hey, what's going on, why am I on the floor — is this another lesson in humility?"

I laughed a bit shakenly, dusting off the end of Elaine's nose.

"I'm sorry, but I'm afraid I forgot for a moment that it was your body, I was so mad at Sally."

"*AT WHO*?!!"

"At Sally. She was insulting about Jesus and declared that she would never bow her knee to Him, and, well, I made her."

"So I see. But what was she trying to do?"

"Kill both of us with the butcher knife."

"Oh boy! Well she didn't succeed I see, though I've certainly seen you looking better."

As Elaine helped me to clean up both myself and the kitchen I asked her:

"Elaine, did you used to do things like that, enter into another person's body and move and talk through them, I mean?"

"Sure, that was simple."

"Were you consciously aware of what you were doing and what was said and done?"

"Yes."

"But how did you do it? I think maybe this is another doorway. How else could she have gotten in?"

"I really don't know *how* I did it, I just did it. It was one of the first things I learned to do. As I grew in power, I could leave my body and go anywhere and do anything I wanted, ail the while still being consciously aware of what was happening and what I was doing with my physical body too."

Suddenly something clicked. The Holy Spirit brought back to my memory a book I had read over a year before. Excitedly I ran to my bookshelf to get it. I told Elaine I thought it might contain the answer to our dilemma. It talked about "soul-power" which is really the power in the human spirit body when under the control of the soul. There are two books that deal with this subject. *The Latent Power Of The Soul*, by Watchman Nee, and *Soul And Spirit*, by Jessie Penn-Lewis. Over the next two days Elaine and I read aloud together through the entire book *The Latent Power Of The Soul*.

We both began to understand just what the strange power was that Elaine had used in addition to demons for so many years. Satan never teaches his people *what* they are using, just how to use the power within them. (The topic of the control of the human spirit by the soul will be explained more fully in chapter 14.) Elaine had been consciously controlling her spirit body.

As we learned about human spirits, I began to get to know many of the witches and warlocks of the area as various ones of them came into Elaine with their spirit body to try to kill both of us. One of the most troublesome of them was code-named David, the high priest of the large and powerful coven in the city in which we lived. He was a physician at the hospital where I was training and he told me that he had sworn to kill me at any cost. The human spirits were much more difficult to fight than the demons as they had no respect at all for God. I was reminded of James 2:19, "Even the devils believe and tremble." and of Jude 8-13:

> "Likewise also these filthy dreamers defile the flesh, despise dominion, and speak evil of dignities. Yet Michael the archangel when contending with the devil he disputed about the body of Moses, durst not bring against him a railing accusation, but said, 'The Lord rebuke thee.'
>
> But these speak evil of those thing which they know not; but what they know naturally as brute beasts, in

those things they corrupt themselves. Woe unto them!
. . . carried about of winds; trees whose fruit withereth,
without fruit, twice dead, plucked up by the roots;
raging waves of the sea foaming out their own shame;
wandering stars, to whom is reserved the blackness of
darkness for ever."

No matter how desperate the battle, the Lord always gave me the physical strength I needed. As we read and learned, the Lord began steadily impressing upon me that Elaine must give up entirely all of her ability to control her spirit body with her soul. He revealed to me that she had been using it to fight with all along. At last I began to understand what had been going on during her time as a patient at the hospital. She and the nurses had been having witchcraft duels under my nose and I hadn't known it. The pieces of the puzzle began to fit together. No wonder the nurses had all been so hostile. Elaine had been winning every time!

It was then that Elaine faced one of the severest tests of her commitment to Christ. The conscious control of her own spirit body not only permitted her to use it, but she was also able to see and communicate with the spirit world whenever she wanted. This, of course, permitted her to see by her spirit whenever an attack was coming. At the Lord's guidance I told her that I thought that the only way that the doorway for human spirits could be closed was for her to ask the Lord to take away all of her power and abilities of witchcraft and the control of her spirit body. To take it all away so completely that even if she were to rebel and decide to use it again that she would be unable to do so.

Elaine agonized over this decision for the better part of the day. She knew only too well that to give up all of her power left her completely defenseless against the many who were trying to torture and kill her. She would then be totally dependent upon the Lord. But her love for, and commitment to the Lord won through and that evening another big step was taken as Elaine and I knelt together and she prayed asking the Lord to take away all of her powers and to sever between her soul and spirit as in Hebrews 4:12.

That night another important lesson was learned. I had just drifted off to sleep when suddenly the Lord awakened me and I ran into the bedroom to find Elaine sitting up in bed under the control of a demon. The demon was pointing with hand and arm outstretched. As the Lord enabled me to hear his guttural, muttered words I was horrified to realize that he was using Elaine's spirit body and directing it at Sally in an effort to kill her. Immediately I reached over and passed my hand up and down in front of the demon's pointing finger saying:

"*NO* demon, I block you with the power of the name of Jesus! You no longer have any right to use Elaine's spirit because she has asked the Lord to seal it." How thankful I was that she had taken that important step. Otherwise the demon would have had legal right to use it.

Furious, he turned on me screaming in rage. "How dare you stop *me*! Her spirit belongs to me, I *will* use it as I please."

"No demon, you can't. It is now under the blood of Jesus and sealed off from anyone's use forever. Now go! I command you in the name of Jesus."

He drew back, eyes glaring pure hatred. "I, Yahshun, the prince will return again, I will kill you for what you have done tonight!" With those words he left.

As he left Elaine's body sagged against me, then she returned to consciousness. I told her of the incident and how Yahshun had been trying to use her spirit.

"Tell me, Elaine, did the demons use your spirit like that before you turned to Jesus?"

"Oh, yes, often. I could not stop them. I was disciplined many times for trying to do so. Yahshun is a very high demon. He and other demons like him use the spirits of cult members as they please. Often this results in much weakness and sickness for the person. Satan never asks, he just takes!"

Later that night I awakened abruptly as Elaine's hands, under the control of Yahshun, closed about my throat. (I was so exhausted I had just dropped off to sleep and had not heard Elaine come into the room.) I struggled frantically to loosen the steel-like fingers that were strangling me. The Lord gave me strength as I silently cried out to Him. Somehow, I managed to break his grip just before passing out from lack of oxygen. We rolled all over the bed and down onto the floor, locked in desperate battle. Waves of fear swept over me. Gasping for breath, I kept saying:

"I *will* defeat you in the name of Jesus. You *will* leave now!"

He fought desperately, cursing, and threatening. But I kept commanding him to go in the name and authority of Jesus and finally with one last enraged shriek he left. Instantly there was a great quietness and a peace in the room such as we had not experienced since the first appearance of the light-cylinder. As always, the Lord had given me the strength that I needed. But the wounds I had received took several weeks to heal. My larynx was damaged so that I had difficulty speaking for some weeks.

Again we both breathed a sigh of relief thinking that our troubles with the doorway for human spirits were over. How wrong we were. Over the next couple of days repeatedly the spirits of the various witches and warlocks came to torment us. After much prayer and searching we realized that there were three levels of the soul which controlled the spirit — the conscious, sub-conscious and a deep third unconscious level (these are, or course, the three levels in the mind). It is this third unconscious level that the demons make so much use of. Elaine had to ask the Lord to deal with all three levels of control of her spirit by her soul. As she did this she was sealed by the Lord. Neither she nor any demon or other person has been able to use her spirit body or enter her through that doorway from that day on.

During the course of our battling I became more and more aware not only of the spirit world but of God's angels as well. One night shortly after the struggle with Yahshun I was particularly ill and exhausted and much weaker than usual. The demons saw this and became much more aggressive in their physical attack. As one of the demons came to the surface, reaching for my throat, bragging that he was stronger than the rest, the Holy Spirit commanded me:

"Do not resist, I will take care of this one."

Immediately I obeyed, hoping fervently that I had heard the Lord correctly as the demon's hands, controlling Elaine's body, began to close about my neck. Suddenly, one-by-one, his fingers were pulled off my throat. Then his hands pulled away from me, pulled down, and his hands and arms crossed in front of him and held firm; rendering him helpless. I could not see the force holding the demon's hands, but he was obviously struggling with something, cursing loudly. As his arms were held firm despite all of his protests, he looked at me and snarled:

"Get those angels off of me, they are hurting me!"

With great joy I praised the Lord for His provision, and gleefully told the demon, "Oh, no, demon, they are not mine to command. Only the Lord gives them orders. If you want them to set you free, you must ask Jesus, not me."

That demon left almost at once. During the next several days I received help from the angels over and over again. Sometimes the demons would address the angels by name. Sometimes they would snarl an answer to a question that I could not hear with my physical ears, but had obviously come from one of the angels. More than once, a demon's hand would be stopped in mid-air as he tried to hit me. I received great comfort and encouragement from the realization that the angels were there.

One night about half-way through the eight-weeks of battling, a new direction was given to us by God. It was about 3 A.M. I had been battling with the demons in Elaine continuously since arriving home from work that afternoon. Exhausted, Elaine had just dropped off to sleep and I was sitting on the couch, knees drawn up, chin resting on my knees, arms about them, pondering the events of the battle of that night. The demons were becoming much stronger and harder to deal with and I was growing much weaker physically. I had been very concerned about this and had, for the past week been asking Father to reveal to me what else I could do to gain strength against the demons.

Suddenly, I felt a "presence" on the couch next to me although no sound had been made. I jumped and looked up. There on the couch next to me sat the tallest and most powerfully built young man I had ever seen. I knew immediately that this man was not a human.

He had shining golden hair, deep blue eyes and the most beautiful smile I have ever seen. He was clean shaven and deep creases slashed his cheeks as he smiled at me. He was dressed in shining white with a golden belt and a huge sword at his side. His tunic-like top was trimmed with gold braid which I had no doubt was made of pure gold. He also wore loose fitting white pants and golden sandals. His skin was bronzed as with a beautiful deep suntan. Light radiated from him with a power that I had never experienced. Immediately he spoke, saying:

"Women, I have a message for you from the Father."

Before he could say any more I interrupted him, not too politely, I'm afraid.

"**STOP**! Who are you?"

"I am your guardian angel."

I was impressed, not only by his size and shining white raiment, but also by a look of such purity in his eyes. However, the verse in II Corinthians 11:14 flashed into my mind:

> "And no marvel for Satan himself is transformed into an angel of light."

I also thought about the scripture verses in I John 4:1-3:

> "Beloved, believe not every spirit, but try the spirits whether they are of God: because many false prophets are gone out into the world. Hereby know ye the Spirit of God; every spirit that confesseth that Jesus Christ is come in the flesh is of God; and every spirit that confesseth not that Jesus Christ is come in the flesh is not of God . . ."

With these scriptures going through my mind I answered curtly:

"Yes, well, I've had demons try to tell me they were my guardians. **WHO** is your master? Whom do your serve?"

"I serve the Lord of Hosts."

"That's not good enough, Satan calls himself that!"

He smiled again and said, "I serve the Lord of Lords and King of Kings. Jesus Christ who was born of a virgin, came to earth in the flesh, died on the cross and rose from the grave three days later. This same Jesus who *is* God and now sits in heaven on the right hand of the Father, *this* Jesus is my Lord and master."

I was relieved, for I knew that he had passed the test given to us by the Lord in I John 4. I knew no demon would dare make such a declaration, Satan would tear him to shreds on the spot if he did.

"Oh, O.K., I'm sorry, but I had to be sure who you were. I was afraid you were a demon manifesting in such a form to try to deceive me."

He nodded, "Father sent me to tell you to be of good courage, do not be afraid or discouraged for we are with you protecting you every step of the way. The battle is going to become even more intense from this point on and Father says you must be sure to always put on the armor of God."

"Do you mean the armor of God spoken of in Ephesians chapter 6?"

"Yes, that is what I am referring to."

Ephesians 6:10-18 says:

"Finally, my brethren, be strong in the Lord, and in the power of his might. Put on the whole armor of God, that ye may be able to stand against the wiles of the devil. For we wrestle not against flesh and blood, but against principalities, against powers, against the rulers of the darkness of this world, against spiritual wickedness in high places. Wherefore take unto you the whole armor of God, that ye may be able to withstand in the evil day, and having done all, to stand. Stand therefore, having your loins girt about with truth, and having on the breastplate of righteousness; and your feet shod with the preparation of the gospel of peace; above all, taking the shield of faith, wherewith ye shall be able to quench all the fiery darts of the wicked. And take the helmet of salvation, and the sword of the Spirit, which is the word of God: Praying always with all prayer and supplication in the Spirit, and watching thereunto with all perseverance and supplication for all saints."

"But tell me," I asked, "how do I put this armor on?"

"Pray like this: 'Father, would you please put your complete armor on me now, I ask and thank you for it in the name of Jesus.'"

"How often should I ask for the armor?"

He sat looking upward for a few seconds, then nodded his head and turned back to me.

"Father says that once every 24 hours will be sufficient. Even as the Lord Jesus told you when He was here on earth that you must take up your cross daily, so must you put on the armor and prepare for battle daily. You **must** understand that this is very important. Don't forget to ask for it each day. If you don't have the armor on you will get hurt."

"But I don't understand, I can't see this armor, and the scripture sounds as if it is rather symbolic. Where does it go?"

"The armor of God goes on your spirit body. God's word plainly states that you are engaged in a spiritual battle, so the armor is also spiritual. You need to search your scriptures further on this."

(The following day, I found a much overlooked verse tucked away in I Corinthians 15:44 which says "There is a natural body, and there is a spiritual body.")

Then the angel's sober expression lightened. He said, "You always have so many questions, Father says you are permitted to ask me any questions you have, I will answer them."

Many questions were buzzing about in my head. But there was one thing that I longed to know most: "Tell me, what is Jesus really like? Please, can you tell me more about Him? I so long to know Him better."

The angel sat back, crossing his legs into a more relaxed position. "Well, Jesus is so beautiful! One flash of His smile lights up the whole universe with warmth and love. Jesus works so intensely and tirelessly for His church. No detail of the care of each one of His people is too small for His undivided attention. He is constantly at work both caring for His people and bringing others into His church. His glory extends out and out, through the whole universe and beyond. It never ends."

I sat pondering his words, trying to picture it all in my mind. "I have often wondered if Jesus' glory was something

126

like a beautiful sunrise. I mean, everything is dark, then the beautiful light and colors begin to creep up over the horizon. The light and colors grow and grow in brightness and beauty as the sun gets closer and closer to popping up over the horizon. Then as it does so, it is so brilliant and beautiful. Would the glory of Jesus be something like that as He would move toward you?"

"Yes, that's it exactly!"

We sat and talked for close to two hours. I will never forget that wonderful experience. The love of God radiated from this creature so strongly I gained a fresh understanding of just how much God loves us. The angel told me that the Lord cares so much for His children that every time one of them cries He sends an angel to hold that person in his arms and bring comfort to him. The people never realize this, of course, but it happens just the same.

The angel also told me that God has created all of his angels with so much love, that every person has a special guardian angel who guards him or her because he has so much love for that individual that he petitioned Father for the job of guarding him from his birth. I was reminded of Hebrews 1:13-14 which says:

> "But to which of the angels said he at any time, Sit on my right hand, until I make thine enemies thy footstool? Are they not all ministering spirits, sent forth to minister for them who shall be heirs of salvation?"

That night I learned in a new depth the meaning of the verse which says:

> "But as it is written, eye hath not seen, nor ear heard, neither have entered into the heart of man, the things which God hath prepared for them that love him. But God hath revealed them unto us by his Spirit: for the Spirit searcheth all things, yea, the deep things of God." I Corinthians 2:9

The angel had pointed out many scriptures to me which, as

127

I prayerfully studied them, revealed much more of the incredible plans God has for His people in the future.

The battle did get much more intense after that meeting with the angel, but I found that each day as I asked Father for the armor, I had more strength and did not suffer in my body so much as a result of the constant conflict with the demons.

During this time of battle I realized that I had reached the point where I no longer cared about possessions or for any of the social activities I used to enjoy. I was growing to be very different from the people around me. I could not share my experiences with anyone, except, occasionally Pastor Pat. I did not know of anyone else who would understand. I worried that I was not staying balanced. I took the problem to Father in prayer, pouring out my doubts and fears. I knew that I would never be smart enough to detect or figure out Satan's deceptions, I had to trust the Lord to show me if I was falling into a trap of Satan's.

At that point the Lord instructed me to read the first epistle of Peter. I must admit that I was rather disappointed as I didn't see how that could help, but, in obedience, I did what Father asked. As I read, the Lord opened a new understanding to me of those precious verses:

> " . . . to the strangers scattered throughout . . ."
> I Peter 1:1
> "Dearly beloved, I beseech you as strangers and pilgrims . . . . "
> I Peter 1:11

Then the Lord brought two other scriptures to my attention:

> "Blessed be the Lord my strength, which teacheth my hands to war, and my fingers to fight: My goodness, and my fortress; my high tower, and my deliverer; my shield, and he in whom I trust; who subdueth my people under me." Psalm 144:1-2
> "For our light affliction, which is but for a moment, worketh for us a far more exceeding and eternal

weight of glory; While we look not at the things which are seen, but at the things which are not seen: for the things which are seen are temporal; but the things which are not seen are eternal." II Corinthians 4:17-18

There is a price to be paid when we fix our eyes (or attention) on what is "unseen." We become aliens and strangers in this world. We do not really have a home here on earth. We will arrive home at last only when Jesus returns to take us home to live with Himself.

As the weeks went by I became increasingly concerned that the intense battle with the demons was destroying Elaine's body. I had many times asked Father how long this must go on and always His answer was, "Until you have learned enough." At last the day came when Father told me to contact Pastor Pat to arrange a time for Elaine's final deliverance. I did so, but did not tell Elaine. I knew that if I did, then the demons in her would hear and do all they could to hinder us.

As the day of Elaine's final deliverance approached both the demons and the spirits of the local witches and warlocks were becoming a greater and greater problem. We could not see them, so had no forewarning of their attacks. Elaine and I were constantly being picked up and thrown across the room, furniture and other objects were frequently being thrown at us — all by unseen beings. We were both bruised from head to toe because of their attacks.

At last the night before Elaine's final deliverance came. We were both completely exhausted and I was very worried as Elaine was also quite ill. We tried to lie down but continuously one or the other of us was pulled off our bed by an unseen spirit and thrown onto the floor or against the wall. There was a growing presence of evil in the house which weighed heavily on my spirit. Even the air seemed so thick with evil that it was difficult to breath.

Late that night I was sitting on the edge of Elaine's bed cradling her in my arms, desperately trying to hold her and shield her with my own body from the continuous attacks. She was so weak by then that she had no strength left to even try to resist the attacks. Tears streamed down my face as I cried out to the Lord for help.

"**FLEE!** " One word was suddenly flashed into my spirit and mind with great force. "**FLEE!** " Then the Lord flooded into my mind the scripture in Matthew chapter 2 where Joseph was instructed by an angel of the Lord in the middle of the night to take Mary and the infant Jesus and flee into Egypt. I knew then that I must take Elaine and run, or we would both be killed.

I asked the Lord to surround us so that the demons and human spirits could not see us leaving. Immediately my spiritual eyes were opened and I saw a ring of powerful warrior angels close about us. Elaine was barely conscious and completely unable to walk. I was not much stronger than she, but knew that we must be obedient to that urgent command. So, I stumbled off the bed with Elaine in my arms. As I began to fall under her weight I heard one of the angels snap a command and immediately two angels lifted us. They essentially carried us out to the car. They put Elaine in the passenger's seat and securely seat-belted her in, then carefully closed and locked the door. She was completely unconscious by then.

I was not sure where to go, so just started out. It was a beautiful clear night, the stars and moon were shining brightly. As I drove down the highway, the Lord permitted me to see through my spirit what was going on back at my house. The demons and human spirits were frantically going all through the house and yard searching for us. I praised the Lord for His goodness and mercy to us. Satan and his servants had no idea where we were. We were completely hidden! Then the Lord instructed me to go to my brother's house. We arrived about 3 A.M. and spent the rest of the night there.

The next morning, I again put Elaine in the car and headed for the church. About a half-mile from the church Elaine turned to me and said:

"Rebecca, you have not told me where we are going. Now please be honest and tell me what in the world is going on?"

"Well, we are headed for the church. Today is the day the Lord has chosen for your final deliverance."

"Great!" That was the only word Elaine managed to get out. Immediately the demons surfaced. They were raging, screaming mad. I was thankful that I had obeyed the Lord and had carefully seat-belted Elaine in and locked the door. Otherwise the demons would have thrown her out of the car. As we rounded the corner into the church drive their struggle to escape became frantic. But the Lord had everything well planned. As I pulled to a stop and turned to try to hang on to Elaine, my friend Judy, who was there to help us, walked quickly to my car, an open Bible in hand. She pulled open Elaine's door and said:

"Just listen to the scripture the Lord has given us for today:

'I will praise thee with my whole heart:
before the gods will I sing praise unto thee.
I will worship toward thy holy temple,
and praise thy name for thy lovingkindness and for thy truth:
for thou hast magnified thy word above all thy name.

'In the day when I cried thou answered me,
and strengthenedst me with strength in my soul.
All the kings of the earth shall praise thee, O Lord,
when they hear the words of thy mouth.
Yea, they shall sing in the ways of the Lord:
for great is the glory of the Lord.

'Though the Lord be high, yet hath he respect unto the lowly:
but the proud he knoweth afar off.
Though I walk in the midst of trouble, thou wilt revive me:
thou shalt stretch forth thine hand against the wrath of

mine enemies,
and thy right hand shall save me.

'The Lord will perfect that which concerneth me:
thy mercy, O Lord, endureth for ever:
Forsake not the works of thine own hands.'"

Psalm 138

As Judy read those beautiful words the demons in Elaine quieted down and came under control. Then Judy and I helped Elaine out of the car. As we came to the church door they began to struggle frantically again. But again, the Lord had everything in hand. Pastor Pat and the assistant pastor met us at the church door. The men each grabbed one of Elaine's arms.

"I see we have some very unhappy demons here," Pastor Pat exclaimed. "Now you demons shut-up and be still. We bind you in the name of Jesus!" If the Lord had not had the men at the door to help us, I doubt that Judy and I would have been strong enough to get Elaine down the hall to the Pastor's study. Immediately, when the five of us entered the study and the door was closed, the battle was on. It raged for the next ten hours. The demons were like caged wild animals and they fought desperately for they knew their final hour had come. But they didn't stand a chance for the power and the presence of the Lord was in that room in a remarkable way.

That day will always remain in my mind as one of the most beautiful experiences I have ever had. The Lord was in complete control and there was absolutely smooth coordination as He used first one of us, then another. We had not been able to completely deliver Elaine before because we did not know all the doorways to close. That day the Lord gave us revelation after revelation.

With a person deeply possessed as Elaine was, the demons must be cleaned out from the inside out. I have listed below the doorways in the order in which they must be closed. The Lord showed us that day, and in many many instances since then that it is much easier and more efficient to clean out a person by areas rather than going after specific demons. Also, in this way the deliverance workers control the demons instead of waiting to see what will manifest. The leader or head over each area is cast out along with all his subordinate demons at the same time. There are just too many demons to try to cast out each one individually — it would take far too much time, causing everyone involved to become too exhausted and discouraged. (For instance the demon Legion may have up to 4,000 subordinate demons with him. Our Lord Jesus set us the example of casting them all out at once in Luke chapter 8.)

1) In most persons involved deeply in the occult there is a doorway for Satan himself. This innermost doorway is held open by a very high demon who refers to himself as a "son of Satan." (Note: this title will change with different geographical areas, and the specific names of these demons also change, and are too numerous to try to list. Specifying the demon by his function will be sufficient to establish authority over him.) This doorway permits Satan himself to enter a person and speak and act through their body at will.

2) The next is the area of the *human spirit*. There is one high demon over the entire spirit. This demon is frequently called a "guiding spirit" but may take different titles in various areas. Mann-Chan was Elaine's guiding spirit. Then there are three areas within the spirit itself, each area has a head demon with many lesser demons under his command. The three areas in the spirit are:

> *conscience* — the ability to discern right and wrong
> *intuition* — the ability to discern the Lord and sense His presence
> *worship* — the area through which we worship the Lord "in spirit" as in John 4:23: "But the hour cometh, and now is, when the true worshipers shall

worship the Father in spirit and in truth..."

3) The *soul* has several areas. The head demon over the entire area of the soul usually refers to himself as a "power" demon. These power demons will be discussed at some length in chapter 14 where we deal with the topic of the soul-controlled spirit. There are 6 areas within the soul. The first 3 have to do with controlling the spirit:

   conscious
   sub-conscious
   unconscious

   Then there are 3 other areas:

   will
   mind
   emotions

   Again, each has a head demon with underlings.

4) Last is the physical *body*. The head demon over the body is usually a "death demon" such as Yaagog. They are powerful and quite capable of bringing about the physical death of the person they inhabit through illness within a very short time if not restrained by the Lord. The areas within the body are:

   brain — meaning the physical organ
   the rest of the *physical body* itself
   sexual — the head demon in that area holds open the door which gives Satan the legal right to have sexual relations with the person, also other demons as well.

There are many scriptures that refer to and confirm the above areas. Time and space does not permit the listing of them all. The one that was the most important to us was:

"And the very God of peace sanctify you wholly; and I pray God your whole spirit and soul and body be pre-

134

served blameless unto the coming of our Lord Jesus
Christic."   I Thessalonians 5:23

If you have further questions about these areas I would
strongly recommend that you read the book *The Spiritual
Man* by Watchman Nee which gives excellent scriptural
references and an explanation of these areas.

The assistant pastor had never experienced a deliverance
session before and had not known about this one until an
hour or so before it started. I was most amused when,
about half way through, as we stopped for a short break, he
made the comment:

"You know, all this makes mowing the grass seem awfully
mundane somehow!" Then he went on to tell us about a remarkable experience he had had the evening before. It was
fairly late and he was sitting in his study at the church reading when:

"Suddenly the Holy Spirit pulled the book out of my hands
and threw my hands up in the air and commanded me to
stand up. As I did so, He told me to get a bottle of oil and
go to the Pastor's study. I was the only person in the church
at the time. The Holy Spirit then instructed me to close and
lock the doors and anoint the door posts and lintels, then
the doors themselves, then all the windows, in the name of
the Father, Son and Holy Spirit, and to ask the Lord to seal
this room. I did so but had no idea why. This room remained closed and sealed until we entered it this morning."

We all praised the Lord for His provision. The sealing of
that room was to provide protection from any outside interference during Elaine's deliverance.

In all, the battle lasted over ten hours. What a time of
praise and rejoicing we had at the end! Once again, the Lord
had remained faithful to His word, and had **SET THE CAP-
TIVE FREE**. From that day on Elaine has remained clear
and free from demons. We cannot praise and thank the
Lord enough for her wonderful deliverance!

CHAPTER 13

Doorways

REBECCA TALKS:

The scriptures are very plain. *Any* dealing with Satan opens a doorway in a person's life for the inflow of Satanic power and/or demon infestation. Whether the person is a Christian or a non-Christian makes no difference. Leviticus 19:31 states, "Regard not them that have familiar spirits, neither seek after wizards, *to be defiled by them:* I am the Lord your God."

Although The Brotherhood is a very strong and fast growing cult, they are but a handful compared to the vast numbers held in bondage by peripheral involvement in the occult and other sins which have opened up their lives to Satan's power. These doorways (created by sin) give Satan legal ground, according to God's word (the Bible), to exert his power in their lives. Christians are not protected because the opening of these doorways involves their conscious participation in sin and/or ignorance.

> "What then? shall we sin because we are not under the law, but under grace? God forbid. Know ye not, that to whom ye yield yourselves servants to obey, his servants ye are to whom ye obey; whether of sin unto death, or of obedience unto righteousness?"
>
> Romans 6:15-16

> "My people are destroyed for lack of knowledge ... "
>
> Hosea 4:6

Not only does every person need to be aware of these areas

of influence in his own life, but also anyone who desires to share the glorious gospel of Jesus Christ with others. Many, many are not able to accept Christ when He is presented to them because their *will* and *mind* is literally bound by the dark powers through some opened doorway in their lives either currently or in the past.

> "But if our gospel be hid, it is hid to them that are lost:
> In whom the god of this world hath blinded the minds
> of them which believe not, lest the light of the glorious
> gospel of Christ, who is the image of God, should
> shine unto them."   II Corinthians 4:3-4

Any dealings with the occult, no matter how lightly or briefly, is a doorway. I am referring to such things as playing with your horoscope, the curiosity visit to a fortune teller, tea leaf reader, palm reader, etc. How many of our school and church carnivals for fund raising have a fortune teller of some sort? *None* of these are harmless! Innocent young children are allowed to go to these people at such events for "something fun to do." How many of these children are then unable in their future life to ever accept Jesus as their personal Savior, or, if they are already a Christian, at some later date lose interest, or are just unable to grow to any depth in their Christianity? We would be appalled if we really knew the number of casualties from this source alone. I have personally seen more than I like to even think about. Again, the scriptures could not be more plain:

> "There shall not be found among you any one that
> maketh his son or his daughter to pass through the fire
> [a form of human sacrifice to a demon], or that useth
> divination, or an observer of times, or an enchanter,
> or a witch, or a charmer, or a consulter with familiar
> spirits, or a wizard, or a necromancer. For all that do
> these things are an abomination unto the Lord: and be-
> cause of these abominations the Lord thy God doth
> drive them out from before thee."
>   Deuteronomy 18:10-12.

Just one visit to a seance out of curiosity is enough to affect the rest of your life. So is studying books on the occult arts, playing with an ouiji board, trying out ESP, psychic experiences, astral projection, meditation of *any* kind that involves blanking out or "clearing" the mind, water witching, or divining for oil or minerals by using a dowsing rod or pendulum. Equally dangerous is participation in magic of *any* kind, using the art of levitation, i.e. movement of objects without touching that object physically, consulting a medium or spiritist in an attempt to locate some missing object, practice of any of the martial arts or yoga. And, of course, *any* practice of witchcraft through spells or incantations, etc. Any of this *will* open a doorway to the inflow of Satanic power and demons.

Any use of, or abuse of street drugs, or repeated drunkenness are also doorways. Child abuse almost always results in demonic infestation. That is why abused children, unless delivered, usually turn out to be child-abusing parents. Any incident of severe emotional and/or physical trauma may serve as a temporary breakdown in the defenses permitting the entrance of demonic spirits. This may occur in both children and adults.

Sexual intercourse is another big doorway. Demons *are* passed from one person to another through sexual intercourse. This is because the two people involved become "one flesh."

> "What? know ye not that he which is joined to an harlot is one body? for two, saith he, shall be one flesh ... Flee fornication. Every sin that a man doeth is without the body; but he that commiteth fornication sinneth against his own body." I Corinthians 6:16 & 18

The word *fornication* means any sexual intercourse between a man and woman who are not married to each other. (Definition from *Vine's Expository Dictionary of New Testament Words,* p. 465.)

This is why God has given His people so many commands not to have sexual intercourse between anyone who is not man and wife. It is for our protection from this source of demonic infestation. Rape and violent sexual assault, particularly in children, is a doorway that I have come across

138

repeatedly in my medical practice. This results in the demonic entrance of some of the strongest demons that I have ever met. Incest within a family and any participation in homosexuality always leads to demonic infestation. Also any of the corrupt sexual practices condemned in the Bible and used in the pornography of today.

I have frequently been asked about problems arising from sexual intercourse between a man and wife when one of the spouses is unsaved and participating in blatant sin. In these cases, I firmly believe that the believing spouse can stand on the promise given in I Corinthians 7:12-16:

> "If any brother hath a wife that believeth not, and she be pleased to dwell with him, let him not put her away. And the woman which hath an husband that believeth not, and if he be pleased to dwell with her, let her not leave him. For the unbelieving husband is sanctified by the wife, and the unbelieving wife is sanctified by the husband: else were your children unclean; but now are they holy. But if the unbelieving depart, let him depart. A brother or a sister is not under bondage in such cases: but God hath called us to peace. For what knowest thou, O wife, whether thou shalt save thy husband? or how knowest thou, O man, whether thou shalt save thy wife?"

In such cases, the Christian spouse need only ask the Lord to sanctify their marriage bed and their unbelieving spouse and close that doorway with the blood of Jesus so that the believing spouse will not become infested with demons from the other through their sexual intercourse.

Hypnosis is another big doorway. The person being hypnotized must so subject his or her will to the hypnotist that he then becomes open to anything the hypnotist chooses to put into him. There are specific demons that hold open the doors for the on-going influence of the hypnotist. Hypnosis to stop smoking or control eating to lose weight is a demonic healing.

Acupuncture also is a form of demonic healing. The Eastern

religions are **all** various forms of demon worship. The public does not know that the needles used in acupuncture are blessed by various leaders of the Eastern religions before use and therefore are direct doorways for demonic entrance. I have seen a number of really strange infections coming from the needles of acupuncturists as well as demonic infestation. Any supernatural healing other than that which comes directly from Jesus Christ himself, is demonic healing and results in demonic infestation and/or bondage. God himself gave men the gift of the knowledge used by our medical doctors today. Remember that Luke, who wrote two books of the New Testament, was himself a physician.

Any involvement in the Eastern religions such as T.M. (Transcendental Meditation), Yoga, etc., will result in demonic infestation and/or bondage. Careful study comparing the teachings of any cult with God's word will quickly show their errors.

Most of the Eastern religions involve meditation. The topic of meditation is much misunderstood by most Christians and Satan has authored much deceptive literature on meditation posing as Christian literature. There are a number of references in scripture to meditation, but there is a big difference between Godly meditation and Satanic meditation. I think it would be well to point out the basic principles here.

One of the major scripture references to meditation is found in Joshua 1:8:

> "This book of the law shall not depart out of thy mouth; but thou shalt meditate therein day and night, that thou mayest observe to do according to all that is written therein: for then thou shalt make thy way prosperous, and then thou shalt have good success."

I wish to emphasize that the meditation referred to in this scripture involved the **active** reading, learning and memorizing of God's law given to the Israelites. Joshua was to learn the law so well that it would become a part of him. David followed the same principle — he wrote about it in Psalm 119:9-11:

> "Wherewithal shall a young man cleanse his way? By taking **heed** thereto according to thy word. With my whole heart have I sought thee: O let me not wander from thy commandments. Thy word have I hid in mine heart, that I might not sin against thee."

Here again David was *actively* doing something — that is, learning and memorizing God's law so that he would not depart from it. At no time in scripture is meditation something *passive*. Satanic meditation is *passive*. Satan wants men to blank out their minds, attempt to clear their minds of all thoughts. This directly opens a door for demonic entrance and influence, because the simple fact is that God commands us to *control our every thought, not blank out our minds!* If *you* don't control your mind, *Satan will.*

> "For though we walk in the flesh, we do not war after the flesh: For the weapons of our warfare are not carnal, but mighty through God to the pulling down of strong holds; *casting down imaginations,* and every high thing [thoughts, in other translations] that exalteth itself against the knowledge of God, and bringing into captivity *every thought* to the obedience of Christ." II Corinthians 10:3-5

> "Thou wilt keep him in perfect peace, whose *mind* is stayed on thee ..." Isaiah 26:3

This scripture clearly demonstrates that we are commanded to *control* our minds, *not blank* them out. *Any* teaching about meditation that tells you to blank out your mind and clear it of all thoughts, or to repeat certain phrases over and over again to enable you to "clear your mind" *is from Satan.*

> "[Jesus speaking] But when ye pray, use not vain repetitions, as the heathen do ... " Matthew 6:7

> "But shun profane and vain babblings: for they will increase unto more ungodliness." II Timothy 2:16

There is a dangerous teaching in some charismatic churches where members are told to repeat a certain phrase over and over, or to "blank out their minds and let the Holy Spirit take over." (This is especially done in reference to an effort to get someone to speak in tongues.) Any blank mind will be taken over by a spirit alright, but unfortunately, an unholy spirit *not* the Holy Spirit.

Another form of occult bondage that is very real, but little recognized, is the placing of a "hex" or "spell" or "voodoo" upon a person by another person. Even a Christian can be terribly damaged by witchcraft of this sort directed toward them. My own experience is a good example of this. I was unaware of what was happening until the Lord gave my pastor the revelation. I have since come across many patients afflicted in this way. Often, they knew a person, or had a person involved in the occult as a friend; then had a quarrel with that person, never suspecting that as an act of vengeance a "hex" or "spell" was sent their way. For this reason it is imperative that Christians walk closely enough with the Lord that He can give them discernment in such cases.

Demons and demonic bondage are inherited. The doorway of inheritance is an often overlooked one. Although we are no longer under the old law because of the new covenant in Christ's blood, we can find some very important principles by studying the Old Testament. We must also bear in mind that any sin not brought under Christ's blood by us *is* legal ground for Satan.

There are many references in the Old Testament to the sins of the fathers being passed down to the sons. Some are found in Exodus 20:5, 34:7, Numbers 14:18 and Deuteronomy 5:9. Exodus 34:6-7 says:

> "And the Lord passed by before him, and proclaimed, The Lord, The Lord God, merciful and gracious, longsuffering, and abundant in goodness and truth, keeping mercy for thousands, forgiving iniquity and

142

transgression and sin, and that will by no means clear the guilty; visiting the iniquity of the fathers upon the children, and upon the children's children, unto the third and to the fourth generation."

We also find that every time there was a major revival in Israel, the people came together in fasting and prayer not only to confess their own sins, but the sins of their fathers also. For example, Nehemiah 9:1-2:

"Now in the twenty and fourth day of this month the children of Israel were assembled with fasting, and with sackclothes, and earth upon them. And the seed of Israel separated themselves from all strangers, and stood and confessed their sins, and the iniquities [sins or evil deeds] of their fathers."

Other references are II Chronicles 29:1-11 during the reign of King Hezekiah, II Chronicles 34: 19-21, and many other references as well.

The sins of our ancestors *do* have a grave effect on our own lives and the doorway of inheritance must be closed by prayer, confession, and the cleansing power of the blood of Jesus Christ. Specific abilities and demons are passed down from generation to generation. A commonly accepted example of this is the ability to "water-witch." Especially damaging is any involvement in the occult, any idol worship which is really demon worship (I Corinthians 10:14-21), any demonic infestation, any oaths taken by parents or ancestors which are binding upon descendants (as are most occult, pagan, Morman, Masonic oaths) etc.

One of Satan's biggest tools in our country today is the occultic role-playing fantasy games which have become so popular. Satan is using these games to produce a vast army of the most intelligent young people of this country; an army that the Anti-Christ will be able to tap into and control in an instant. Through their involvement in these games, people can be controlled demonically without them ever realizing what is happening. In many states such games are used as a part of the school curriculum for the more intelligent students. Almost every school has extracurricular clubs formed to play the games. In essence, such games are crash courses in witchcraft. Unfortunately the participants usually do not realize this until it is too late.

Most games have a leader who plans the over-all outline for each game. The game is an adventure in which many battles are fought with various "monsters" and "beings," each one having certain abilities and characteristics. There are numerous thick manuals available with pictures and many details about the abilities of the various characters. The players are supposed to "visualize" the action of the game in their minds. The better they become at "seeing" the action and therefore anticipating the moves of the various "monsters" and the other players, the more advanced they become in the game.

What people don't realize at first is that these monsters are actually real demons. What they think they are visualizing in their minds, they are in actuality beginning to see in the spirit world. The better they become at "seeing" the game, the more in-tune they are with the spirit world. The imagination is a key stepping stone to contact with the spirit world. I do not know at what point the players become infested with demons, but I have worked with many young people involved in the games and I have yet to meet anyone on the level of a game leader who was not indwelt by demons and *knew it.* They will, of course, lie about this. A number have told me that the demons would come and talk to them, and, to gain more power, they invite the more intelligent of the demons to come into them.

The more advanced manuals detail spells, incantations, and satanic writing that is used and taught to the witches and warlocks of The Brotherhood itself. All who play the games feel the strange fascination and power of them. Few realize what a trap it is, they are completely deceived. How many of our young people who were once active and enthusiastic

144

Christians have lost interest in the Lord as a result of playing this type of game? Untold numbers more will never come to a saving knowledge of Jesus because of the demonic bondage they have come under by playing these games.

Occultic influences are rampant in toys for small children as well as the cartoons on TV. Small children are naturally very imaginative. Satan knows that if he can direct their imagination to the spirit world they will quickly learn to see and communicate with his demons. Parents need to be extremely careful what toys they permit their little ones to play with, and what cartoons they permit them to watch on TV.

Biofeedback has literally exploded onto the medical scene within the last few years. Its growth has been phenomenal. It is used mainly for pain control, blood pressure control and to control drug and alcohol abuse. The Brotherhood used biofeedback for many, many years before it ever came into public use. They found that it was the most rapid method of training witches to gain conscious control of their spirit bodies and thereby to contact the spirit world. In essence, biofeedback trains a person to control those bodily functions and areas God has not ordained that we should control. It teaches him to consciously control his spirit body, which then controls and alters what is happening in his physical body. Again, very few people entering such programs ever realize what they are becoming involved in. Christians should *never* have anything to do with biofeedback. It is nothing more than modernized Yoga, satanic meditation and witchcraft.

Another area often overlooked, but very powerful, is that of rock music. Rock music is Satan's music. Like so many other things, the whole movement of rock music was carefully planned and carried out by Satan and his servants from its very beginning. Rock music didn't "just happen," it was a carefully masterminded plan by none other than Satan himself.

As mentioned earlier in the book, Elaine has personally met a great number of the rock stars. They have *all* agreed to serve Satan in return for money and fame. They have received all they wanted, but also much they didn't expect. Their very lives and souls are destroyed. These rock stars *know* exactly what they are doing. They are, step by step, teaching untold millions of young people to worship and serve Satan.

Elaine attended special ceremonies at various recording studios throughout the U.S. for the specific purpose of placing satanic blessings on the rock music recorded. She and others did incantations which placed demons on EVERY record and tape of rock music sold. At times they also called up special demons who spoke on the recordings — especially in the various backmasked messages. *Also*, in many, many of the recordings, the satanists themselves were recorded in the background (masked by the over-all noise of the music) doing chants and incantations to summon up more demons every time one of the records or tapes or videos is played. As the music is played, these demons are called into the room to afflict the person playing the music and anyone else who is listening.

The purpose of all of this? *Mind control!* Mind control not only to give the listeners understanding of the messages about Satan conveyed to them by the music, but also to prevent them from recognizing their need for Jesus and the salvation He died on the cross to give us.

Many of the song lyrics are themselves actual incantations calling up demons when the song is sung. The purpose of this is two fold: to exert control over the listener and to provide the listener with actual incantations he or she can use to send demons upon another person. This is done to gain revenge by afflicting them with illness, accidents, etc. and also to help influence another person into the bondage of rock music itself.

146

We highly recommend the book *The Devil's Disciples — The Truth About Rock*, by Jeff Godwin, published by Chick Publications, Inc., for an in-depth study of rock music. This book is an excellent tool for parents to use to gain an understanding of the rock music their children are involved in.

All these doorways must be closed.

> "If we confess our sins, he is faithful and just to forgive us our sins, and to cleanse us from all unrighteousness."
> I John 1:9.

If you have participated in any of these things you can simply close the door by a prayer such as the following:

> "Father, I confess to you my involvement in _____ . I recognize that such a thing(s) is an abomination to you and detestable in your sight. I humbly ask your forgiveness for my sin in this area(s). I ask you to lift out any demonic entrance as the result of my actions and to cleanse me from my sins and close the doorway(s) forever with the precious blood of Jesus. I ask for this and thank you for it, in Jesus' name ."

Then I recommend that you address Satan and his demons out loud in a manner similar to the following:

> "Satan and you demons, I have asked my heavenly Father for forgiveness for participating in _____ and have received it. I now by faith close the doorway of that area of my life to you forever through the blood of Jesus Christ shed on the cross for me. In the name of Jesus I command you to go away!"

Cases of infestation with the stronger demons will often need to have help from another person or persons for deliverance. If you pray earnestly and desire deliverance regardless of the cost, the Lord will instruct you as to what you need to do, and He *will* set the captive free.

I will give some examples of people whom I have dealt with in my medical practice who have been terribly affected by the opening of such doorways. All names have been changed to protect those involved. We Christians must understand an important principle that I have never heard clearly taught in any church. Many of the people with whom we share the gospel are literally bound by demonic spirits, either from within or without, so that their wills are not free. They cannot will to accept Jesus as their Savior and their minds are similarly bound so that they cannot understand the gospel message.

> "But if our gospel be hid, it is hid to them that are lost: In whom the god of this world hath blinded the minds of them which believe not, lest the light of the glorious gospel of Christ, who is the image of God, should shine unto them."   II Corinthians 4:3-4

These people will not tell you that they are bound, indeed, the binding is so complete, that in most cases they don't even know that they are bound. The excuses you will hear when you directly ask someone if they will pray with you to accept Jesus are: "I'm not ready yet," or "I'll do it later," or "I just can't right now, don't push me," and many, many more.

But Jesus came to set the captives free.

> "The Spirit of the Lord God is upon me; . . . to proclaim liberty to the captives, and the opening of the prison to them that are bound."   Isaiah 61:1

We Christians need simply to take that power and authority that Jesus has given to us and use it to set such captives free. The following are some examples from my own experience.

1)   Jane is a 35 year old nurse from my home town. I worked with her about 10 years before when I was myself still a nurse. I ran into her again some time ago. She was amazed by the change she saw in me and as a result I was able to sit down one afternoon and share with her what the Lord had done in my life. Her response was:

"You know, I have had two other friends over the past five years who also committed their lives to Christ and changed dramatically from being dissatisfied and unhappy to joyful and filled with peace. I have often thought I would like to do the same, but I just can't, so I don't think about it anymore."

"Why can't you commit your life to Christ?" I asked.

"Well, I can see the benefits, but I just can't. In fact, I find myself getting very anxious and restless as we talk about it. I think we had better stop now, I don't want to talk about it anymore."

Not long before I would have stopped there. But, praise the Lord, thanks to His training, I easily recognized all the symptoms. So I persisted.

"Let me ask just one more question — when you try to think about Jesus, is it kind of like you run up against a blank wall and it becomes such an effort to continue thinking about it that you just give up?"

"Yes that's it! How did you know?"

"Well, I have been in God's training school. Tell me, what occult activities have you been involved in?" She reacted with shocked surprise.

"How did you know about that? I haven't done much, but I did visit a palm reader about eight years ago just for kicks. I've been back to palm readers and fortune tellers several times since then and recently have been doing my horoscope. But nothing really serious."

"Well, Jane, that 'superficial' involvement in the occult has been enough to put you into demonic bondage so that you can't accept Jesus. But I have good news for you. Jesus came to set the captives free and because I am His, He has given me His power and authority over Satan and his demons. Now, you demons who are binding and blinding Jane, I bind you right now in the name of Jesus, you may no longer operate in her life!"

Jane looked startled as if she wondered if I had taken leave of my senses. But I merely changed the subject and talked about something else for about 10 minutes. Then I asked:

"Jane, I asked you once before about accepting Jesus as your Lord and Savior awhile ago. You know that's what you need to do, how about praying with me now?"

She looked surprised, then relief flooded over her face.

"You know, I would like to pray with you now. I *can* accept Jesus. I don't know why I didn't do so earlier."

We both knelt down together, and another captive was released from Satan's kingdom of darkness and entered into God's kingdom. I then told her about the doorways she had opened, and she prayed and closed them to Satan forever with the precious blood of Jesus.

2)   A 20 year old girl came into the emergency room where I was working one evening. Her complaint was that she was afraid that if she didn't get help she would commit suicide. She was depressed and afraid, she felt as if she had nothing left to live for, her life was empty and without meaning. After talking with her for awhile I told her plainly that what she needed was Jesus Christ and shared the gospel with her. She responded, "My parents are Christians and I was raised in a church. I know that what you say is true, but I'm just not ready for that yet."

"You demons binding this girl, I bind *you* now in the name of Jesus, you may no longer operate in her life!" As I said this she looked at me as if I were crazy, but quickly forgot about it as I changed the subject and talked about something else for a few minutes. Then:

"Susy, you just admitted a few minutes ago that you knew that what I was saying was the truth, that you need Jesus in your life. How about praying with me now and asking Him to become your Lord and Savior and Master?"

"Yes, I'd like to do that. No one really asked me to do so before. Will you help me? I don't know what to say."

So Susy prayed with me and started on the road to eternal life. On further gentle questioning I discovered that the doorway opened in her life had been a brief, one weekend experimentation with street drugs at the age of 13 at a slumber party. That's all it took to bind her mind demonically. From the way she described her life I have no doubt that prior to the time I met her she had had many opportunities given to her to accept Jesus but was bound from doing so.

3)   An 80 year old man was admitted to the intensive care unit with a very severe heart attack during the time I was the medical resident in charge of the unit. After examining him I knew he probably wouldn't live for very long. He asked me how he was doing and I told him that he wasn't doing very well that he had had a very severe heart attack. He turned away and started to cry. The conversation went as follows:

"Oh doctor, please don't tell me that, I can't take it!"

"Sir, what is the matter, are you afraid to die?"

"Yes."

"Do you know what will happen to you after you die?"

"Yes young lady, I'm going straight to hell!"

I was most surprised, as very few people are so straight forward. "Please, Sir, let me tell you how you can avoid going to hell."

"NO, NO! I've heard it all before and it does no good. Don't bother."

"Well, want to or not, you ARE going to hear about Jesus one more time." I then shared the gospel in about four sentences. Brevity is a must in such situations.

"I know it all, I know that's right, but I just can't."

"Sir, just repeat three words after me: Jesus save me."

"I can't, I can't. Go away!"

"Sir, I know that you are being blocked, you're right, you can't say those words. Tell me, do you know who is blocking you?"

At this point he turned and looked me straight in the eye and said, "Satan and his demons!"

"I have good news for you. Jesus came to set the captive free and you surely are a captive. But I am a child of the King and I have been given His authority over Satan and the demons."

I then, out loud, addressed Satan and his demons and in the name of Jesus bound them. I will never forget the joy that came over that old man's face. He took my hand and tears streamed down our faces as he prayed to Jesus asking Him to be his Lord and Savior. I could see the peace spread over him. He looked up and said, "Young lady, I have been longing and searching and wanting to come to Jesus for 50 years, but could not."

As I talked to him for awhile he told me that at about the age of 30 he was working as a sailor. His ship stopped in the Philippines for awhile and during shore leave he had become involved in an argument with some of the local people. They had placed a voodoo curse on him with the result that he had been seeking Jesus for fifty long years, but was bound from accepting him because no one he had talked with knew to make use of the tremendous power and authority Jesus has given to us or to recognize what had happened to him. The next day when I went in to see him he was much worse physically but he was radiant. His last words to me were: "Young lady, I have perfect peace." He went into a coma and died shortly after that.

 # 4)   A 44 year old woman was brought to my office by her friends because she was on the verge of committing suicide. Her friends brought her to me because they knew that I was a Christian physician and they hoped that perhaps I could help her. Her story was no different than so many I have heard. She was born to Christian parents who loved her and she knew that they did. But somehow, in her teens, her life began to go wrong. She began to run around with the wrong crowd at school, getting into all kinds of illicit sexual relationships. She remarked:

"I knew that what I was doing was wrong and deep down I really didn't want to do those things but I couldn't seem to help myself. I had been raised in church and I knew what was right and wrong. I never seemed to be able to bring myself to actually accept Jesus and commit my life to Him as my brothers and sisters did — I never knew why, I just wasn't ready I guess."

By the time she was 17 she had already had a baby out of wedlock which her parents made her give up for adoption. Later that year she nearly succeeded in committing suicide and spent three months in a psychiatric hospital. The rest of her life had been spent in and out of psychiatric institutions, going to numerous psychiatrists and psychologists, taking innumerable drugs and tranquilizers. Nothing helped. She was unable to make any stable relationships or experience any love. She had a second child out of wedlock and ran away from home at the age of 19, fearing that her parents would make her give the second child up for adoption also. Finally, two years before she came to see me, she started attending a church and eventually accepted Jesus. Life improved then over the next year. She stopped drinking, and was able to hold a steady job. She found true Christian friends who spent much time with her, helping her to change and clean up her life. Her joy was reading the Bible and praying. Then suddenly one day:

"I felt as if someone had slammed a door shut and all was darkness. I could no longer read the Bible or pray. I could no longer sense the Lord's presence. I was in great distress. I kept going to church because I knew that that was the only answer. I no longer had any joy. I have talked to many ministers who all told me that there must be some unconfessed sin in my life or that the Lord is putting me through a test. But I know that I'm being destroyed. I no longer have any desire to go on living. The only way out for me is suicide."

I asked her if she had ever felt as if there was something inside of her that was not her, but that controlled her actions and often her thoughts. She brightened.

"Oh yes, I often have. I really think that there *is* something inside of me that isn't me. I have asked several ministers if I could have a demon but they told me that 'Christians can't have demons.' I guess I'm just crazy anyway. The psychiatrists told me that I was schizophrenic when I tried to tell them about this 'thing.'"

Alas, how ignorant so many people are! Sarah did indeed have a demon in her, a very powerful one with many lesser demons under him. The Lord instructed me to search for the key, the doorway that had been opened to the demon. At the Lord's leading I asked Sarah if she remembered any incident from her early childhood that was very traumatic for her. After thinking a few moments she said:

"You know, it's funny that you ask such a question. I do vaguely remember that my mother mentioned to me once that I was raped when I was a little girl. She would never talk to me about it, said it was best forgotten. I remember a man grabbing me and throwing me to the ground, but all I remember is lying on the ground looking up into a beautiful flowering crab tree. I don't remember anything else about the incident."

That was the doorway. The demon which entered into her while she was being raped had remained in her undetected for many, many years and had destroyed her life. He was of a particular class which I will discuss later, that can inhabit body, soul, and spirit, all at the same time. He has thousands of tentacles which he winds and entwines deep down into each area. He it was who slammed shut the door in her spirit so that she could no longer sense God's presence. The growth and take-over of the Holy Spirit was something that he could not tolerate so he tried to turn Sarah away from her commitment to the Lord.

But the Lord had held onto Sarah and over the next two hours, that demon and many others which were his subordinates, were cast out. At last, after many, many years, Sarah was set free. Again she experienced the sense in her spirit of the Lord's presence, read His word joyfully and for the first time in her life, began to live a normal, healthy life and experience the love of Jesus Christ our Lord. I was again reminded of Hosea 4:6 which says, "My people are destroyed for lack of knowledge . . . "

5)   A well built, 35 year old man came to my office with the following complaint:

"My life is being destroyed, it is falling in pieces around me. I can't put my finger on any particular thing, but I know it is happening. I am dying."

I talked with him and questioned him for over an hour seeking the key. His health was excellent. He had no medical problems, did not feel ill in any way. He was a Christian, although he did not have a deep walk with the Lord. His marriage was happy, his children well, his relationship with his entire family good. He had a good job in which he was happy. Finally, as I questioned him about every body system he said:

"I did used to have trouble with my sinuses until about

155

three years ago, but haven't had any since."

Interestingly, he had told me that it was over the last three years that he had had the feeling that his life was falling apart.

"What happened three years ago to cure your sinuses?"

"Oh, I went to Dr._____, and had acupuncture. It really worked. I've had no trouble since."

That was the key! During the physical examination I ran an electrocardiogram (EKG) on him. While the EKG machine was tracing out his heart beat, I suddenly felt an overwhelming presence of evil in the room. Immediately the young man's heart stopped! I wasn't exactly sure what I was dealing with, but I rebuked the evil in the name of Jesus and his heart spontaneously started beating again. His heart had stopped beating for over one full minute! Afterwards the Lord revealed to me that the evil I had felt was the spirit of the acupuncturist. He was drawing strength from the patient, even to the extent of stopping his heart briefly. The Lord had allowed this to happen at that particular time for my instruction. Demonic doors had been left in this young man through the acupuncture needles to leave him open to the control of the acupuncturist similar to a hypnotist. The acupuncturist was drawing strength from this young man for his own use. That is why he had the feeling his life was being destroyed. It was! I could not tell him what was happening. He would have thought I was crazy. He was a superficial Christian, not yet ready to accept the fact that demons even existed. I asked the Lord what I could do in such a situation.

"Use the most powerful tool you have," was His answer, "pray mightily for that young man."

Over the next year I fasted and prayed for that young man many times. Finally after a year the Lord spoke to me one day and told me that in response to my prayers He had delivered him without him ever knowing what had happened. Shortly after that I saw him again for a minor problem and he told me that he was feeling much better. Again, Jesus had set the captive free!

 # 6)   A 24 year old young man came under my care because he had tried to commit suicide. Rick had been raised in a Christian home in a loving family. He fully committed his life to Jesus during his teens and had had a very close walk with the Lord, hearing Him speak to him in his spirit. He was a very intelligent young man and after college had entered graduate school at a seminary to become a minister. The Lord was the joy of his life.

Suddenly, about a year before I first met him, he was no longer able to commune with the Lord. He found it almost impossible to read his Bible or pray and was completely unable to sense the Lord's presence. He counseled and prayed with a number of people but received no help. He began to have much difficulty concentrating on any of his studies and his grades fell drastically. He finally became so despairing that he had dropped out of school entirely about a month before the suicide attempt. He felt he had nothing left to live for.

I questioned him, trying to find the doorway. Finally, as I asked him to tell me about everything he had done shortly before the trouble began, he related the following story to me.

"Shortly before school started in the fall a year ago, I drove out to Denver, Colorado. My mother had called and asked me to come because her mother was critically ill in the hospital out there. I took a few days off from work and drove out. On arrival in the city I headed straight for the hospital. As I was driving through the city to the hospital I suddenly had the sensation of something dark, like a cloud, dropping down over me. It lasted for only a few seconds and then was gone. I didn't think anything more about it. When I got to the hospital I found out that my grandmother had died just a short time before I arrived. I stayed for the funeral, then returned home."

On further questioning he told me that his grandmother had been deeply involved in witchcraft. Many members of the family had tried to bring her to see her need for Jesus without success. That was the doorway — inheritance. At the death of the grandmother, the powerful demons that inhabited her were passed on to another member of the family. Of course Satan would choose Rick as he was preparing to enter full time service for the Lord. After deliverance he was again restored to full and free communion with the Lord. A simple prayer in faith by his parents breaking any lines of inheritance from Rick's grandmother would have protected him from such a thing — *but* they lacked knowledge.

I know that many people will say that Rick should have been protected from such a thing because he was a Christian. But the Bible states plainly that the sins of the parents will be passed down to the children even to the third and fourth generations. That is why God so strongly warned the Israelites against any involvement in the occult. Christians need to be aware of this. If they are aware of anyone in their family that has been involved in the occult in any way, they should ask the Lord to close that doorway of inheritance with the precious blood of Jesus both for themselves and their children.

. . . .

I want to outline below the four basic steps a Christian can take to fight for the salvation of someone who is demonically bound. Many parents face this problem with their unbelieving children who are involved in rock music, occultic games, drugs, alcoholism, etc. These steps can also be applied by any Christian to anyone for whom he/she has a burden and is willing to fight for, to bring them to the Lord Jesus Christ.

 # 1)   If the unsaved person is living in the same house as the Christian, the first step must be to clean out the house, that is, if the Christian is in a position of authority in the household. Children cannot, obviously, do this if they are minors still living at home with their parents. This situation will be handled at the end of this section.

All objects used in the service of Satan (occult objects, rock records, occultic role-playing fantasy game material, etc.) are "familiar objects." (See chapter 20.) These must be removed from the house as they provide legal ground for the demons to use to bring a continuing evil power into the house.

In the case of Christian parents dealing with their rebellious teenagers, I would warn you that you cannot just go into your child's room and make a clean sweep of everything that you feel is a familiar object. You must *communicate* with them first. Bind the demons in them, then sit down and talk with them. Listen to their rock records with them, carefully examining the lyrics. I guarantee your kids will be embarrassed because they know in their hearts that rock music is rotten. If they are into occultic games, sit down and look at the manuals and study the game with them so that you gain an understanding of what they are doing and can then point out to them scripturally why it is wrong. After you have done all this, then destroy all the records, tapes, game materials, etc.

As mentioned above, Christian children who are minors can, in faith, ask the Lord to seal such familiar objects so that the demons can no longer operate through them.

 # 2)   You must realize that your loved ones are demonically bound and blinded. You can talk to them for years telling them of their need for Jesus, but they just won't understand you. They can even repeat back to you what you are saying, but it is as if there is a "scrambler" between what you are saying and their brain so that they cannot really understand the concepts. The "scrambler" is a demon. Also their wills are bound so that even if they do understand their need for Jesus' salvation, they cannot will to ask Him to become their Savior and Lord.

If they are living in the same house as you, each day, out loud, take the aggressive against the demons in them. You can do this in another room where they cannot hear you. Don't forget, demons have *very* sharp ears. Say something like this:

> "You demons binding _____ , I take authority over you in the name of Jesus Christ my Lord. I bind you in the name of Jesus, you may not afflict _____ today. My house is committed to the Lord and is holy ground. You are a trespasser and may not function here. I bind you and command you to leave in the name of Jesus!"

This battle will be a daily thing. I cannot tell you how long the battle will take, only the Lord knows in each case. Be alert to the fact that the demons can speak through the other person, often being very rude and insulting to you to try to drive you away. In many cases it becomes necessary to rebuke the demon directly as he is speaking through the other person and command him to be silent. The Lord will guide you.

 # 3)   You can ask the Lord to let you "stand in the gap" for the unsaved person. This will be discussed in more detail in Chapter 14. See Ezekiel 22:30-31. Ask the Lord to let you stand in the gap for this person in order that their eyes may be opened and their will set free to accept Jesus.

 # 4)   Lastly, you must understand the wonderful position of power our Lord Jesus has placed us in. Hebrews says:

> "Let us therefore come boldly unto the throne of

> grace, that we may obtain mercy, and find grace to
> help in time of need." Hebrews 4:16

Scripture shows us that Satan comes before God and petitions Him for people. The account given in Job chapter 1 clearly demonstrates this. Also Satan obviously petitioned God for Peter.

> "And the Lord said, Simon, Simon, behold, Satan
> hath desired to have you, that he may sift you as
> wheat: But I have prayed for thee, that thy faith fail
> not: and when thou are converted, strengthen thy
> brethren." Luke 22:31-32

Satan is not finally thrown out of heaven until the 12th chapter of Revelation.

> "And there was war in heaven: Michael and his angels
> fought against the dragon; and the dragon fought and
> his angels, and prevailed not; neither was their place
> found any more in heaven. And the great dragon was
> cast out, that old serpent, called the Devil, and Satan,
> which deceiveth the whole world: he was cast out into
> the earth, and his angels were cast out with him. And I
> heard a loud voice saying in heaven, now is come
> salvation, and strength, and the kingdom of God, and
> the power of his Christ: for the accuser of our brethren
> is cast down, which accused them before our God day
> and night." Revelation 12:7-10

You must understand that Satan stands before the throne of God petitioning our heavenly Father for our unsaved loved ones. Satan points the accusing finger and says, "See, so-and-so is participating in rock music (or whatever), therefore I have a legal right to his/her soul and to influence his/her life and to send my demons into him/her."

Because God is absolutely just, He must grant Satan his petition *if* it is uncontested. *But* we as heirs and joint heirs with Jesus Christ have *more* right to petition God the Father than Satan does. We must "boldly" go before the throne and counter-petition Satan. We can pray something like this:

> "God and Father, I counter-petition Satan. I come to

you in the name of Jesus Christ my Lord and lay claim
to this person. I claim him/her as my inheritance which
you promised to give to me (if the person is your child,
or spouse). Satan may *not* have him/her. I ask you to
open his/her eyes so that they can see the light of the
gospel of Jesus Christ."

If the person you are petitioning for is not a relative, you
can petition on the basis that Jesus Christ commanded us to
make disciples of the whole world and we can claim that
person for a disciple of Jesus Christ.

Again, you must understand that this is a *real battle.* You
will not win overnight, but you do have the power and authority in Jesus Christ to win in the end.

CHAPTER 14

The Human Spirit, Standing In The Gap, And The Spirit World

REBECCA TALKS:

HUMAN SPIRITS

Throughout this book many references have been made to human spirits. This is a very important concept that Christians should understand. This is the power that Elaine and many others like her developed and used. Let us look at the scriptures that touch on this.

> "And the very God of peace sanctify you wholly; and I pray God your whole *spirit* and soul and body be preserved blameless unto the coming of our Lord Jesus Christ."   I Thessalonians 5:23.

Paul teaches us here that we humans are tripartite beings. That is, we have three separate parts — the body, the soul (which is our conscious intellect, will, and emotions), and the *spirit.* He plainly states that all three must be cleansed and committed to Jesus, and that Jesus himself must enable us to keep all three parts "blameless" until His return.

Genesis 2:7 says,

> "And the Lord God formed man of the dust of the

> ground, and breathed into his nostrils the breath of
> life; and man became a living soul."

That is, Adam lived, and became aware of himself. In essence our self is our soul which manifests in our mind, our will, and our emotions.

> " . . . There is a natural body and there is *a spiritual*
> *body.*"   I Corinthians 15:44

This is a much overlooked verse. Our spirits have a form or shape, a body corresponding to our physical body. Few people other than the satanists or those involved in such things as astral projection realize this. *(See figure A.)*

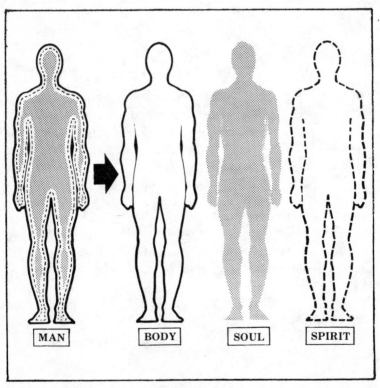

Figure A

> "I knew a man in Christ above fourteen years ago, (whether in the body, I cannot tell; or whether out of the body, I cannot tell: God knoweth;) such an one caught up to the third heaven. And I knew such a man, (whether in the body, or out of the body, I cannot tell: God knoweth;) How that he was caught up into paradise, and heard unspeakable words, which it is not lawful for a man to utter." II Corinthians 12:2-4

> "After this I looked, and, behold, a door was opened in heaven: and the first voice which I heard was as it were of a trumpet talking with me; which said, Come up hither, and I will shew thee things which must be hereafter. And immediately I was in the *spirit:* and, behold, a throne was set in heaven, and one sat on the throne." Revelation 4:1-2

These scriptures and others show an experience perceived in the person's spirit, and that the spirit body was separated from the physical body. Notice that when John stated that he was in the "spirit" that it is spelled with a small "s" signifying his own human spirit. Every time the Holy Spirit is referred to in scripture it is spelled with a capital "S" as in Revelation 1:10:

> "I was in the *Spirit* on the Lord's day, and heard behind me a great voice, as of a trumpet ... "

> "For the word of God is quick, and powerful, and sharper than any two-edged sword, piercing even to the dividing asunder of soul and *spirit*, ... "
> Hebrews 4:12

Did you ever wonder why it is necessary to divide between our soul and spirit? According to the above verse there can be a division made (or separation of) the soul and the spirit.

The first Adam, before the fall, could relate to, and see the spirit world as easily as he could the physical world. How? By the use of his spiritual body. This is demonstrated by the ease with which he could walk and talk with God in the garden of Eden. He had a conscious awareness of his spiritual body the same as he had a conscious awareness of his physical body. His *soul* (conscious intellect and will) controlled both his spiritual and physical bodies. But, at the fall, spiritual death took place — that is, Adam and his descendants were no longer consciously aware of their spiritual body, and thus could not commune with the Lord as he had once done. *(See figure B & C.)*

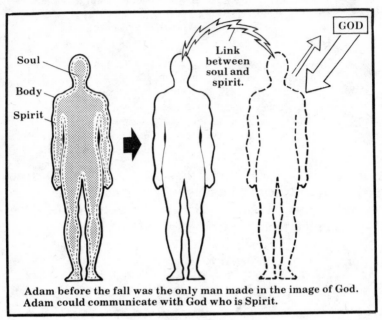

Adam before the fall was the only man made in the image of God. Adam could communicate with God who is Spirit.

Figure B

At the fall it was disaster. The mysterious link was destroyed. This ended Adam's free communication with God.

(See Hebrews 4:12.)

Figure C

As the Holy Spirit comes in at rebirth when we accept Jesus as our Lord and Savior, our spiritual body is re-born, or rejuvenated so that we can commune with and worship the Lord as Adam did before the fall. The fact that it is through our human spirit that we commune with God (with the help of the Holy Spirit) is clearly demonstrated in the following verse:

> "[Jesus is speaking] But the hour cometh, and now is, when the true worshipers shall worship the Father in *spirit* and in truth: for the Father seeketh such to worship him. God is a Spirit: and they that worship him must worship him in *spirit* and in truth."
>
> John 4:23-24

Please note in these two verses that when God is referred to as being a "Spirit" the word is spelled with a capital "S." However, the human spirit is clearly differentiated by spelling it with a small "s." Therefore, only a spirit can commune (that is communicate with) with the spirit world, in this case, worshiping God the Father who is a Spirit. *(See figure D.)*

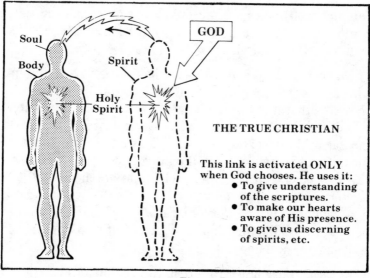

Figure D

Angels are also clearly defined in the Bible as being spirits:

"Who [referring to God] maketh his angels spirits;"

Psalm 104:4

This verse is also quoted by Paul in Hebrews 1:7.

"But to which of the angels said he at any time, Sit on my right hand, until I make thine enemies thy footstool? Are they not all ministering spirits, sent forth to minister for them who shall be heirs of salvation?" Hebrews 1:13-14

Satan and his demons are also spirits, they were once angels in God's service before they rebelled. Jesus himself defines these creatures as angels and thus spirits. One scripture reference for this is in Matthew 25:41:

"Then shall he say also unto them on the left hand, Depart from me, ye cursed, into everlasting fire, prepared for the devil and his angels." Matthew 25:41

So we see from these scriptures and many others that not only is God a Spirit, but there are other spirit beings as well called angels — some in God's service, some in Satan's service.

Our spiritual bodies are the link between us and the spirit world because the spirit world cannot be seen or measured with anything physical.

Through the Holy Spirit, our spirits are able to commune with and worship God, but the scripture in Hebrews 4:12 shows us that it is *not* God's will for us to regain the conscious control of our spirit bodies while we remain here on the earth in our sinful condition. This is why the sword of the Spirit severs between the soul and spirit. Once this severing has taken place the soul (mind, intellect, will) can no longer control the spirit body. This is also why the Lord is so adamant in I Thessalonians 5:23 that our spirit *must* be under the total mastership of Jesus Christ, as well as our soul and physical body.

There is an intriguing scripture in Revelation 18:11 & 13:

[Referring to the fall of Babylon] "And the merchants

168

> of the earth shall weep and mourn over her; for no
> man buyeth their merchandise any more: . . . and
> sheep, and horses, and chariots, and bodies, and souls
> of men."

Why the difference made between bodies and souls of men? Because there is a phenomenal amount of power and intelligence in the spirit bodies of humans especially when those spirit bodies are under the control of their soul. Satan has been working steadily down through the ages since the fall of Adam to gain the use of these spiritual bodies for his own evil schemes. Men's physical bodies are weak and really are of little use to Satan, but their spiritual bodies under the conscious control of their souls, are very different.

Satan's goal is to teach humans to again regain the conscious control of their spiritual bodies. Many do. Once this is achieved, these people can perceive the spirit world as well as the physical world. They can talk freely with demons, leave their physical bodies with their spirit bodies, and with full conscious awareness go places and do things with, what seems to the average human, supernatural power. It was with their spirit bodies that the various witches and warlocks, without being physically present, would pull Elaine and myself out of bed, throw us across the room, etc. We were unable to see them because our physical eyes cannot see the spirit world. God does not want His people to control their spirit bodies in such a manner. If we did so, not only would we be open to overwhelming temptations to sin, we would not need to be so dependant upon Him and we would *also* be constantly aware of Satan and his kingdom.

There is a special class of demons who frequently refer to themselves as "power demons" who seem to provide the "glue" so to speak, to establish the link between the soul and spirit body enabling the person involved to gain conscious control of his spirit body. The imagination is a key

169

stepping stone to develop the link between soul and spirit. That is why it is so important to bring every thought into captivity to Christ (2 Cor. 10:3-5). A good example of the imagination as a link with the spirit world is found in the occultic role-playing fantasy games. *(See figure E, F, G & H.)*

We have found that we can save ourselves much time and effort in the area of deliverance if we make it clear to a person requesting deliverance (who has been involved in the occult) that this power demon is the first demon we will ask the Lord to cast out. If someone is not really serious about desiring deliverance, or is trying to deceive us, they will back off quickly when they find out that with the removal of this demon they will instantly lose all their ability to use their spirit body.

I have also found that this is a very overlooked area in deliverance and frequently this doorway is left open. The result is much suffering as Satan and his demons will continuously harass the person. If the person being so tormented will simply pray and ask the Lord to remove all their ability to perceive the spirit world and ask the Lord to sever between his soul and spirit (as in Hebrews 4:12), they will gain tremendous relief from such torment by the evil spirit world. After this the person will perceive the spirit world *only* when the Lord chooses to give them such perception. Their spirit will, from that point on, be totally under the mastership of Jesus Christ.

We Christians also must be very careful to ask the Lord to take complete control of our spirits. Many Christians fall into the trap of learning to control their own spirits. I have heard many say "I meditate until I have a spiritual experience, or, experience God." Christians *do* have experiences in the spirit — visions and revelations — but these are *always* under the control of our Lord Jesus Christ and *never* controlled or initiated by the person

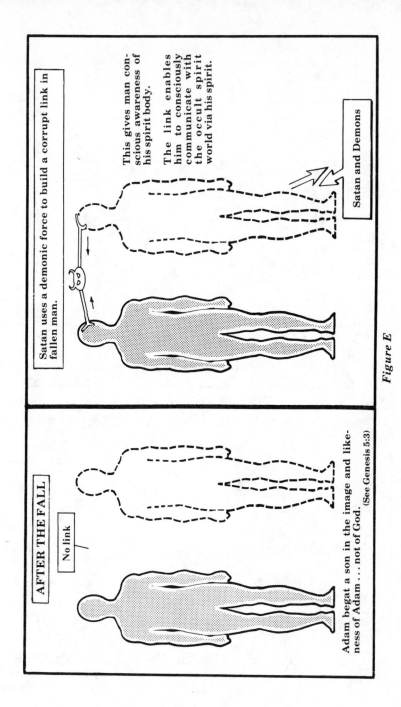

Figure E

171

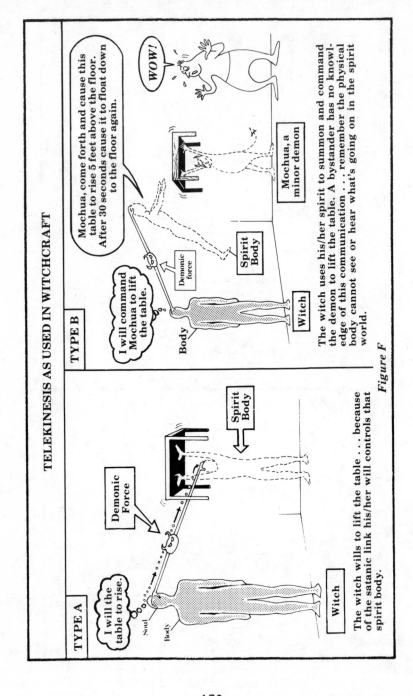

TELEKINESIS AS USED IN WITCHCRAFT

Figure F

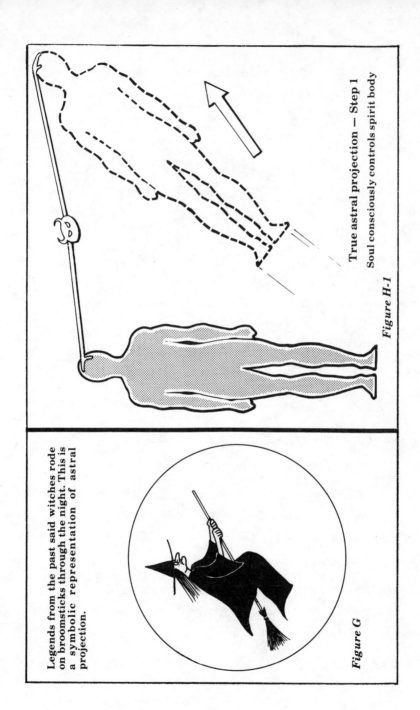

True astral projection — Step 1

Soul consciously controls spirit body

Figure H-1

Legends from the past said witches rode on broomsticks through the night. This is a symbolic representation of astral projection.

Figure G

173

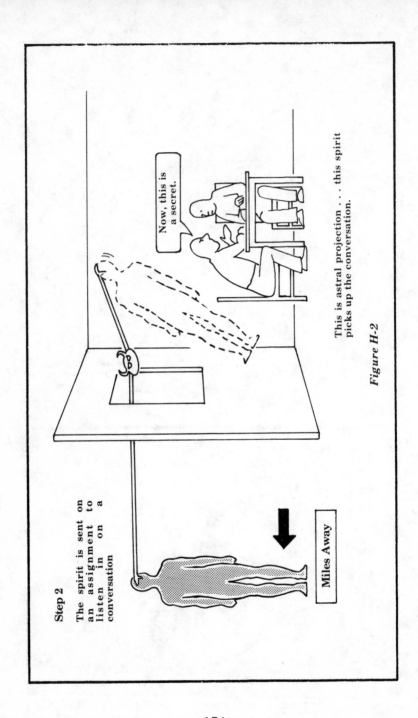

Figure H-2

himself. If a Christian is able to control when he has such spiritual experiences, then I would have to say to him that I would seriously doubt that his experiences came from God. Most likely they came from Satan.

Too many Christians think that they must "blank out" their minds so that the Holy Spirit can speak through them, or "control" them. The Bible clearly shows us that we are to *actively* cooperate with the Holy Spirit. Any time we blank out our minds, the spirit speaking through us is most likely *not* the Holy Spirit. Multitudes of Christians are, and have been, mislead because of their lack of knowledge of God's principles regarding their spirits. Many so called prophecies given by people who blank out their minds thinking this gives control to the Holy Spirit are demonic prophecies. Too many Christians are mislead in this area and accept such prophecies because the person prophesying knows facts about them or their life that they think only God could know. They forget that Satan knows every detail of our lives, the only thing he doesn't know is the thoughts and intentions of our hearts.

There is currently a growing teaching amongst the Christians of America which I consider to be very dangerous. That is, that "Our soulical man should be placed under the authority of our spiritual man because once indwelt by the Holy Spirit our spirits are without sin." There are two things wrong with this teaching. First, the only way the soul can be placed under the authority of the spirit is to establish conscious contact between the soul and spirit. This is pure witchcraft. I Peter 1:22 says:

> "Seeing that ye have purified your souls in obeying the truth through the Spirit unto unfeigned love of the brethren..."

Note here that in this verse "Spirit" is spelled with a capital "S" referring to the Holy Spirit. Our souls are "purified" by staying in subjection to and obeying the Holy Spirit, *not* our own human spirits.

175

Second, I Thessalonians 5:23 clearly shows us that our spirits *are* vulnerable to fall into sin because Jesus must *keep* them blameless until His return. The keeping is an ongoing thing. Look at that verse again:

> "And the very God of peace sanctify you wholly; and I pray God your whole spirit and soul and body be preserved blameless unto the coming of our Lord Jesus Christ." I Thessalonians 5:23

I John 1:8-9 certainly doesn't agree with this teaching. It says:

> "If we say that we have no sin, we deceive ourselves, and the truth is not in us. If we confess our sins, he is faithful and just to forgive us our sins, and to cleanse us from all unrighteousness." I John 1:8-9

Please note, God does not exempt our spirits from the vulnerability to fall into sin in this verse, or in any other verse that I have been able to find. The purpose of the severing between the soul and spirit is to separate our spirit from the influence of any of our natural "self" desires which reside in our souls. If a Christian walks in submission to God, he will not originate anything. Instead, he will wait quietly for the voice of the Holy Spirit to be heard in his spirit and then act only according to the directions of the Holy Spirit. A Christian who is in conscious contact with his own spirit will not wait in submission for the Holy Spirit to speak to him. He will be taking the initiative, and thus the voice he hears in his spirit will most likely *not* be that of the Holy Spirit.

There is one other major area regarding our spirits that has a terrible impact upon many people, but is not taught about in our churches. This is the fact that, whenever he has the chance, Satan will use a person's spirit body without his awareness.

> "Whosoever hateth his brother is a murderer . . ."
> I John 3:15

I often wondered about this verse before I understood the spirit body. How could one be a murderer through an

·emotion, hatred, if he did not physically do something to bring about the death of the person he hated?

Hatred is a conscious sin. As such, it gives Satan legal ground in our lives if we permit it to dwell in our hearts. If you hate someone, Satan can step in and use your spirit body to attack the person you hate. Such an attack can produce all sorts of illness, accidents, emotional problems, and even physical death. The person doing the hating usually is never aware that Satan is using his spirit body. The person being hated usually has no idea where his trouble is really coming from. That is why we must be so careful to ask Jesus to cleanse and keep pure all three parts, body, soul, and *spirit.* That is why the Lord Jesus gave us so many commands to forgive one another. Forgiveness puts a stop to hatred. We Christians should ask the Lord regularly to clean out our hearts of any sin.

> "Create in me a clean heart, O God; and *renew a right spirit* within me." Psalm 51:10

Again, please note the small "s" in the word spirit here. Obviously the sin in David's heart had affected his spirit also.

An excellent description of the personal experiences of some Christians being terribly affected by the hatred of other Christians is found in the book *The Latent Power Of The Soul,* by Watchman Nee.

STANDING IN THE GAP

Are you willing to stand in the gap for someone?

> "And I sought for a man among them, that should make up the hedge, and stand in the gap before me for the land, that I should not destroy it: but I found none. Therefore have I poured out mine indignation upon them; I have consumed them with the fire of my wrath: their own way have I recompensed upon their heads, saith the Lord God." Ezekiel 22:30-31

"Standing in the gap" can be done in several different ways. Often it is necessary to ask the Lord to let you stand in the gap for a particular person so that he can have an opportunity to hear the gospel free from demonic interference. Again remember II Corinthians 4:3-4:

> "But if our gospel be hid, it is hid to them that are lost: In whom the god of this world hath blinded the minds of them which believe not, lest the light of the glorious gospel of Christ, who is the image of God, should shine unto them."

In Ezekiel 22:30-32 God was looking for someone who would be willing to stand and fight Satan and his demons to stop them from blinding the people so that they could see their need for a savior. Because the Lord could not find such a person He said that He would have to pour out His wrath and punishment upon the people for their sins.

We as Christian warriors must be willing to stand in the gap and fight in the spiritual realm to break the demonic forces blinding the unsaved. Paul makes it very clear in Ephesians 6:12 that:

> "For we wrestle not against flesh and blood, but against principalities, against powers, against the rulers of the darkness of this world, against spiritual wickedness in high places."

We often pray a prayer such as the following:

> "Lord, please let me stand in the gap for _____ and fight for him so that his eyes will be opened and he will be freed from demonic bondage so that he can see his need for Jesus."

The Lord has shown us yet another way to stand in the gap. Look at the following scriptures:

> "Is not this the fast that I have chosen? to loose the bands of wickedness, to undo the heavy burdens, and to let the oppressed go free, and that ye break every yoke? ... "   Isaiah 58:6

> "Bear ye one another's burdens, and so fulfill the law of Christ."   Galatians 6:2

"Greater love hath no man than this, that a man lay
down his life for his friends."   John 15:13

The above scriptures clearly show that the Lord expects us
to help bear the burdens and hurts of our Christian brothers
and sisters as well as to fight whenever necessary to free
them from oppression. Standing in the gap is one way of
doing this.

Are you willing to stand in the gap for your minister? *If* he
is really teaching Jesus *and* exposing Satan as he should,
he will come against much opposition. Servants of Satan
posing as Christians will be attacking him with their spirit
bodies and many demons every time he gets up to speak,
and at many other times also. These Satanic servants are
often in high positions within the church. There is a real
need for strong, healthy young people to be willing to stand
in the gap for their minister and ask the Lord to let them
fight for him. In other words, any demonic powers directed
towards the minister must get past you first. This will mean
suffering for you — both physical and emotional. You may
not always be able to get to church every Sunday as a result
because you will be too ill to get there. This may mean false
accusation against you from members of your church
saying, "You are sick because you don't get to church."
Are you willing to take this kind of accusation and keep
silent as to the real reason why you weren't there? Standing
in the gap for someone is a way of "laying down your life
for a friend."

You can't put yourself in the gap. Only the Lord can do that
because only the Lord controls your spirit body. What you
must do is ask Father to put you there *if* it is within His will
to do so. You must be willing to allow Father to use you in
any way He wants for the benefit of another person. *You*
cannot decide how you are to be used.

Let me make one point clear. You will rarely be consciously
aware that you are "in the gap." This is because the Lord
has complete control of our spirit bodies. We do not "see"

179

the spirit world at all times like we do the physical world. Only on special occasions does the Lord allow individuals to see the spirit world and then usually only in glimpses or for short periods of time. You know you are, or have been, in the gap only when the Lord reveals it to you, or by the various problems in your physical body, which the Lord will confirm to you is from what has happened to your spirit body in the gap.

Have you ever experienced a time of intense intercessory prayer after which you felt completely exhausted? That is because while you were praying with your physical body and mind, God had taken your spirit body and put it into combat with the demonic forces you are praying against on the battlefield of the spirit world. The fatigue you felt is mostly a reflection of the stress your spirit body experienced. Wounds inflicted in your spirit body are often manifested by various symptoms in your physical body as well.

I have come to realize that our physical bodies have been so altered by the onslaught of sin that they can cope with the conscious awareness of the spirit world for only very short periods of time without becoming excessively weakened. Witches and warlocks grow old in their physical bodies at a much accelerated rate. They pay dearly in their physical bodies for their frequent intercourse with the spirit world.

There are a number of interesting references in the Bible that confirm this. Some are in the book of Daniel. For instance, in Daniel chapter 8, Daniel starts out by telling us that he had a vision where he saw the spirit world and spoke with the angel Gabriel. At the end of his time of experiencing the spirit world Daniel says:

> "And I Daniel fainted, and was sick certain days; afterward I rose up, and did the king's business; and I was astonished at the vision, but none understood it."

Also in chapter 10:

> "And I Daniel alone saw the vision: for the men that

180

were with me saw not the vision; but a great quaking fell upon them, so that they fled to hide themselves. Therefore I was left alone, and saw this great vision, and there remained no strength in me: for my comeliness was turned in me into corruption, and I retained no strength. Yet heard I the voice of his words: and when I heard the voice of his words, then was I in a deep sleep on my face, and my face toward the ground. And, behold, an hand touched me, which set me upon my knees and upon the palms of my hands. And he said unto me, O Daniel, a man greatly beloved, understand the words that I speak unto thee, and stand upright: for unto thee am I now sent. And when he had spoken this word unto me, I stood trembling. Then said he unto me, Fear not, Daniel: for from the first day that thou didst set thine heart to understand, and to chasten thyself before thy God, thy words were heard, and I am come for thy words. . . . And when he had spoken such words unto me, I set my face toward the ground, and I became dumb. And, behold, one like the similitude of the sons of men touched my lips: then I opened my mouth, and spake, and said unto him that stood before me, O my lord, by the vision my sorrows are turned upon me, and I have retained no strength. For how can the servant of this my lord talk with this my lord? For as for me, straightway there remained no strength in me, neither is there breath left in me. Then there came again and touched me one like the appearance of a man, and he strengthened me . . . ''

Daniel 10:7-18

Battling by our spiritual bodies takes a tremendous toll on our physical bodies as well. As we come against demonic forces we do so with our spiritual bodies rather than our physical bodies. That is why Paul makes so many references to the fact that our battle is not against flesh and blood. We cannot, obviously, fight in the spirit world with physical bodies. But the two are linked together by God so that what happens to our spiritual bodies inevitably has an effect on our physical bodies.

We have touched on the topic of our spirits battling in the spirit world several places in the book already — particularly when discussing the concept of "standing in the gap." This is a difficult concept to grasp because it is something that is completely out of our control and rarely perceived.

Please understand that we ourselves are still learning about this whole area. There are many deep things written about in the scriptures. We are still searching and seeking God's enlightenment, we do not consider ourselves "experts" but are simply following our Master's command to share here what we have learned so far.

Once you understand that your spirit is a living, active part of you which can walk, talk, sing, think, pray, praise the Lord and fight in the spirit world, many puzzling portions of scripture begin to be more understandable. For instance, keeping in mind the fact that for a large portion of each day we must give our mental and physical efforts to the business of being righteous and earning a living, caring for families, etc., how then can we carry out the following scriptures?

> "For this cause also thank we God without ceasing . . ."　　　　　　　　　　I Thessalonians 2:13
>
> "Pray without ceasing."　　　　I Thessalonians 5:17

Our minds simply cannot pray or thank God without ceasing 24 hours a day, but when our minds cannot, our spirits can.

> ". . . but live according to God in the spirit." I Peter 4:6

Again, please note here the small "s" signifying the human spirit. How can we live in the spirit in this manner? By committing our spirit to God to be used by Him in any way He chooses.

Our spirit bodies can move, think and talk just the same as our physical bodies, but they take their character and way of thinking from our physical bodies and souls. For instance, if you do not know the scriptures with your mind, neither will your spirit body, with the exception, of course, that it is much more in tune with the Holy Spirit. Several times Paul tells us that our battle is not "against flesh and blood," but against spirits. Since our physical bodies cannot fight against spirits in the spirit worlds, our spiritual bodies must do the fighting. That is why it is so important to daily ask God to put His armor on us. This battle is continuous and unrelenting and if we don't have the armor of God on our spirit bodies as they fight we will receive many terrible wounds from the "fiery darts." (Ephesians 6)

We cannot put ourselves on the spiritual battlefield as our spirits are completely under the control of our master, Jesus. We simply tell the Lord that we are willing for our spirits to be used in this way if He wants. Frequently I petition Father to let me stand in the gap and fight for a particular person, but the final decision is Father's. You will soon learn to recognize the symptoms of fatigue, pain, depression or other illness in your physical body which indicates that your spirit body is fighting hard.

The concept of our spirits being separated and geographically away from our physical body is strange and difficult to accept. There is a fascinating scripture in which Paul describes just such a circumstance.

> "It is reported commonly that there is fornication among you, and such fornication as is not so much as named among the Gentiles, that one should have his father's wife. And ye are puffed up, and have not rather mourned, that he that hath done this deed might be taken away from among you. *For I verily, as absent in body, but present in spirit, have judged already, as though I were present,* concerning him that hath so done this deed, In the name of our Lord Jesus Christ, *when ye are gathered together, and my spirit, with the power of our Lord Jesus Christ."*   I Corinthians 5:1-4

Notice here that Paul uses a small "s" denoting his own spirit, not the Holy Spirit. Also of utmost importance is the fact that Paul's spirit was there in Corinth *only* with the "power of our Lord Jesus Christ." (I Cor. 5:4) Paul's spirit was completely under the control of the Lord, *not* his own soul.

Normally the human spirit resides within the physical body. However, many scriptures show that the human physical body can still live when the spirit is separated from it. This is not true of the soul. Once the soul leaves the physical body, the body dies. That is why the many scriptures referring to physical death refer also to the soul. However, there is a peculiar drain on the physical body when the spirit is not actually within it.

Through the years I have been involved in this ministry, the Lord has shown me that the drain on our physical bodies is a peculiar one in that it creates an acute loss of protein. If we are not careful to increase our intake of high quality protein during times of intensive spiritual battle we will become weak. The scriptures have much to say on this subject.

Ever since God's covenant with Noah in which he commanded Noah to eat meat, Satan and his demons have been trying to stop humans from eating meat. It is interesting to note that today's Hindus and many other Eastern religions (all of which are forms of demon worship), believe that the success of either a medium or an adept whose powers come from the demons possessing them, depends on the presence in their bodies of a subtle fluid called "akasa," which is soon exhausted, and without which the demons are unable to act. This fluid, the Hindus say, may be regenerated only by a vegetarian diet and chastity.

If we stop to think a moment, we will see that the final straw, so to speak, which brought about God's judgment in the flood, was the intercourse occurring between humans and demons. (Genesis chapter 6) I do not believe it was any accident that God commanded Noah to start eating meat after the flood, knowing full well the spiritual battle Noah and all his offspring would have to go through to keep demons from controlling them and their lives.

As we study the Old Testament and the laws God gave to his people the children of Israel, we will find that the spiritual warriors of those days were the Levites of Israel. Their diets were clearly high in beef and lamb.

If beef is so harmful, then why did Abraham prepare beef for God himself to eat when He came to visit him? Abraham would obviously prepare the best he had. (See Genesis 18:1-7)

If we look at the various spiritual warriors of renown in the Old Testament, we will find that every time, before they engaged in a great battle, God prepared them with the eating of meat. For instance, Elijah. Please note the menu provided for him personally by the Lord during his period of preparation just before he faced all the prophets of Baal.

> "And the word of the Lord came unto him, saying, Get thee hence, and turn thee eastward, and hide thyself by the brook Cherith, that is before Jordan. And it shall be, that thou shalt drink of the brook; and I have commanded the ravens to feed thee there. So he went and did according unto the work of the Lord: for he went and dwelt by the brook Cherith, that is before Jordan. And the ravens brought him bread and *flesh* [meat] in the morning, and bread and *flesh* in the evening; and he drank of the brook."   I Kings 17:2-6

The Lord speaks very directly through Paul to this point in the New Testament.

> "Now the Spirit speaketh expressly, that in the latter times some shall depart from the faith, giving heed to seducing spirits, and doctrines of devils; Speaking lies in hypocrisy; having their conscience seared with a hot iron; Forbidding to marry, and **commanding to abstain from meats,** which God hath created to be received with thanksgiving of them which believe and know the truth. For every creature of God is good, and nothing

to be refused, if it be received with thanksgiving: For it is sanctified by the word of God and prayer."

I Timothy 4:1-5

I have searched the medical literature carefully, and, despite all the publicity, there simply are *no* good studies that conclusively show that red meat is harmful. (Please note I am referring to the lean meat, not the fat, which the Lord told the Israelites not to eat when He gave them the law.) In fact, much work has been done showing the merits of protein supplements in a very wide range of illnesses. But Satan has such control of the medical field that it is extremely difficult to get the average physician to pay any attention to the merits and necessity of protein.

If you will stop to evaluate, you will find that the bottom line in any health food teaching or fad is the abstinence from meat. This is no accident. It is a carefully masterminded plan by Satan, because he knows very well the protein needs our bodies have and the tremendous protein drain caused by involvement in spiritual warfare. If Satan can keep God's warriors from eating meat, he can cause much weakness and illness among them from the lack of protein. The physical body rapidly loses its ability to fight infections when deprived of protein. Many people die unnecessarily in these days of "modern medicine" because their doctors don't supplement their protein intake.

During times of intense battling we often find it necessary to eat meat at least twice daily. If we do not, we rapidly lose strength and often become physically ill. I have worked with many people who, when under intensive attacks by witchcraft, became excessively weakened and even ill, simply because they did not know about God's simple principles regarding the needed protein intake. All of them were much improved when they increased the amount of meat in their diets.

When you are experiencing pain, depression and exhaustion from being on the battlefield, (or at any other time), don't forget one of our key weapons — praise. I will never forget the night Father taught me that lesson. I had just gone to bed and was tossing and turning, unable to sleep. I was deeply depressed. I was exhausted, in much pain and everything seemed so impossible. Actually, what I was doing was having a pity party for me.

Suddenly, Father allowed me to see through the eyes of my spiritual body and I saw that I was on the battlefield, (that is, my spirit body) but I was not fighting. I was down on the ground, surrounded by many demons who were all jeering and throwing stones at me. I did not care. I was so tired that I hoped those demons would kill me, I did not want to live. There was no where to run, no way out of the situation except to stand up and fight, but at that point I was too tired and depressed to do so.

I do not know how much Elaine knew of what was happening, but I do know that it was in response to a command from Father that she came into the bedroom at that point and put on one of our tapes of Christian music. I was in no mood to listen to music, especially not the tape of all praise hymns she chose. Elaine did not say anything to me. She simply sat and listened to the music. Gently and persistently the Holy Spirit showed me how wrong my indulgence in self-pity was. Once again, I marveled at how loving and gracious the Lord is when we fail and fall. I could not help but respond to so great love. So, as I started singing along with the tape in my physical body, in the spirit world I struggled to my feet and told the demons I did not care what they did, that I was going to praise my Lord for His incredible love. I lifted my head and hands and arms toward heaven and sang my heart-felt love and worship and praise (in both my physical and spiritual bodies). As I did so, suddenly, in the spirit world, a brilliant white light shown around me. I saw all of the demons fall flat on the ground and then one by one they slunk away into the darkness.

Satan and his demons cannot stand in the presence of praise to the Lord. I am sure that is why Paul wrote that much debated scripture in I Thessalonians 5:16:

> "*In* everything give thanks ... "

Please note the word is "In" not "For." The worse our circumstances are, the more sure we can be that Satan and his demons are all around us. As we give praise to the Lord, the source of our problems, Satan, will rapidly lose strength and we will gain much blessing.

As you fight in the spiritual realm remember that every weapon and tactic of warfare mentioned in the Bible is available to us. The Psalms are especially helpful. Don't forget to ask Father to put your feet on "The Rock" which is Jesus, and your back to "The Rock." The Lord will show you and teach you step by step what you need to know.

Are *you* willing to serve the Lord in this way??

CHAPTER 15

Why Should We Fight?

REBECCA TALKS:

The question we get from so many people is "Why should we fight?" So many Christians today are living exceedingly comfortable lives and quite naturally they don't want their comfort disturbed. They say, "Why should we even have to fight? After all, Christ won the complete victory for us on the cross. So why should Christians have to think about becoming soldiers and warriors? All Christians have to do is claim the victory Jesus has already won." This is the issue I wish to address here.

Let us first look at what Jesus Himself had to say about this subject when He was here on earth. I don't think we can go to a better source.

> "Think not that I am come to send peace on earth: I came not to send peace, but a sword. For I am come to set a man at variance against his father, and the daughter against her mother, and the daughter-in-law against her mother-in-law. And a man's foes shall be they of his own household. He that loveth father or mother more than me is not worthy of me: and he that loveth son or daughter more than me is not worthy of me. And he that taketh not his cross, and followeth after me, is not worthy of me. He that findeth his life shall lose it: and he that loseth his life for my sake shall find it."
> Matthew 10:34-39

Please note where Jesus said in verse 34 "Think not that I am come to send peace on earth: I came not to send peace, but a sword." This cuts directly across the "peace and love gospel" that is being taught so widely. Then in verse 39 Jesus says "He that findeth his life shall lose it: and he that loseth his life for my sake shall find it." Christianity involves violence *if* we practice it the way God wants us to. Losing our lives does *not* involve peaceful co-existence with the world.

> "Behold, I send you forth as sheep in the midst of wolves: be ye therefore wise as serpents, and harmless as doves. But beware of men: for they will deliver you up to the councils, and they will scourge you in their synagogues; And ye shall be brought before governors and kings for my sake, for a testimony against them and the Gentiles. But when they deliver you up, take no thought how or what ye shall speak: for it shall be given you in that same hour what ye shall speak. For it is not ye that speak, but the Spirit of your Father which speaketh in you. And the brother shall deliver up the brother to death, and the father the child: and the children shall rise up against their parents, and cause them to be put to death. And ye shall be hated of all men for my name's sake: *but he that endureth to the end shall be saved.* But when they persecute you in this city, flee ye into another: for verily I say unto you, Ye shall not have gone over the cities of Israel, till the Son of man be come. The disciple is not above this master, nor the servant above his lord."
>
> Matthew 10:16-24

We *must* "endure to the end." Jesus certainly doesn't promise us a "free ride" as so many people think.

> "For we wrestle not against flesh and blood, but against principalities, against powers, against the rulers of the darkness of this world, against spiritual wickedness in high places."   Ephesians 6:12

Here Paul is placing the emphasis of our fighting in the spiritual world. In Matthew 10:14-16 Jesus is talking about the physical world and physical persecution. Paul here is emphasizing the spiritual world. The two are linked, but in our day and in this country, physical persecution is not yet very strong in most areas. I have no doubt that such persecution is coming shortly. In the meantime our battle is primarily in the spiritual realm.

> "Thou therefore endure hardness, as a good soldier of Jesus Christ. No man that warreth entangleth himself with the affairs of this life; that he may please him who hath chosen him to be a soldier."   II Timothy 2:3-4

> "Beloved, when I gave all diligence to write unto you of the common salvation, it was needful for me to write unto you, and exhort you that ye should earnestly contend [to fight for] for the faith which was once delivered unto the saints."   Jude 3

Why should we fight? The obvious answer is because God wants us to. These and many, many other scriptures make God's will plain. But, many people ask, "Why would God want us to fight when He has already fought the battle for us?"

I have sought the Lord earnestly for the answer to this question. Of course, in thinking about all of this, I had to ask myself the same question. Why have I suffered and lost so much to fight in this battle if it is not necessary? I wish to submit to you here the answer the Lord gave to me for this question.

The basic reason, is because I have made a commitment. You see, unfortunately, when the gospel is preached in this day, it's preached "Jesus died for your sins, ask Him to forgive your sins, and everything will be wonderful." Nothing is said about the fact that you can't get Jesus to forgive your sins without making a commitment to Him. The way the gospel has been preached for so many years is that salvation is a one-way street. Jesus does it all and you don't have to do anything.

That's not true. That's not what Jesus Himself said. He said that if you do not take up your cross and deny yourself, and perhaps even get killed for your belief in Him, you're not worthy of Him. He says He's going to give salvation to those who endure to the end. He makes no promise to give salvation and eternal life to those who don't endure. This

191

concept is repeated by Paul many times in the book of Hebrews. For example:

> "But Christ as a son over his own house; whose house are we, *if* we hold fast the confidence and the rejoicing of the hope firm unto the end."   Hebrews 3:6.

> "For we are made partakers of Christ *if* we hold the beginning of our confidence stedfast unto the end."
>   Hebrews 3:14

We can't be saved by works, but salvation is more than just saying "Jesus please forgive me" and then going on our merry way. It is a total and complete commitment to Jesus. We literally sell ourselves to God just as much as people in Satanism sell themselves to Satan. We are then a debtor. We are bought and paid for and we no longer belong to ourselves. We no longer have any rights. We are servants. The word *commitment* is neither taught nor practiced today, most people don't even know what the word commitment means.

Commitment is not a "work." Commitment is a contract, it is a literal selling of yourself. Paul says in Romans that he is a debtor. (Romans 1:14) Christ bought Paul even as He bought us. Salvation is a sale, it is a transaction. Commitment is not a work, it is actually a sale. Jesus bought and paid for us, otherwise we would belong to Satan and would go to hell. The only way out is through a sale. What a terrible price Jesus had to pay for us!

I don't think enough people understand this. The amount Satan attacks us seems to be directly dependant upon how we abide by this sale — that is, the level of our commitment to the Lord.

Job was totally committed. Only God can know the degree to which you have sold out to Jesus. God knew Job's heart, He knew Job was totally committed to Him. That's the reason God was willing to take up Satan's challenge because God knew that Job would stand. God knew that Jesus would stand, because when Jesus was here in human form, (Phil. 2) He was totally committed to the Father. Therefore God the Father knew that His son Jesus Christ would stand to the point of death, which He did, and not just His own death, but He suffered terribly for all the rest of us.

Satan hates Jesus more than anything else because Jesus now has the legal ownership of the world and shortly will take up that ownership and will dispossess Satan of his kingdom. We don't have any concept of just how intense and deep Satan's hatred for God is. You see, the instant we make a conversion, a commitment asking Jesus to purchase us, we become Jesus' property — then Satan hates us the same as he hates Jesus. That's the reason why, the moment we are truly saved, we are head-over-heels in a phenomenal battle. Satan plans to destroy us. Jesus told us that.

> "If the world hate you, ye know that it hated me before it hated you. If ye were of the world, the world would love his own: but because ye are not of the world, but I have chosen you out of the world, therefore the world hateth you. Remember the word that I said unto you, The servant is not greater than his lord. If they have persecuted me, they will also persecute you; if they have kept my saying, they will keep yours also. But all these things will they do unto you for my name's sake, because they know not him that sent me. If I had not come and spoken unto them, they had not had sin: but now they have no cloke for their sin."
>
> John 15:18-22

There are two key points here. Jesus is telling us very clearly that the instant we become identified with Him as we will when we become His property (i.e. servants), then the world, which is currently under Satan's control, will hate us in exactly the same manner as it hates Jesus. Secondly, so many people say, "Why should I have to suffer or die, after all, Jesus won the victory on the cross and suffered for me, therefore suffering is not necessary for me." But what did Jesus say? He said, "I have said unto you, the servant is not greater than his lord. If they have persecuted me, they will also persecute you . . ." (verse 20) Anyone who tells me that he should not have to suffer because Jesus did it all on the cross is *really* saying that he is greater than his master! The master in this instance being Jesus Christ. He is absolutely going against the words Jesus himself spoke. This "no suffering, health and wealth" doctrine which is being taught across our land is a doctrine of demons; let's label it for what it is.

The gospel is not really being presented in full. When have you heard any evangelist get up and say "You can have salvation, but only under one condition, that you are totally committed, totally sold to Christ, you don't have any personal rights, you no longer belong to yourself, you no longer have any right to anything. You will become a servant. You are in essence signing your own death warrant because Satan will hate you and try to kill you. You ARE gaining eternal life and citizenship in heaven. You give up your life here on earth to gain eternal life in heaven." How many preachers do you know who present this? How many tracts present this? *NONE!*

Why does Satan and the world hate Jesus so much? Because once He came they " . . . now have no cloke for their sin." (vs. 23)

> "[Jesus speaking] And this is the condemnation, that light is come into the world, and men loved darkness rather than light, because their deeds were evil."
>
> John 3:19

We must understand that when we accept Jesus as our Savior, our Lord and our Master, we are accepting citizenship in heaven *and death* here on earth. I personally don't believe we can really have salvation under any other conditions. Total commitment is what Jesus demands over and over again throughout the gospels. I'm afraid that there are an awful lot of people who are going to find out that they are not really saved. The gospel has never fully been

194

presented to them.

This is why you cannot separate warfare from salvation. True salvation is going to put you into direct conflict with Satan. I know I came into direct conflict with Satan the day I made a total commitment to Christ in my freshman year of medical school. Four years later when the Lord asked me if I was willing to commit my life to Him to be used in any way *HE* chose to directly fight against Satan, I really wasn't making a different commitment. The Lord was challenging me as to how willing I was to stand by the commitment I had originally made. He was opening my understanding to what was involved in that commitment. By identifying myself with Christ, I had made Satan my bitter enemy.

Over and over and over again Jesus tells us that we must follow Him to the point of dying. Let us look at a couple more scriptures.

> "If any man come to me, and hate not his father, and mother, and wife, and children, and brethren, and sisters, yea, and his own life also, he cannot be my disciple. And whosoever doth not bear his cross, and come after me, cannot be my disciple." Luke 14:26-27

Now what does it mean to bear your cross? Most people interpret this as putting up with "bad" things that come their way, if they think about it at all. Let's look at Matthew 16:

> "Then said Jesus unto his disciples, If any man will come after me, let him deny himself, and take up his cross, and follow me. For whosoever will save his life shall lose it: and whosoever will lose his life for my sake shall find it. For what is a man profited, if he shall gain the whole world, and lose his own soul? or what shall a man give in exchange for his soul? For the Son of man shall come in the glory of his Father with his angels; and then he shall reward every man according to his works." Matthew 16:24-27

I submit to you that *the cross is an instrument of death.* It's not just bearing trials here on earth, the cross means literally our death. So then what does it mean to die? To me this means that in making this commitment to God I have committed everything that matters to me into His hands. *All* belongs to Him. The instant I do this I know that Satan is going to petition God for it and, as in Job's case, Father may very well grant Satan his petition. To me, dying daily means that I am literally, day-by-day, going to lose everything that I love on the face of this earth. God does not always require that of everyone, but most people are simply not *willing* for this sort of commitment, they are not *willing* to take up their cross.

Once Christ purchases us we become aliens here on earth and there is a barrier between us and everything here on earth — Jesus Christ. Nothing here on earth belongs to us. This is very painful. The cross is probably *the* most painful method of dying. So what we are doing is committing ourself to a life of pain, taking up our cross daily is painful; it is just that simple. This is not the way most people wish to present the gospel, but this is how Jesus presented it. Let me make one point clear, *you* cannot do the work of the cross, only *God* can. In other words, those people who inflict pain upon themselves thinking this is the way of the cross are completely in error. We are servants, we simply obey the commands of our master, we do *not* decide what suffering we must bear.

I suggest that everyone making a commitment to the Lord sit down and take a sheet of paper and write down every area of his or her life that they can think of. Such things as schooling, career, who your friends will be, if you will have any friends, what will happen to your family, what will happen to your physical body, where and how you will live, what will happen to your reputation, if you will have any money, etc. This is not an easy commitment to make. As soon as you make a commitment like that you are going to be tested and tried on it.

You're not really going to grow in faith if you don't make a commitment. Yet, faith is a pure gift from God so that you

196

can make such a commitment in the first place. The two are strangely interrelated. As you stand on your commitment throughout testings I'm convinced that God gives you more and more faith as you go along. Your faith grows and is strengthened. Faith is really saying "I have made this commitment, I have entered into this contract, and I'm going to stand by it."

You cannot permit Satan's doubts to dwell in your mind regarding your commitment. You must throw out any doubts immediately. As you are being tested and tried, you need to understand that everything that happens here in the physical world has an effect in the spirit world. For every time Satan says "I petition for this girl's parents" for example, and Father says "Alright, go ahead and take them." (this means bringing about their physical death, Satan cannot touch their souls) and *I still* serve the Lord, then there is a victory won in the spiritual world which drives back the spiritual forces of darkness so that more souls can come to Jesus Christ. There is always an effect on the spirit world. We have no idea what happened in the spiritual world because of Satan's defeat in the case of Job.

Job had everything wiped out at once. Satan does not usually work in that manner. When everything is taken away in one day's time it is clearly a supernatural act. Satan doesn't usually work that way in our lives. He takes one thing here, one loved one there, you just begin to get recovered from the grief of it and then he takes another one. He is a master at causing agony.

As you stand firm, no matter what the circumstances and continue to serve God, understand that this is a part of the literal physical dying brought about as a result of daily carrying your cross and being a hated alien in this world. We are living a literal living death from the moment we accept Jesus Christ because our life is now established in the spiritual realm and we have eternal life through our soul and our spiritual bodies. But this physical existence is now all dying to us. That's why the instant you become saved you're in warfare against Satan. There is no other choice.

> " . . . as dying, and, behold, we live . . . "
>
> II Corinthians 6:9

People will say, "You're really coming across hard." God says in Isaiah:

> "For my thoughts are not your thoughts, neither are your ways my ways, saith the Lord. For as the heavens are higher than the earth, so are my ways higher than your ways, and my thoughts than your thoughts."
>
> Isaiah 55:8-9

The plain fact is **GOD IS GOD.** We cannot question Him.

> "Many therefore of his disciples, when they had heard this said, This is an hard saying; who can hear it? . . . From that time many of his disciples went back, and walked no more with him." John 6:60 & 66

What happened to Job? After all of this had occurred to him, what happened to him? You see, through all of this Job had an opportunity to catch a glimpse of God, and immediately when he did, **NOTHING ELSE MATTERED.**
Once Job caught a glimpse of God he did not care anything at all about everything that had happened to him. In the book of Revelation where it says that Father is going to wipe away every tear from our eyes, I know, from personal experience, that when we get one glimpse of God himself absolutely nothing else will matter. It is an incredible thing. God himself is vastly wonderful and great beyond anything we can imagine. God is pure power, pure love, pure justice, pure holiness, pure greatness, pure beauty. With one glimpse of Him our relationships, everything we might have or hold dear fades into insignificance. Nothing pertaining to us matters to us once we glimpse God.

> "Then Job answered the Lord and said, 'I know that thou canst do every thing, and that no thought can be withholden from thee. Who is he that hideth counsel without knowledge? Therefore have I uttered that I understood not; things too wonderful for me, which I knew not. Hear, I beseech thee, and I will speak: I will

> demand of thee, and declare thou unto me. I have
> heard of thee by the hearing of the ear: but now mine
> eye seeth thee. Wherefore I abhor myself, and repent
> in dust and ashes.'"   Job 42:1-6

Note here where Job says "I have heard of thee by the hearing of the ear: but now mine eye seeth thee. Wherefore I abhor myself, and repent in dust and ashes." (vs. 5-6) Job didn't have anything to repent for. The earlier part of the book makes it very plain that in everything Job did not sin.

> "In all this Job sinned not, nor charged God
> foolishly."   Job 1:22

> " . . . In all this did not Job sin with his lips."   Job 2:10

But the instant Job got a glimpse of God as He really is, nothing else mattered. It just didn't matter.

My prayer is that the Lord will reveal Himself as only HE can do, both to myself and to everyone reading this book. We could not possibly receive a greater blessing. The Lord calls many people into many different types of service, but all of us will, one day, be attacked viciously by Satan. When that day comes we must be prepared to stand up and fight. If we do, and if we endure to the end, Jesus *will* give us that crown of life and we will have the indescribable blessing of seeing God just as He is in all of His glory.

> "And I heard a great voice out of heaven saying,
> Behold, the tabernacle of God is with men, and he will
> dwell with them, and they shall be his people, and God
> himself shall be with them, and be their God. And
> God shall wipe away all tears from their eyes; and
> there shall be no more death, neither sorrow, nor
> crying, neither shall there be any more pain: for the
> former things are passed away."   Revelation 21:3-4

CHAPTER 16

How To Fight

REBECCA TALKS:

God called us to be soldiers not pacifists.No where does the Bible give room for "soft" Christians. As discussed in the previous chapter we are to be fighters and soldiers, and that, primarily, in the spirit world. We are living in a world ruled by Satan and time is running out. Satan is becoming bolder and bolder.

> "For we wrestle not against flesh and blood, but against principalities, against powers, against the rulers of the darkness of this world, against spiritual wickedness in high places."   Ephesians 6:12

> "For though we walk in the flesh, we do not war after the flesh: For the weapons of our warfare are not carnal, but mighty through God to the pulling down of strong holds."   II Corinthians 10:3-4

> "Thou therefore endure hardness, as a good soldier of Jesus Christ. No man that warreth entangleth himself with the affairs of this life; that he may please him who hath chosen him to be a soldier."   II Timothy 2:3-4

> "Cursed be he that doeth the work of the Lord deceitfully, and cursed be he that keepeth back his sword from blood."   Jeremiah 48:10

As we take up the power and authority Jesus has given us in His name and take the offensive in warfare against Satan, the persecution that inevitably will come will not come in the way we think. People will not stand up and say, "We are slandering you because of your stand for Jesus." No, you will be accused of doing all sorts of wrong things that you did not do, of being too radical and of becoming unbalanced in your mind. Schizophrenia and paranoia are favorite accusations of Satan's. You will be discredited by your *fellow Christians* more than by avowed non-Christians. Satan always deceives and lies, nothing is ever as it seems. His most effective servants are those who are supposedly the strongest Christians, the regular church goers, the financially successful and respected and revered members of your community. They are the ones who will accuse and persecute those fighting in spiritual warfare for Christ. But fight we *must* if souls are to be saved and brought to Jesus.

> "Blessed are they which are persecuted for righteousness' sake: for theirs is the kingdom of heaven. Blessed are ye, when men shall revile you, and persecute you, and shall say all manner of evil against you falsely, for my sake. Rejoice, and be exceeding glad: for great is your reward in heaven: for so persecuted they the prophets which were before you."
>
> Matthew 5:10-12

Do not be surprised when the persecution comes from within your own church, from those who you thought were your Christian brothers and sisters and from your family. The scriptures are plain:

> "For I know this, that after my departing shall grievous wolves enter in among you, not sparing the flock. Also *of your own selves* shall men arise, speaking perverse things, to draw away disciples after them."
>
> Acts 20:29-30

> "For such are false apostles, deceitful workers, transforming themselves into the apostles of Christ. And no marvel; for Satan himself is transformed into an angel of light. Therefore it is no great thing if his ministers also be transformed as the ministers of righteousness; whose end shall be according to their works."
>
> II Corinthians 11:13-15

There is one point that we both wish to make clear. We are *not* trying to dictate to you, nor control you in any way.

201

We are simply sharing with you what the Lord has taught us. You must ultimately get your guidance directly from the Lord. You must learn to hear the Lord in your spirit and mind. Only the Holy Spirit can teach you this, but you must ask for it and seek such communication earnestly. In fact, you must realize that you are responsible as an individual before the Lord to carefully study *everything* anyone tells you, to see if it is consistent with the scriptures. That includes this book as well as anything your pastor says. Paul himself instructed the Corinthians to do this:

> "Let the prophets speak two or three, and let the other judge." [Carefully weigh, evaluate, etc.]
>
> I Corinthians 14:29

The reader would do well to read this whole chapter as it contains much neglected and overlooked commands applying to our church services of today.

Anyone involved in spiritual warfare must be prepared to fight in more than one area. But please remember, *you* do not control how or where you fight. Only the Lord controls that. We simply make ourselves available to Him to use as *He* chooses. He is our commanding officer. Our goals are always to do the will of Jesus Christ, to bring glory to His name and to bring others to a saving knowledge of Jesus. Remember always, *Jesus Is God!* Anyone who would say He is anything less is *false* .

Be careful who you confide in, be wise, be alert to the Lord's guidance always. Our Lord warned us:

> "Lay hands suddenly on no man . . ."   I Timothy 5:22

Wait to see the fruits of a person's life; wait until the Lord gives you a complete peace with them.

> "Beloved, believe not every spirit, but try the spirits whether they are of God: because many false prophets are gone out into the world."   I John 4:1

Remember, Satan and his demons will always try to deceive you. Especially in spiritual matters.

There are at least 8 steps that should be taken by anyone seriously entering spiritual warfare. They are as follows.

#1) You must accept *total* mastership of Jesus in every area of your life.

#2) You must be willing for a *total* dealing of the cross in your life. This must be an on-going day-by-day experience. There is a book by Dr. A.W. Tozer called *The Pursuit Of God*, which I think every Christian should read. The following quote explains this dealing of the cross in your life better than I could.

> "Everything in the New Testament accords with this Old Testament picture. Ransomed men need no longer pause in fear to enter the Holy of Holies. God wills that we should push on into His presence and live our whole life there. This is to be known to us in conscious experience. It is more than a doctrine to be held; it is a life to be enjoyed every moment of every day . . .
>
> "Similarly, the presence of God is the central fact of Christianity. At the heart of the Christian message is God Himself waiting for His redeemed children to push into conscious awareness of His presence. That type of Christianity which happens now to be in the vogue knows this Presence only in theory. It fails to stress the Christian's privilege of present realization. According to its teachings we are in the presence of God positionally, and nothing is said about the need to experience that Presence actually . . . What hinders us?
>
> "The answer usually given, simply that we are 'cold,' will not explain all the facts. There is something more serious than coldness of heart . . . What is it? What but the presence of a veil in our hearts? A veil not taken away as the first veil was, but which remains there still shutting out the light and hiding the face of God from us.
>
> "Self is the opaque veil that hides the face of God from us. It can be removed only in spiritual experience, never by mere instruction. We may as well try to in-

struct leprosy out of our system. There must be a work of God in destruction before we are free. We must invite the cross to do its deadly work within us. We must bring our self-sins to the cross for judgment. We must prepare ourselves for an ordeal of suffering in some measure like that through which our Savior passed when He suffered under Pontius Pilate.

"Let us remember that when we talk of the rending of the veil we are speaking in a figure, and the thought of it is poetical, almost pleasant, but in actuality there is nothing pleasant about it. In human experience that veil is made of living spiritual tissue; it is composed of the sentinent, quivering stuff of which our whole beings consist, and to touch it is to touch us where we feel pain. To tear it away is to injure us, to hurt us and make us bleed. To say otherwise is to make the cross no cross and death no death at all. It is never fun to die. To rip through the dear and tender stuff of which life is made can never be anything but deeply painful. Yet that is what the cross did to Jesus and it is what the cross would do to every man to set him free.

"Let us beware of tinkering with our inner life, hoping ourselves to rend the veil. God must do everything for us. Our part is to yield and trust. We must confess, forsake, repudiate the self-life, and then reckon it crucified. But we must be careful to distinguish lazy 'acceptance' from the real work of God. We must insist upon the work being done. We dare not rest content with a neat doctrine of self-crucifixion. That is to imitate Saul and spare the best of the sheep and oxen.

"Insist that the work be done in very truth and it will be done. The cross is rough and it is deadly, but it is effective. It does not keep its victim hanging there forever. There comes a moment when its work is finished and the suffering victim dies. After that is resurrection glory and power, and the pain is forgotten for joy that the veil is taken away and we have entered in actual spiritual experience the presence of the living God."   pp. 46 & 47

#3)   A willingness to lay down both your *own* life *and* the lives of your loved ones if the Lord so chooses. You can probably expect a total change in your life situation.

"He that loveth father or mother more than me is not worthy of me: and he that loveth son or daughter more than me is not worthy of me. And he that taketh not his cross, and followeth after me, is not worthy of me." Matthew 10:37-38

" . . . he that loseth his life for my sake shall find it." Matthew 10:39

#4) You must learn to hear the Lord speak to you in your spirit. By "hearing the Lord speak to you in your spirit," I do **not** mean an audible voice which you hear with your physical ears. What I mean is, the Lord says something to your spirit and then suddenly it is flashed into your mind in the form of a thought. That is one reason why it is so important to scrutinize our thoughts and ask the Lord to keep our minds and hearts pure.

"I [Jesus] have yet many things to say unto you, but ye cannot bear them now. Howbeit when he, the Spirit of truth, is come, he will guide you into all truth: for he shall not **speak** of himself; but whatsoever he shall hear, that shall he **speak**: and he will shew you things to come. He shall glorify me: for he shall receive of mine, and shall shew it unto you." John 16:12-14

"Whereof the Holy Ghost also is a witness to us: for after that he had said before, This is the covenant that I will make with them after those days, saith the Lord, I will put my laws into their hearts, and **in their minds** will I write them;" Hebrews 10:15-16

The Holy Spirit will put thoughts into our minds, that is how He speaks to us and is a witness to us. Satan can also flash thoughts into our minds, but remember, the Holy Spirit will confirm to your heart and spirit what is from Satan, and what is not. The Bible is our safeguard here. The Lord will **never** tell you anything that is not consistent with His word, the Bible. Also, if you are praying and talking with the Lord silently, Satan cannot read your mind and thus will not be able to put in thoughts that are in context with what is currently going on in your mind as you pray. This is another important reason why you must learn to control your mind so that it does not wander while you are in prayer and communion with the Lord.

> "I love them that love me; and those that seek me
> early shall find me." Proverbs 8:17

The literal translation of the Hebrew word for "early" means "diligently, with the implication of earnestness" according to Strong's Exhaustive Concordance of the Bible. You must seek such a relationship with the Lord diligently.

Only the Holy Spirit can teach you to hear His voice. You may have to seek this type of relationship with much fasting, tears and prayer. Remember, the Lord never does anything in a hurry and He will probably test you to see how sincere you are. If you have not asked the Lord to do the work of a total dealing of the cross in you as described in the quote from Tozer, you will not be able to develop such a relationship with Him. Also if you are not totally committed to Him you will not be able to develop such a relationship.

When the Lord does speak to you and you have checked to see that what was said is consistent with the Bible, and the Holy Spirit confirms to your heart that you did indeed hear His voice, then you must stand in faith that this is so. Otherwise Satan will try to persuade you that you did not really hear from the Lord, that you were only imagining things.

> "The Spirit itself beareth witness with our spirit, that
> we are the children of God:" Romans 8:16

> "Wherefore as the Holy Ghost saith, To day *if ye will
> hear his voice*, Harden not your hearts, as in the
> provocation, in the day of temptation in the
> wilderness:" Hebrews 3:8-9

The Holy Spirit will speak to us *if* we will hear His voice. Then when we do, we must not harden our hearts, but step out in faith and obedience in accordance with what the Holy Spirit said to us. Usually the Holy Spirit starts speaking to a believer by bringing to his or her attention something that is not pleasing to the Lord. The temptation is to ignore this communication and continue doing whatever it is the Lord is not pleased with. If you do this you are "hardening your heart" and will stop further communication from the Lord.

The Holy Spirit will bear witness with your spirit that what you have heard is from Him. If what you hear is not from Him learn to be sensitive to the hesitation or check you will feel. Too often we are anxious to go ahead and do something and pay no heed to these checks. We must learn to be patient and wait for confirmation before taking any action. Impulsiveness cannot have any part in spiritual warfare.

#5) You must learn absolute mind control. This will probably be one of the hardest things you will ever do. The Lord's command is clear:

> "For though we walk in the flesh, we do not war after the flesh: (For the weapons of our warfare are not carnal, but mighty through God to the pulling down of strong holds;) Casting down imaginations, and every high thing that exalteth itself against the knowledge of God, and bringing into captivity every thought to the obedience of Christ." II Corinthians 10:5

> "And be not conformed to this world: but be ye transformed by the renewing of your mind . . . "
>
> Romans 12:2

The mind is a major battlefield, Satan attacks everyone in their mind more than any other way. This battle is unceasing, unrelenting and will continue as long as we live here on the earth. No longer can you lazily allow thoughts to run through your mind willy-nilly. We are responsible before God to stop and scrutinize *every* thought that goes through our minds to decide if it is obedient to Christ.

Let's face it, basically we are lazy creatures. I can tell you that when God first began bringing this to my attention it was one of the most difficult things He ever asked me to do. To get through medical school, I had to study for hours on end. I knew how to maintain absolute concentration on something, but I still did not control my thought life.

Everyone has a continual "thought-life" going on in his or her mind, that is the way we are created. We are responsible to bring every one of those thoughts captive to Jesus Christ.

You must understand that Satan can inject thoughts into your mind just the same as a doctor can inject medicine into your body. Satan and his demons can do this from *outside* your body. They do not have to be inside you to do it. However, they cannot read your mind. Only God can know your thoughts and intentions. (See Hebrews 4:12-13 and Jeremiah 17:9-10.) Therefore, as in the example Jesus set for us when He was here on earth in human form, we must rebuke Satan and his demons out loud.

Satan will put thoughts into your mind starting with the word "I" to make you think the thought was originated by you. For instance, a thought may come such as "I sure would like to do _____," something which you know is sin. As soon as you realize such a thought is in your mind, you need to attack the real source. Out loud say something like this: "Satan and you demons, I rebuke you in the name of Jesus Christ. I will *not* accept that thought. Go away!" Then force yourself to think about scripture, recite a passage out loud if necessary to control your mind.

> "Finally, brethren, whatsoever things are true, whatsoever things are honest, whatsoever things are just, whatsoever things are pure, whatsoever things are lovely, whatsoever things are of good report; if there be any virtue, and if there be any praise, think on these things."   Philippians 4:8

This is another example of controlling our minds. We must literally re-train and renew our minds as in Romans:

> "And be not conformed to this world: but be ye transformed by the *renewing* of your mind, that ye may prove what is that good, and acceptable, and perfect, will of God."   Romans 12:2

This takes time and persistence, *and hard work!*

> "Put on therefore, as the elect of God, holy and

> beloved, bowels of mercies, kindness, humbleness of
> mind, meekness, longsuffering;"   Colossians 3:12

Did you ever wonder how you would go about "putting on" such things as kindness, mercy, etc? I did, many many times. Finally the Lord gave me the answer. We must train our minds before-hand so that when situations arise in which people do us harm, we will not just react in our natural emotions of the moment. We will *choose* to act with God's mercy and return good for evil.

The well known Chinese Christian author Watchman Nee describes the battle for the mind as follows: (Please note, his works have all been translated from Chinese and therefore might be a little difficult to read.)

> "According to the Bible the mind of man is unusual in that it constitutes a battlefield where Satan and his evil spirits contend against the truth and hence against the believer. We may illustrate as follows. Man's will and spirit are like a citadel which the evil spirits crave to capture. The open field where the battle is waged for the seizure of the citadel is man's mind. Note how Paul the Apostle describes it: 'though we live in the world we are not carrying on a worldly war, for the weapons of our warfare are not worldly but have divine power to destroy strongholds. We destroy arguments and every proud obstacle to the knowledge of God, and take every thought captive to obey Christ.' (II Cor. 10:3-5) He initially tells us of a battle — then where the battle is fought — and finally for what objective. This struggle pertains exclusively to man's mind. The Apostle likens man's arguments of reasonings to an enemy's strongholds. He pictures the mind as held by the enemy; it must therefore be broken into by waging war. He concludes that many rebellious thoughts are housed in these strongholds and need to be taken captive to the obedience of Christ. All this plainly shows us that the mind of man is the scene of battle where the evil spirits clash with God . . . When firmly held by Satan the mind of man becomes 'hardened;' man follows the desires of body and mind (as) 'children of wrath' and so 'is estranged and hostile in mind' be-

cause 'the mind that is set on the flesh is hostile to God.' (II Cor. 3:14; Eph. 2:3; Col 1:21; Rom 8:7)

"Upon reading these various passages we can see clearly how the powers of darkness are especially related to man's mind, how it is peculiarly susceptible to Satan's assault. With respect to man's will, emotion and body, the powers of evil are helpless to do anything directly unless they first have gained some ground therein. But with man's mind they can work freely without initially persuading man or securing his invitation. The mind appears to be their possession already. The Apostle in comparing men's minds to an enemy's strongholds seems to imply that Satan and his wicked spirits already have established a deep relationship with the minds of men, that somehow they are using them as their bastions in which to imprison their captives. Through man's mind they impose their authority and through the mind of their captives they transmit poisonous thoughts to others so that these too may rise up against God. It is difficult to estimate how much of the world's philosophy, ethics, knowledge, research and science flow from the powers of darkness. But of one point we are certain: all arguments and proud obstacles against the knowledge of God are the fortresses of the enemy.

"Is it strange to behold the mind in such close proximity to the authorities of wickedness? Was not the sin which mankind first committed that of seeking the knowledge of good and evil, and that at the instigation of Satan? Hence man's mind is especially related to Satan. If we were to peruse the Scriptures carefully and to observe the experiences of the saints we would discover that all communications between human and satanic forces occur in the organ of thought. Take for instance, Satan's temptation. Every temptation with which he entices man is presented to his *mind*. It is true that Satan often uses the flesh to secure the consent of man, yet in each instance of enticement the enemy creates some kind of temptation and thought. All temptations are offered us in the form of thoughts ...

"The original definition of repentance is none else than 'a change of mind.' ...

"But even following repentance the believer's mind is

not liberated totally from the touch of Satan. As the enemy worked through the mind in former days, so today will he work in the same manner. Paul, in writing to the Corinthian believers, confided that he was 'afraid that as the serpent deceived Eve by his cunning, your thoughts will be led astray from a sincere and pure devotion to Christ.' (II Cor. 11:3) The Apostle well recognizes that as the god of this world blinds the mind of unbelievers so will he deceive the mind of the believers . . . The mind is the easiest avenue for them to accomplish their purpose. Eve's heart was sinless and yet she received Satan's suggested thoughts. She was thus beguiled through his deception into forfeiting her reasoning and tumbling into the snare of the enemy. Let a believer accordingly be careful in his boast of possessing an honest and sincere heart, for unless he learns how to repulse the evil spirits in his mind he will continue to be tempted and deceived into losing the sovereignty of his will. pp. 7-10

"God wishes to restore our thought life to the excellent state it had when He created it so that we may not only glorify God in our walk but may glorify Him in our thinking as well. Who can estimate the multiplied number of God's children who, due to neglecting their mind, grow narrow, stubborn and obstinate, and even sometimes defiled. They fall short of the glory of God. The Lord's people need to know that if they want to live a full life their mind must be renewed. So whenever a child of God notes that he is no longer able to govern the mind, he ought to perceive at once that it is the enemy who is managing it . . . God's intention is for man to control himself. Man has the authority to regulate his every natural endowment; hence his mental processes should be subject to the power of his will. A Christian ought to inquire of himself: Are these my thoughts? Is it I who am thinking? If it is not I thinking, it must then be the evil spirit who is able to work in man's mind. The person should know that in case he has not intended to think and yet there are thoughts arising in his head, he must conclude that these are not of him but of the evil spirit." pp. 12-13

The Spiritual Man, Volume III, by Watchman Nee.

Let me give you some examples.

A. There are 3 sources of the thoughts that come into the mind of a true born again believer. The person himself, the Holy Spirit, and, Satan and/or his demons. Nearly everywhere we go to speak we always have people criticize us and tell us that we must not speak about Satan because in so doing we are giving glory to him, etc., etc. Why? Because there are almost always some witches in every audience. They sit back and with a simple incantation send a demon to every person in the audience (please note, the demons do *not* go into the people). The demon shoots in the thought that "These women should not talk about Satan because in so doing they are giving glory to Satan." The person assumes the thought is their own and therefore must be true.

B. The roommate I lived with at the time I met Elaine was not a Christian, and frankly I did not like her at all. I had reluctantly agreed to let her stay with me for the school year hoping to bring her to the Lord but I had a *most* difficult year. Our personalities were very different, and she irritated me most of the time. During this time the Lord was teaching me to control my mind. One of the first things the Holy Spirit showed me was that most mornings as I was preparing to go into work, I had not even seen Sue yet, but in my mind I was going around and around with her having a fight in my mind so that by the time I did see her I was so mad at her I couldn't even say a civil "Good morning." Now where did those thoughts come from? Not from me. I had such a struggle to control them, there were times when I would say to myself, "Rebecca, *shut-up!*" But this wouldn't do any good, the angry thoughts would just keep on going. Why? Because by telling myself to shut-up I was resisting Satan with my own strength. When we try to withstand Satan with our own strength we lose the battle before we even get started.

But as the Holy Spirit taught me and trained me to recognize that those thoughts were from outside of me and from

Satan, I began to have victory as I rebuked Satan out loud in the name of Jesus. Soon I learned that the instant that first negative or angry thought would come into my mind about Sue, I immediately out loud said, "Satan and you demons I rebuke you in the name of Jesus! I will not accept those thoughts about Sue," and would force myself to think about some portion of scripture and recite it out loud. Then I had victory because I was then resisting Satan with the power of Jesus, and my whole relationship with her improved immensely. How many marriages and families and churches and whole communities have been destroyed by this one simple tactic? *(See Figures I, II and III.)*

#6)   Scripture memory is another important point.

> "Wherewithal shall a young man cleanse his way? By taking heed thereto according to thy word . . . Thy word have I hid in mine heart, that I might not sin against thee." Psalm 119: 9 & 11

The way to hide God's word in your heart is to *memorize* it. I cannot emphasize this strongly enough. Believe me, when you are fighting with demons, you do not have time to go thumbing through your Bible. You may well lose your life or the life of the one you are trying to deliver if you have to take the time to even open your Bible.

There is an easy way to memorize scripture. Set aside a certain time each day. For me, it is the 20 minutes or so I spend each morning blow-drying my hair. Write the section you want to memorize on a 3 X 5 card. I have my cards taped on my mirror. Write the section of scripture you want to memorize with the reference both before and after the verses. Usually it is best if you limit it to no more than 2-3 verses. Then, *out loud* say the verses and reference over and over until you can say it through once or twice perfectly with your eyes closed. For example:

> "John 3:16 — For God so loved the world, that he gave his only begotten Son, that whosoever believeth

Figure I

214

Figure II

215

Figure III

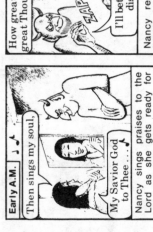

216

in him should not perish, but have everlasting life. —
John 3:16"

Do this once each day. Add a new section of scripture once per week. If you do this faithfully each day for 3 months you will have that scripture locked into your memory forever. You will soon find that the Holy Spirit will bring these verses back to your mind many times per day. You will find this a quick, easy, painless way to memorize scripture.

#7) Authority. God always puts his people under authority. This is a lesson we must learn early if we are to survive in spiritual warfare. Unless we learn to obey delegated authority we will never truly obey God's direct authority and thus we will lose many battles because we will neither hear or obey our captain, Jesus Christ. I think it would be wise here to quote a section from the book *Spiritual Authority*, by Watchman Nee (Christian Fellowship Publishers, Inc., 1972).

> "God's children should not only learn to recognize authority, they should likewise be looking for those to whom they ought to be obedient. The centurion spoke to the Lord Jesus saying: 'I also am a man under authority, having under myself soldiers.' (Matt. 8:9) He was truly a man who knew authority. Today, even as God upholds the whole universe with His authority, so He joins His children together through His authority. If any one of His children is independent and self-reliant, not subject to God's delegated authority, then that one can never accomplish the work of God on earth. Each and every child of God must look for some authority to obey so that he or she may be well coordinated with others. Sad to say, though, many have failed this point." page 115.

If you are unable to come under the authority of a boss at your work, how, then, can you ever really come under God's authority? Also, be very careful who's authority you place yourself under. Do not be in a hurry to become a member of a particular church until you know without a

217

doubt that that is where the Lord wants you. Once you place yourself under such authority God considers it very serious if you then disobey that authority. If you are disobedient to such authority you are then giving Satan legal ground in your life.

The same holds true for women. So many young women feel that they cannot survive without getting married, therefore they tend to marry any man who shows an interest in them. I have seen so many tragedies of young women earnestly desiring to serve the Lord who are tied in a marriage with a husband who is not interested in serving the Lord. However, because they have committed themselves to the marriage relationship, God will **not** honor any rebellion by them against their husbands. They will **never** be free to serve the Lord in the way they would have been had they not married the man.

If the time comes when you must obey God's authority rather than the governmental authority you have been placed under you must do so, but openly and willing to take the punishment coming. For example, Daniel refused to obey the decree by King Darius which forbid anyone to pray to God for a period of 30 days, but he did not do so in secret.

> "Now when Daniel knew that the writing was signed, he went into his house; and his windows being open in his chamber toward Jerusalem, he kneeled upon his knees three times a day, and prayed, and gave thanks before his God, as he did afore time."   Daniel 6:10.

Daniel obeyed God before the government, but he did so openly, willing to take the punishment. God honored Daniel in this and saved him from the lions in the den into which he was thrown. Many martyrs have given their lives for obeying God over their governments. How many of you reading this book would be willing to lose your job rather than agree to refrain from praying or sharing the gospel at work?

I strongly recommend that anyone involved in any way in spiritual warfare read the book *Spiritual Authority*, by Watchman Nee.

#8) *Never* under estimate Satan's power, or treat him with disrespect, or think that he cannot or is not active in your life.

> "Likewise also these filthy dreamers defile the flesh, despise dominion, and speak evil of dignities. Yet Michael the archangel when contending with the devil he disputed about the body of Moses, durst not bring against him a railing accusation, but said, 'The Lord rebuke thee.' But these speak evil of those things which they know not ..."　　　　Jude verses 8-9

> "Be sober, be vigilant; because your adversary the devil, as a roaring lion, walketh about, seeking whom he may devour."　　　　II Peter 5:8

Never forget that the battle is *real.* If you get on the front lines you are more likely to get shot down. In almost every disaster I have ever seen where someone who was fighting for the Lord and then became deceived by Satan, the first step was their loss of respect for their enemy. We are *not* giving any glory or honor to Satan! But he *is* a formidable foe. He is much more intelligent than we. Don't forget what God said when he created Satan:

> "Thou sealest up the sum, full of wisdom and perfect in beauty."　　　　Ezekiel 28:12

Satan is the most beautiful and intelligent creature God has created. We cannot hope to overcome Satan with our small human intelligences, or to figure out his deceptions. We must remain totally dependent upon the Lord to reveal to us Satan's tactics. We can stand against and overcome Satan *only* with the power of Jesus Christ.

As soon as someone stops respecting Satan, he becomes careless and the doorway is opened for pride and a multitude of other deceptions by Satan.

. . . .

We will discuss here five areas of battle. We certainly do not claim that the following is complete, but the Lord has directed us to share with you what we have learned so far. It is our earnest prayer that the Lord Himself will lead you into all spiritual understanding. The areas are: demons, human spirits of satanists, physical creatures such as the wer animals (the word lycanthrope refers only to werwolves, not to other wer animals), humans, and directly on the spiritual battlefield in your spiritual body.

Two special sources of instruction on how to fight in spiritual warfare is the Psalms and the book of Joshua. Every weapon mentioned in the Bible is available for us to use in the spirit world. Study the scriptures. Get a notebook and write down everything the Lord reveals to you as you read. That way you will have the information so that you can go back and review frequently. Otherwise you will have to waste a lot of time re-learning things you once knew but had forgotten.

DEMONS

Demons are very intelligent creatures. They are spirits, and do not normally have physical bodies although they can, for certain periods of time manifest as a physical body that we can see and feel. They were once angels in God's service. Satan, their leader, was once an archangel. His is one of the most powerful and intelligent creatures God ever created. Man's intelligence is nothing compared to Satan's. Many, many ages ago Satan chose to rebel against God and tried to exalt himself above God. A large number of angels followed Satan to be in his service instead of God's. These angels are often referred to as "fallen angels" and are the various demons. They are *all* evil and liers. They go by different names in various parts of the world. They have a wide range of strengths and abilities and can be defeated *only* with the power of Jesus. In Jesus we are in a remarkable position of authority over demons and we should make use of that authority, but always respectfully.

The number and various types of demons are so vast that we could never name them all. Also, the same demon will take different names depending on what geographical area he is in. Satan's kingdom is highly organized and very efficient. Very high demons referred to in the Bible as princes rule over various areas of the world.

Demons know the Bible very well, that is why we must also know the Bible thoroughly. Demons are expert at twisting the scriptures to try to make them mean something other than what God said. If we do not know the scriptures we will be easy prey for them.

We find no need to attempt to list or name demons because not only is this an impossible task, but each time we need to deal with them the Holy Spirit gives us the wisdom we need.

Time and space does not permit us to talk much about deliverance here other than the details given in Elaine's case and the other cases I have given. We approach deliverance by areas of the person, and by the known doorways that have been opened in their lives. Later publications will deal with this in more detail.

HUMAN SPIRITS OF SATANISTS

Dealing with the human spirits of the satanists is about the same as dealing with demons except you must always remember that it is a human life and spirit you are dealing with, therefore the primary goal is salvation. We accept a lot more torment from human spirits without fighting back than from demons because we do not wish to injure them, and we always preach the gospel to them.

I remember on evening shortly after Elaine's final deliverance when I was standing in the kitchen after dinner doing the dishes. I was alone and crying into my dish water while praying to Father. It had been a particularly rough day. Elaine and I were being continuously tormented by the satanists' spirits. Nothing seemed to control them. We were almost constantly being picked up by these unseen forces and thrown against a wall or onto the floor or objects were thrown at us. We were exhausted and battered. We could stop the demons rather easily by simply rebuking them in the name of Jesus, but these human spirits could not be stopped in the same manner. I cried out to the Lord in desperation, "Father please, what can we do? I feel like my house is an open thoroughfare to any power or spirit of evil that wants to come through. You know how these spirits are tormenting us. I just can't stand it anymore!"

At that point the Holy Spirit flooded into my mind the story of the passover lamb in Exodus chapter 12. Then He said, "Since the death of Jesus, there are no more blood sacrifices. So, what would you say is the counterpart of the blood today?"

"The oil?" I asked.

"That is right." Then the Lord also reminded me of the scripture in Exodus chapter 40 where he had instructed Moses to use the anointing oil also.

> "And thou shalt take the anointing oil, and anoint the tabernacle, and all that is therein, and shalt hallow it, and all the vessels thereof: and it shall be holy."
>
> Exodus 40:9

As I pondered these scriptures, the Lord showed me that I must take oil and anoint my house and sanctify it holy unto the Lord. So I took the oil I had on hand (cooking oil) and placed some on the doorposts and lintels of all the doors, the doors themselves, and on each of the windows. As I did so, I asked the Lord to sanctify my home holy unto Himself, and to seal it with a shield of His precious blood. Then, leaving the doors open I went back into the house

222

and stood in the middle of it and asked the Lord to cleanse it and drive out all the evil spirits currently in the house. The change was immediate and dramatic. My house was sealed and no demons or human spirits could get in from that point on.

When we are involved in particularly heavy warfare and, as usual, have many people in and out of our house constantly, we sometimes find it necessary to re-anoint and cleanse our house occasionally. Anyone involved in spiritual warfare will find this most helpful. The Lord has also taught us that whenever we move to a different home we should walk around the edge of the property and claim that property for the Lord asking Him to sanctify it holy to Himself, and to seal and protect it.

If the Lord shows you that you personally are being afflicted by a human spirit (not only that of a satanist, but even of a fellow Christian who has hatred in his heart for you) you will find it most helpful to be anointed with oil by a Christian brother or sister, praying and asking the Lord for special shielding not only from demonic powers, but also from human spirits as well.

Be alert for the possibility of human spirits speaking and acting through an undelivered person. As for the rest, the Holy Spirit will give you personal guidance for each occasion as it arises.

WER BEASTS AND PHYSICAL MANIFESTATIONS OF DEMONS

Vampires and werwolves have been legend for many, many years. Much has been written about them and many movies and stories have centered around them. Unfortunately, most everyone believes they are simply "make-believe" fantasy creatures, and almost everything told about them is inaccurate.

These creatures **do** exist. Let me define what I mean by wer beasts and vampires, then let us look at some interesting scriptural references.

> "Behold, I was shapen in iniquity; and in sin did my mother conceive me." Psalm 51:5

Ever since the fall of Adam, humans have been born sinful, and their physical bodies shaped in and peculiarly affected by iniquity. (Iniquity means wickedness.) Because of this the demons have great power over our physical bodies. People totally committed to Satan can and do ask certain demons to live in them that are capable of bringing about tremendous physical changes in their bodies. It is well known that demons can give humans unusual strength. Remember the demoniac of Gadarah in Luke 8. Wer beasts are produced by these demons. The demons bring about the physical changes in the person's body that change them into animal-like shapes and also gives them super-human strength and characteristics.

There are some very interesting scriptures on this subject. Of course the term wer animals or wer beasts is not used as that is a fairly modern term. But let us look at the following:

> "And I will give peace in the land . . . and I will rid evil beasts out of the land." Leviticus 26:6

> "I will also send wild beasts among you . . . " Leviticus 26:22

In these two references a clear distinction is made between evil beasts and wild beasts. God is here telling the Israelites that if they obey His commandments that He will rid the land of the Canaanites of *evil beasts,* but that if they do not keep His commandments He will send in *wild beasts* to kill them. Earlier on when God gave Moses the law, He designated certain animals clean and unclean among both wild and domestic animals. So evil beasts clearly means something different from unclean beasts.

> " . . . [God speaking] the wild beasts of the field are mine . . ." Psalm 50:11

There are numerous references to wild beasts belonging to the Lord, but never to evil beasts belonging to Him.

Then we find a most interesting scripture in Ezekiel. Here, the Lord is instructing Ezekiel to go into the temple at Jerusalem to see the evil that was being practiced there. At this time the Israelites were practicing demon and Satan worship with all the perversions that accompany it.

> "And he [God] said unto me, go in, and behold the wicked abominations that they do here. So I went in and saw; and behold every form of creeping things, and abominable beasts, and all the idols of the house of Israel, portrayed upon the wall round about."
>
> Ezekiel 8:9-10

In a previously referenced scripture in I Corinthians 10:19-20, it is clearly stated that these idols were images of the demons that were worshiped. I believe that the drawings which Ezekiel saw were not only of demons, but also of wer beasts. Israel has been in Egypt for over 400 years prior to this time. The hyroglyphics found throughout Egypt contain drawings of creatures part human part beast, especially of human bodies with wolf heads. There are many references in scripture to show that the Israelites carried the Egyptian traditions and forms of worship with them.

References to evil beasts are also made in the New Testament. I believe the following scriptures are referring to what we call wer beasts today.

> "One of themselves, even a prophet of their own, said, 'The Cretians are always liars, evil beasts, slow bellies.' This witness is true."   Titus 1:12-13a

> "Even as Sodom and Gomorrah, and the cities about them in like manner, giving themselves over to fornication, and going after strange flesh, are set forth for an example, suffering the vengeance of eternal fire. Likewise also these filthy dreamers defile the flesh, despise dominion, and speak evil of dignities [demons]. . . But these speak evil of those things which they know not: but what they know naturally, as brute beasts, in those things they corrupt themselves. Woe

225

unto them! for they have gone in the way of Cain, and
ran greedily after the error of Balaam . . . [The error of
Balaam was demon worship, specifically Baal.]"

An almost identical passage is found in II Peter 2:10-12.
This passage shows how men are corrupted and turned into
beasts by lacking respect for and consorting with and
worshiping demons. There is also clear reference to a special
defiling of the flesh and a reference to "strange flesh."

Much is hidden in the scriptures and we must seek wisdom
from the Lord to understand all this, but we believe these
scriptures make reference to the phenomenon of human
beings literally turned into evil beasts with actual temporary
physical changes brought about by demons.

Most people consider such things as werwolves, vampires
and zombies pure fantasy. Christians need to understand
that Satan and his servants are deadly serious about these
creatures and that they *do* exist. The satanic activity in the
Dark Ages was so intense because the light of the gospel of
Jesus was almost extinct. Witchcraft was rampant during
that time until God brought the Reformation and the
gospel was preached again. The only accurate writings
about the existence of wer animals we have been able to
find are translations of writings by a few German Christians
during the start of the Reformation period. Our Lord Jesus
told us that in the last days before His return that evil would
increase tremendously, far more than that of the Dark
Ages. Satan is on the move and we are going to see more
and more manifestations of his power. The explosion of
occult movies, satanic rock music, satanic role playing fantasy games, occult literature, Eastern religions and lukewarm
uncommitted Christians should give us a good indication of
the times we are in.

"[Jesus speaking about the last days before His
return.] For then shall be great tribulation, such as was
not since the beginning of the world to this time, no
nor ever shall be. And except those days should be

> shortened, there should no flesh be saved: but for the
> elect's sake those days shall be shortened . . . For there
> shall arise false Christs, and false prophets, and shall
> shew great signs and wonders; insomuch that, if it
> were possible, they shall deceive the very elect."
>
> Matthew 24:21-24

Let us look at some of the lore that surrounds wer beasts —
werwolves in particular. First of all, it is commonly said that
if a person is bitten by a werwolf that he will become a
werwolf. I feel this is completely in error. First of all, the
scriptures indicate that a man must be in a God-forbidden
relationship with demons to be so affected. Secondly, from
my own experience and that of others, a person is most un-
likely to simply be bitten by a werwolf. These demon-
humans desire one thing only — destruction of others. If a
werwolf or other wer beast gets close enough to bite
someone it will most likely tear them apart, not stop with
just one bite. Satan uses these wer beasts for discipline. I
think that during the tribulation they will multiply greatly.

Other lore about these creatures includes such things as
claims that they can turn into their beast shape only at night
and only during the full moon. I know both of these claims
are false, because I have personally met a werwolf fully
turned during daylight and also at a time of the month
when the moon was not completely full.

The obvious question is how can we effectively fight against
these creatures? In the name and power and authority of
Jesus Christ. I have not, to this date, known of the deliverance of any wer beasts, but, the work of Christ on the cross
was so complete, that I am sure it is possible *if* the person
involved is willing to lay down his life to obtain deliverance.
These people have so given over their physical bodies into
the control of the demon that apart from a total miracle of
the Lord I doubt that the demon can be cast out without resulting in the physical death of the person.

As I mentioned, I have, myself, encountered a werwolf

face-to-face once so far. Perhaps it would be helpful to describe that experience here. One evening at dusk I was driving from my office back to the hospital to see a patient who had taken a turn for the worse. I was alone in the car and was driving down a stretch of isolated country road where there were no houses or buildings within at least a one mile radius. Suddenly, about a block ahead of me a huge werwolf stepped out into the middle of the road. As I approached closer, he raised up and stood on his hind legs. I put my foot down hard on the accelerator intending to swerve around him but the car didn't respond. It glided to a stop, motor still running, despite all my prayers and attempts to make it go. I sat there staring in horror at the most incredibly ugly and fierce creature I had ever seen. I felt as if I was drowning in the pure evil power that radiated from him. He threw back his head and howled — a terrifying sound which I shall never forget.

Then he looked straight into my eyes and told me, "You can't go anywhere — see, I have stopped your car and there's nothing you can do about it. Now I'm going to enjoy ripping your throat out and drinking your blood. You have been interfering with Satan too long; I am going to punish you. You cannot stand against my power." Ending in a deep growl, he started walking from the front of the car toward my door.

Fear rolled over me in waves, but I knew I must stand, as I was certain it was not the Lord's will for me to die at that point. I knew I had work yet to do. The Lord had taught me well during my near fatal illness 3 years previously. As I made my decision to stand my ground, the Holy Spirit flooded such calm and peace and strength into my soul. He (the Holy Spirit) also flashed the understanding into my mind that the werwolf was trying to frighten me into panicking and running. If I had done so, he would have been able to kill me.

Taking a deep breath, I extended my right hand to point

directly at him and cried out, "*STOP!* In the name of Jesus *STOP!* you foul servant of Satan! I am a servant of Jesus Christ who is God almighty! It is not my master's will for me to die now. You may not touch me for I have work yet to do." The werwolf stopped in his tracks, unable to move, snarling and growling in fury.

Pointing at him again, I looked straight into his eyes and said, "In the name of Jesus I command you to get out of my way and be gone! My hour of death has not yet come. *NOW GO!*" He howled once more, then dropped onto all fours and disappeared off the edge of the road into a field of tall corn.

I was shaking so hard in relief that I could hardly drive. But as my car gathered speed I drove away praising the Lord for once again "Extending his right hand against the anger of my foes." Psalm 138:7. (I stopped about a mile down the road and had a "nervous breakdown" before going on to the hospital.)

If only people would realize the power available to them in Jesus. Much has been written about various methods of effectively killing werwolves while they are in their wolf form. I would never consider even trying such a thing because in so doing I would be killing a human who's salvation is my deepest concern. Also, once such a person is killed, the demon would leave the body immediately and then the body would return to its human form. That, of course, would present a most awkward situation because who would believe that the dead body was ever in a different form? The killer would most certainly be accused of murder, and rightly so.

Vampires also exist. This, too, is a relatively modern term. Essentially, a vampire is a person who drinks blood, with a particular liking for human blood. Vampirism is a current rapidly growing fad amongst heavy metal Rock stars and fans. Many songs are written about the subject, blood drinking by Rock stars during stage performances is common and the altering of their teeth to become sharp pointed spears is also a growing fad amongst these people. Recent publications show pictures of Dee Snider, singer in the Rock group Twisted Sister, whose front teeth are now pointed. There is a fascinating reference to this in scripture.

> "My soul is among lions: and I lie even among them that are set on fire, even the sons of men whose teeth are spears and arrows . . . "   Psalm 57:4

When we remember that most of David's writings in the Psalms referred to spiritual warfare, and the fact that he says his soul, not physical body, was being attacked, makes me wonder if he could be referring to people inhabited by these same demons of vampirism?

Again, most all the lore concerning vampires is wrong. They certainly can function in the light of day, do not need to sleep in a coffin, etc. I have never personally met a vampire, but I have talked with several people who claim they have. In this case also, we must stand firm in the power and authority of Jesus Christ.

Demons can and do manifest in a physical form. The forms they chose to take can range from exquisite beauty to horrifying ugliness. Demons can also manifest in a physical appearance identical to an existing human being. These demons are frequently referred to by satanists as changelings, incubi, or dopple-gangers. We must also stand against these the same as any demon, in the name of Jesus.

PHYSICAL BATTLE

There is not much I can tell you about the inevitable conflict you will have with actual humans as a result of your involvement in spiritual warfare. You must earnestly petition the Lord to teach you to hear His voice clearly and you must obey, no matter how ridiculous it sounds at the time. *Faith* and *immediate obedience* are two keys.

I will never forget one afternoon in the month of July (just after Elaine's final deliverance) when I arrived home early from work. I went into the house and dropped off some things. As I had about 45 minutes before I had to go pick Elaine up from work I decided to run over to the grocery store. I did so and arrived back home in about 20 minutes. As I reached to put my key in the lock of the front door the Holy Spirit flashed one word into my spirit and mind. *"NO!"* I looked around. Everything seemed peaceful. The birds were chirping, a gentle breeze rustled the leaves on the trees, my two cats were sleeping on the front porch swing. I looked in the window next to the door but could see nothing unusual.

"I must be crazy!" I thought. "I haven't been away for more than 20 minutes and it's broad daylight." Immediately the command came again: *"NO!"*

"But Lord," I said, "I have ice cream and it will melt quickly in this heat."

"Do not go in" was the last command. Then silence. I knew in my heart that that was the last the Lord would say to me on the subject. The Lord will *never* argue with us. So, with a shrug, I turned and went back to the car and went to wait until Elaine finished at work. I had been too well schooled by the Lord to disobey. Half an hour later when Elaine and I and the melted ice cream arrived home we found that the back part of the house had been ransacked! Whoever had been there must have been in the house at the time the Holy Spirit had stopped me from going in. We praised the Lord for His guidance. I might well have been killed if I had gone in earlier. I could give many other similar experiences, but the Lord will lead you in your own life.

Be very careful who you trust. Do not confide in anyone unless they have had time to prove themselves. What are the fruits of their life and Christian walk? Always wait until you have complete peace in your spirit and heart from the Lord before you take anyone into your confidence. Pray constantly asking the Lord to reveal to you Satan's servants and lies. We can *never* outsmart Satan. Only the Lord can show us his traps.

BATTLING IN THE SPIRIT WORLD

This area of battle was discussed in chapter 14 for better continuity. However, as with all the other areas of battle, the eight steps outlined in the beginning of this chapter apply here equally.

CHAPTER 17

Destruction Of Christian Churches

ELAINE TALKS:

During my years in The Brotherhood I was carefully trained, and I in turn trained others, how to infiltrate and destroy the various Christian churches. Satan's goal is to make every Christian church like the church of Laodicea described by our Lord Jesus Christ in Revelation 3:15-16:

> "I know thy works, that thou art neither cold nor hot: I would thou wert cold or hot. So then because thou art lukewarm, and neither cold or hot, I will spue thee out of my mouth."

Churches full of passive people who never bother to read or study the Bible, who "Having a form of godliness, but denying the power thereof . . . " as so well described in II Timothy 3:5, are *not* a threat to Satan.

We were taught a basic eight-point plan of attack that could be adapted to whatever denomination of church we were sent to. The fact that most all high ranking satanists regularly attend Christian churches should not be a surprise to anyone. That is, anyone who takes the time to read God's word. We Christians are very clearly warned that Satan's attack will come from within the churches — especially in times of prosperity.

As Paul was saying "good-by" to the Ephesian elders he gave them this warning:

"And now, behold, I know that ye all, among whom I have gone preaching the kingdom of God, shall see my face no more. Wherefore I take you to record this day, that I am pure from the blood of all men. For I have not shunned to declare unto you all the counsel of God.

"Take heed therefore unto yourselves, and to all the flock, over the which the Holy Ghost hath made you overseers, to feed the church of God, which he hath purchased with his own blood. For I know this, that after my departing shall grievous wolves enter in among you, not sparing the flock. *Also of your own selves shall men arise, speaking perverse things, to draw away disciples after them*. Therefore watch, and remember, that by the space of three years I ceased not to warn every one night and day with tears."   Acts 20:25-31

"For such are false apostles, deceitful workers, transforming themselves into the apostles of Christ. And no marvel; for Satan himself is transformed into an angel of light. Therefore it is no great thing if his ministers also be transformed as the ministers of righteousness; whose end shall be according to their works."
                                    II Corinthians 11:13-15

"For there are certain men crept in unawares, who were before of old ordained to this condemnation, ungodly men, turning the grace of our God into lasciviousness, and denying the only Lord God, and our Lord Jesus Christ."   Jude 4

These scriptures make it very plain that Satan's attack will come from *within* our churches. We are not trying to start a witch hunt, rather our desire is to show you the main tactics Satan uses so that you can stop any such activities within your own churches. Each individual is responsible before God to be vigilant and alert, to read and prayerfully study God's word (the Bible), to carefully listen to what is being taught within their church. Any teaching that does not agree with God's word *must* be challenged, no matter *who* is teaching it. But the challenging *must* be done *in love*, and gently, but firmly. Paul gave some very good advice to Timothy on this subject:

> "Rebuke not an elder, but intreat him as a father; and the younger men as brethren; the elder women as mothers; the younger as sisters, with all purity."
>
> I Timothy 5:1

The word intreat means to ask earnestly, beseech; implore, with respect. Never forget that Jesus loves these people and died for them just the same as He did for you and me. Your purpose is not to expose them, but to control them and get them saved.

Please do not forget my own experience. The little church I was sent to destroy knew that I was a witch, but they did not publicly expose me or challenge me. If they had done so I would have been killed immediately. Instead, they loved me, controlled me so that I could not bring in destructive doctrine and prayed for me until finally I was saved.

Here are the basic 8 points of attack taught by Satan to his servants to be used in the destruction of Christian churches:

#1)   Profession of Faith

First of all the satanist must make a "profession of faith." He or she must pretend to be saved in order to gain credibility with the church people. In churches who have altar calls, the person will go forward, usually with tears, and pretend to "get saved." If the particular church is a charismatic church which places great emphasis on the gift of speaking in tongues, the satanist will speak in tongues. This is no problem, demons can speak in tongues very easily. Remember that when I was indwelt by Mann-Chan I was able to address any of the foreign dignitaries in their own language fluently. This is why the Lord places such emphasis on interpretation:

> "When ye come together . . . If any man speak in an unknown tongue, let it be by two or at the most by three, and that by course; and let one interpret. But if there be no interpreter, let him keep silence in the church; and let him speak to himself, and to God."
>
> I Corinthians 14:26-28

Alas, how much damage is done because churches do not heed this simple warning. It is the custom in charismatic churches for many people to speak and pray in tongues at the same time without interpretation during their services and prayer meetings. Satanists take great advantage of this. During the time I served Satan, I spoke in tongues regularly in all the meetings and prayer meetings, so did the other satanists I was working with. *No one interpreted.* We were cursing the church, the pastor, the members, and God! And *No one knew!* We challenge churches everywhere to take heed of this scripture. When you come together as a group, restrict your speaking in tongues as the scripture directs. If you do so, you will have taken a major step in restricting Satan's attack on you.

Three other scriptures most churches overlook are:

> "Beloved, believe not every spirit, but try the spirits whether they are of God: because many false prophets are gone out into the world. Hereby know ye the Spirit of God: Every spirit that confesseth that Jesus Christ is come in the flesh is of God: And every spirit that confesseth not that Jesus Christ is come in the flesh is not of God: and this is that spirit of antichrist, whereof ye have heard that it should come; and even now already is it in the world."   I John 4:1-3

> "And he said, take heed that ye be not deceived: for many shall come in my name . . . "   Luke 21:8

> "Not every one that saith unto me, Lord, Lord, shall enter into the kingdom of heaven; but he that doeth the will of my Father which is in heaven. Many will say to me in that day, Lord, Lord, have we not prophesied in thy name? and in thy name have cast out devils? and in thy name done many wonderful works? And then will I profess unto them, I never knew you: depart from me, ye that work iniquity."   Matthew 7:21-23

This seems to be one of the areas of greatest confusion amongst Christians. Satanists *can* and *do* use the name of Jesus. They can teach and preach about Jesus, they can use the name of Jesus in prayer, etc. The scriptures just quoted in Luke and Matthew clearly show this. The one thing they can't do is pass the test given in I John 4. They cannot look you square in the eye and say, "Jesus Christ who is God, who came in the flesh, died on the cross and three days later arose from the grave and now sits at the right hand of God the Father, this Jesus *is* my Lord and Savior and Master." Oh, they can say "Jesus saved me." But *which Jesus* are they talking about? Jesus Himself said that many would come claiming to be Him. They can also read or repeat a confession or profession of faith in Jesus Christ. They can and do read the scriptures. If you ask them if Jesus Christ who came in the flesh is their Savior, they can lie and say "Yes." But they cannot, with their own mouth, make the declaration as given above. God gave us a test to use, dear brothers and sisters in Christ. Let us *use* God's word.

#2)   **Build Credibility**

Satanists build credibility within the Christian churches in many ways, depending upon the particular church. They are regular attenders. They can be counted upon to always be ready and willing to help in any project. Not only do they build credibility in this way, but they also get to know the church and its members. It doesn't take long for them to find out who is truly committed to Christ and who is not.

Money is another big tool. If the church is a large and wealthy one they give regularly, gradually increasing the amounts they give until they are one of the main supports of the church financially. In small churches where the members are mostly poor, they do not flash around a lot of money, but gradually and carefully increase their giving until many of the programs within the church become dependant upon their financial support. Of course The Brotherhood provides the money they give, and money talks! Unfortuantely this is true even in our Christian churches. Rarely will you find poor people on the board of

237

directors of any church.

#3) Destroy the Prayer Base

> "Praying always with all prayer and supplication in the
> Spirit, and watching thereunto with all perseverance
> and supplication for all saints;"   Ephesians 6:18

The single most important goal of the satanists is to knock
prayer out of the church. There are so many scriptures
about prayer that we could not begin to list them all. A
strong church is a praying church. Prayer requires self-
discipline, and unfortunately the majority of Christians
spend very little time in prayer. Let me give you a true
story of how a satanist destroyed the power of the very
church in which I was delivered. Rebecca and I are broken
hearted over what happened, but we could not get the leaders of that church to listen to us.

Shortly after I was completely delivered, we were horrified
to see that the high priest of the large and powerful coven
of the city in which our home church was located, started attending our church. I knew the man and his family personally while I was still in Satanism, and he personally threatened
both Rebecca and myself on more than one occasion.
Within two short years, he and his co-workers completely
destroyed this wonderful and powerful church! Many times
Rebecca and I pled in tears with the pastor and some of the
elders to stop what was happening within the church, but
they would not listen to us. We could not accuse "Roy"
(not his real name) of being a satanist because, of course,
we had no proof. It would have been our word against his.
But we did try to show the pastor and a couple of the elders
on more than one occasion that the fruits of his life were
not scriptural. Here is what he did.

Roy was very wealthy. He joined the church shortly after he
started attending it. He claimed to be well grounded and
knowledgeable in the scriptures, which he was. He con-
tributed large sums to the church, attended every meeting

and activity, and joined the choir. At that time our church had an extremely powerful prayer meeting every Wednesday night. Every week 200-300 people attended the prayer meeting and prayed as a unified body. We have been in prayer meetings so powerful that the power of the Holy Spirit literally shook the church building. These people were serious about prayer.

Then, as would be expected, the church began to experience tremendous growth. Its membership grew from 300 to over a thousand in less than a year. This is an exceedingly dangerous time for any church. The pastor and the elders were no longer able to know every member personally. Instead of dividing the church into a sister church to keep down the number of members to a manageable number, they built an addition onto the church, and the church keep on growing rapidly. Everyone thought they were being richly blessed by God — and so they were. *But* many of the newcomers were satanists posing as Christians.

Less than 6 months after joining the church Roy stepped forward and told the church that God had put a great burden on his heart for America. He said that God wanted the men of the church to start coming once a week at noon to spend an hour in prayer for our country. He was willing to lead the group. Everyone thought this was wonderful, and Roy was much looked up to within the church. Within a couple of months he was made an elder, and shortly after that elected to the board of directors.

About 4 months after establishing the "Prayer for America" group, he launched his next two-pronged attack. He and his wife and about 20 choir members tearfully told the choir leader that they must stop attending choir because it "took too much time away from their families." They claimed that it was too much of a burden to have to attend the Wednesday night prayer meeting, then go to choir practice *after* the prayer meeting. Needless to say, it didn't take long for the choir director to approach the elders about having choir practice *during* the prayer meeting, and "Of course having their own prayer just before practice." The elders agreed, and the 20 members rejoined. The first attack had been a success. Because the choir was large, a significant portion of the church members were now neither praying nor benefiting from those powerful prayer meetings. Most of the other church members began to wonder if the prayer meeting was so terribly important after all.

About a month after the victory with the choir, Roy attacked at a meeting of both the elders and board of directors. Roy told them that because of the fast rate of growth of the church that not enough time was being spent teaching individuals to grow in the Lord, or about how to share the gospel with others. He said that the Sunday schools just couldn't do the job. He also pointed out the fact that people did not know each other personally as they used to when the church was smaller — all valid points. BUT his solution to the problem was to stop the large unified prayer group and split everyone up into small "discipleship groups" where they could be "individually taught" how to "grow and evangelize" and get to know one another better. The pastor, the elders and the board of directors swallowed the bait hook, line and sinker.

The prayer meeting was disbanded and small discipleship groups formed. Of course, Roy was in charge of forming the groups. The people he chose to lead them were mostly satanists. The prayer and the power of the church was destroyed!

Rebecca and I went to the pastor and some of the elders in tears, trying to show them scripturally that those powerful prayer meetings were the backbone of the church. They refused to listen to us. From each one we heard the same excuse, "Roy is the first one to know about the importance of prayer. Look how he started the 'Pray for America' group."

Many of the strongest Christians in the church shortly left to attend other churches. Within a year the church was in a shambles. The pastor became discouraged and left the church, the older and strong members of the church left, the power of the church was gone.

Do you see how easy it is? Is, or has, this happened within your own church? Don't just leave the church, please stand and fight Satan. Put prayer back into your church!

#4) Rumors

Once the prayer base of the church has been destroyed, the satanists are free to do about anything they want. One of the easiest things to use is rumors. Gossip is Satan's prime tool. Very few people are strong enough not to pass along a rumor they have heard. Satanists can easily destroy the credibility of the pastor and the true Christians within a church by starting rumors.

We urge all church leaders to be very careful. *Never* go alone to the home of a member of the church of the opposite sex to help or counsel them. You can be framed so easily. Even if you did nothing unseemly or wrong, who can prove it? Many a pastor's career had been destroyed by just such set-ups. I Thessalonians 5:22 says, "Abstain from all appearance of evil." Every Christian would do well to carefully follow that scripture.

#5) Teach and Change Doctrines

Satanists particularly covet teaching positions within the churches. They can do tremendous damage in these positions. Do you really know where all of your Sunday school teachers stand with the Lord? Do you really know just what they are teaching to your children? Or to anyone else for that matter. I taught Sunday school in a large Bible-believing charismatic church in my home town for several years, and led and taught the youth choir, while at the same time serving Satan. My heart breaks now as I think of the many young lives I destroyed by recruiting them into Satanism through those classes, and the countless others whose time I wasted by not teaching them the true gospel of Jesus Christ.

Do not be deceived. A number of ministers of large and wealthy churches in our country are satanists. Their influence is far reaching, and they get away with doing what they do because Christians everywhere are too lazy to study their own Bibles to check out what they are saying!

There are three basic areas satanists teach most about:

(a) Prayer. They make prayer a very complicated procedure. They often teach that there are a number of steps the believer must go through to be sure they are in a "right" relationship with God before they have any power in prayer, or even before God will hear them. They use and twist many scriptures to make their false doctrines look legitimate. Untold numbers of people are discouraged from praying at all because prayer is presented as such a burdensome and complex thing. We encourage everyone to study Hebrews 4:14-16:

> "Seeing then that we have a great high priest, that is passed into the heavens, Jesus the Son of God, let us hold fast our profession. For we have not an high priest which cannot be touched with the feeling of our infirmities; but was in all points tempted like as we are, yet without sin. Let us therefore come boldly unto the throne of grace, that we may obtain mercy, and find grace to help in time of need." Hebrews 4:14-16

(b) One of the most destructive Satanic doctrines of today is the health-and-wealth message. One of the best ways to keep people from being willing to suffer anything to help out a brother and to discourage a true Christian undergoing persecution (it *does* happen in our country every day) is the teaching that *every* Christian should be healthy all the time, and wealthy. Anyone who is not is failing in some area of his or her life. The scriptures showing that the falsehoods of this doctrine are too numerous to list. One brief verse that about covers it all states:

> "Yea, and all that will live godly in Christ Jesus shall suffer persecution."   II Timothy 3:12

Please take note that there are no limitations on just what kind of persecution the believer will suffer — it could be financial, physical, or emotional.

(c) The love doctrine — "We can't judge anybody." Satanists protect themselves by this doctrine, and passive Christians don't want to step on anyone's toes. They just don't want to be bothered because if they did, their quiet little well-planned prosperous lives might not be so quiet and prosperous any longer.

#6)   Break Up Family Units

Satan knows that if he can successfully break up the family unit, he will also break up the unity of the church, and, I might add, of our nation. Satanists within Christian churches work hard to separate families. They start all sorts of programs for teenagers, school age, and preschool children. They develop separate programs for women and men, so as to keep the parents separated as much as possible also.

Children need to listen to the sermons and join in the prayer meetings just as much as the parents. All through the Bible the principle of learning by joining in with parents is shown. Children learn respect both for God and the church by learning to sit quietly in church and listening to the pastor. Immediately after programs are provided for young people separating them from the main church services, they lose respect for the pastor and the church. THEY don't have to sit and listen to the pastor, he is just too boring. This is the attitude they quickly develop.

What better way for children to learn to pray than by joining in with their parents? Husbands and wives are constantly under attack by Satan. In this day of easy divorce, couples need to spend time together to stay unified. Separating them within the church, and for such things as retreats, etc. is a big step towards driving wedges between husbands and wives.

#7)   Stop All Accurate Teaching About Satan

"Lest Satan should get an advantage of us: for we are not ignorant of his devices."   II Corinthians 2:11

"My people are destroyed for lack of knowledge: because thou hast rejected knowledge, I will also reject thee, that thou shalt be no priest to me: seeing thou hast forgotten the law of thy God, I will also forget thy children."   Hosea 4:6

"Be sober, be vigilant; because your adversary the devil, as a roaring lion, walketh about, seeking whom he may devour."   I Peter 5:8

"And this is the condemnation, that light is come into the world, and men loved darkness rather than light, because their deeds were evil."   John 3:19

One of the major goals of Satan and his servants is to prevent any teaching about him or his activities. As long as people remain ignorant about Satan he is relatively unhindered in anything he chooses to do. Satanists are *always* commanded to prevent any teaching about Satan within the churches they attend.

The excuses are many. They say that any teaching about Satan gives glory to him, takes people's minds off of the Lord, tempts people to turn to Satan, etc., etc., ad infinitum. God's word clearly teaches much about Satan, and warns us that if we are ignorant about our enemy he will surely gain an advantage over us.

One simple incantation by a high satanist will assign a demon to every person attending the church in which he is involved. The purpose of the demon is to stand guard and the instant anyone says anything about Satan, to beam thoughts into the person's mind that he or she should not be listening to anything about Satan.

Beware, the very church members who complain the loudest about any teaching about Satan and his tactics, will probably turn out to be satanists themselves.

#8) Direct Attacks By Witchcraft Against Key Members of the Church

This is another reason why prayer is so important. Any pastor and church leaders and/or church members who are really taking a stand for the Lord and against Satan will come under tremendous attack by witchcraft.

They will be afflicted with all sorts of physical illness, difficulties in concentrating, confusion, fatigue, difficulties in praying, etc. The leaders of any church must be continuously upheld in prayer and interceeded for by the members of the congregation. Once such a prayer base is lost, the pastor and leaders face these attacks alone. Often they are overcome. That is why Paul asked his fellow Christians to pray for him at the end of almost every letter he wrote.

. . . .

The incredible number of powerless, dead Christian churches in our land today is a testimony to the success of Satan's carefully planned tactics. Our prayer is that every Christian reading these words will go to the Lord in prayer and seek guidance as to how to fight such attacks within his or her own church.

CHAPTER 18

Demonic Illnesses

REBECCA TALKS:

The issue of demonic involvement in illnesses afflicting the physical human body is a much debated and misunderstood one. I am not trying to settle any debates here because I know that is impossible. I wish to present to you, the reader, some scriptures and personal experiences as a physician in this area, and share with you what the Lord has taught me about this problem.

I am well aware that some church leaders teach that *all* physical illness is a direct result of demonic infestation and that the only route to healing is through deliverance. Others, of course take the opposite extreme and say that Christians cannot be touched by demons. Let us look at God's word.

I, as a physician, especially enjoy reading the gospel of Luke, because I see so many areas where Luke brings a physician's view point to his writing. He is careful to show differences in the areas of illnesses where others did not have the same awareness.

> "And he [Jesus] came down with them, and stood in the plain, and the company of his disciples, and a great multitude of people out of all Judaea and Jerusalem, and from the sea coast of Tyre and Sidon, which came to hear him, and to be healed of their diseases; and they that were vexed with unclean spirits: and they were healed."   Luke 6:17-18

Please note the clear distinction made here that some of the illnesses were healed, and some were healed as a result of the unclean spirits being cast out.

> "And in that same hour he [Jesus] cured many of their infirmities and plagues, and of evil spirits; and unto many that were blind he gave sight." Luke 7:21

Again, the same distinction is made. There are two clear cases also given in Luke which demonstrate the same point — that is, some diseases are purely physical, and some are caused by demons.

> "And as he [Jesus] was yet a coming, the devil threw him down, and tare him. And Jesus *rebuked the unclean spirit*, and healed the child, and delivered him again to his father." Luke 9:42

> "And he [Jesus] arose out of the synagogue, and entered into Simon's house. And Simon's wife's mother was taken with a great fever; and they besought him for her. And he stood over her, and *rebuked the fever*; and it left her: and immediately she arose and ministered unto them." Luke 4:38-39

The emphasized portions show the clear difference. In the first case Jesus healed by rebuking the unclean spirit, in the second He healed by rebuking the physical fever.

Demons can, and do, cause illness. *Not all* illness is demonic, but a significant amount is. We must remember that physical as well as spiritual death was the result of Adam's fall. The alteration in our physical bodies caused by sin makes us vulnerable to an array of physical illnesses. The Lord has taught me much in this area. Demons are expert in handling bacteria and viruses and do cause much illness by placing these into human bodies, but they can also do damage directly.

Demons tear apart a physical body on the molecular level. They do this in such a way that devastating damage can be done to the various organs without altering the appearance of the cellular structures under our microscopes. The damage they do usually requires treatment with physical medicines, nutrition, etc., but the physician can know *only* by direct revelation from the Lord, what is really wrong with such a patient and what treatment to use. Few Christian physicians are willing to take the risk of depending on the Lord so completely. I am *not* advocating treating a patient without all the appropriate diagnostic tests, but every physician, whether he will admit it or not, sees an uncomfortable number of cases in which all the diagnostics do not give the answer as to what is wrong with the patient. In these cases it is the responsibility of the physician to specially seek the Lord's guidance with fasting and prayer.

One of the most striking illustrations of this type of demonic damage was a case that happened close to the end of my training. I was, at the time, the internal medicine resident in charge of the intensive care unit. A 35 year old man, Bob, was brought into the unit one day from a hospital in one of the smaller outlying cities close by where he had been hospitalized for a week. He had taken ill suddenly and was running extremely high fevers. His doctors had been unable to find the cause. As I examined him the day he was admitted, I could not find any specific thing wrong either, but he was obviously profoundly ill. As we started the usual battery of tests, and asked other specialists to see him also, I started praying intensely asking the Lord to reveal to me what was wrong with him.

The next morning he suddenly jumped out of bed declaring that he was going to leave the hospital that very minute, that if he didn't, he would be killed. No amount of talking could change his mind. Finally his private doctor got a 72 hour restraining order from the court to keep him in the hospital. When the restraining order was served on Bob he immediately "flipped out," and lay on the bed staring at the ceiling muttering incoherently, unresponsive to any stimulus. He remained in this condition over the next 2 days while his physical condition rapidly deteriorated.

Finally on the third morning as I was getting ready for

248

work, Father spoke to me and told me that Bob was actually a high priest from a nearby town. His illness was satanic discipline because he had displeased Satan in some way. Bob had wanted to leave the hospital because he had run into the demonic power of "David" the local high priest who was a physician at Memorial Hospital. Two high priests never get into the same territory, except by mutual agreement, without dueling to the death. Bob knew that in his weakened condition that he did not stand a chance against David. Father told me to go and bind the demons of Mind-binding and Confusion and then tell Bob that I knew who he was and what was going on and share the gospel with him. Fervently hoping that I had heard the Lord correctly, I went to do His bidding that morning.

As I entered Bob's room early that morning I made sure no one else was in the room and closed his door. I tried to see if I could get him to respond to me, but was unsuccessful. He continued his incoherent muttering. Then, leaning my arms on the rail of his bed I said:

"You demons of Mind-binding and Confusion, my master Jesus has sent me to bind you, and I now do so in the name of Jesus Christ. You may no longer afflict this man."

The result was dramatic. Instantly Bob's muttering stopped and he turned his head and looked at me, completely lucid. "Good morning," he said, "did you want something?"

"Yes, I have a message for you from the God most high." I went on to tell him the things Father had told me. Then I briefly shared the gospel with him.

"Bob, you must realize that your *only* hope is Jesus. Satan is determined to kill you. To continue to serve him will only bring destruction to you, and what is worse, an eternity in hell."

He looked at me with feigned surprise. "Who are you?! You are crazy! I don't know what you are talking about!"

249

"Oh yes you do, *my* God does not lie."

"Oh go away, I want nothing to do with Jesus!"

"So be it. That is your choice."

With that, I left his room. From that time on Bob remained completely alert and oriented. I must admit, I did have some fun pushing the specialists that morning, asking them to give me an explanation for Bob's sudden return to alertness when his physical condition had not improved. None of them could give me a reasonable explanation.

I continued to fast and pray intensely for Bob, asking Father to give him at least one more chance. Four days later Bob was very near death. His kidneys had stopped working two days before, his liver was hardly working at all, he was in heart failure and his lungs were filling up with water. His blood pressure was so low that he was on medication in his I.V. (intravenous) to try to maintain his blood pressure at a reasonable level. I knew that within a very short time he would have to be put on a machine to breath for him. He had pain continuously that we could not control. Then Father spoke to me again, telling me to go once more and share the gospel with Bob.

As before, I made sure I was alone in his room. "Bob, you are dying! Don't you realize that? Don't you think maybe it's time to be honest with me?"

"Yes, perhaps you are right."

"Do you remember our conversation four days ago?"

"Yes, very well. You were right, I am a high priest, and I did want to leave because I knew David would kill me."

"Bob, you *must see* that your *only* hope is Jesus. Won't you ask Him to forgive you and to become your master instead of Satan?"

"Yes, but I don't think I would be permitted to do so."

250

"Why?"

"Because of Satan standing there." He motioned with his hand to the opposite side of the bed from which I was standing. I could not see anything, but my spirit sensed his presence.

"No, the Lord has bound him. Do you need a sign that this is so?" (The Lord had told me I could cast out the demon of pain as a sign that what I was saying was true. The casting out of this demon would have brought immediate relief from his pain.)

"No, just the fact that you are crazy enough to take the chances you are by coming in here like this is enough to show me."

Then, with tears streaming down his face he took my hand and with a quavering voice asked Jesus to forgive him and to be his master. Then he turned toward the other side of the bed and addressed Satan directly and told him that he would no longer serve him, no matter what happened.

At the Lord's direction I cast out several demons responsible for his fever, pain, kidney failure, etc. His pain stopped immediately and he was pain free for the first time in many days. Within two hours he was off the medicine for his blood pressure. Within two days he was out of the intensive care unit and within less than two weeks he was discharged from the hospital completely well! (The specialists attributed his illness to a "virus." That is a diagnosis often used when no one really knows what the problem is.)

I sometimes wonder how many patients I have seen in the past who have died of devastating illnesses without ever really being diagnosed. Usually such cases are attributed to a "virus." Christian physicians should earnestly, with much prayer and fasting seek the Lord's guidance and revelation about such cases. Also, James chapter 5 is too often overlooked by both churches and doctors. Often the only way demonic wounds and illnesses can be healed is by prayer in faith and anointing with oil.

Another common way demons afflict the physical bodies of human beings is with pain. Pain that varies in severity but usually is devastating and for which no cause can be found medically. Any time I see a patient who is experiencing significant pain for which I can not find a physical cause, I immediately begin to seek the Lord for a revelation as to the source. It is usually demonic. When satanists fight with their witchcraft powers the loser frequently ends up in the emergency room of some hospital with severe pain for which no cause can be found. Demons do not always inflict physical damage at the same time as they cause pain, and they do not have to be inside the body to cause pain.

Often Christians are also afflicted with this type of pain. Usually they have no idea that the problem is demonic, or where the demons came from. Demons sent by witches usually afflict a person from outside their body — especially born again believers. Also, human spirits (as described in figure F of chapter 14) can afflict from without just as demons do, although demons are usually the cause except when the doorway of hatred is involved. I have seen a number of cases where the patient's affliction was the result of hatred directed toward them by another person. In these cases a simple anointing with oil and prayer by the afflicted person asking the Lord to shield them from any hatred directed toward them has been effective when all other measures failed.

A good example of such pain is the case of a young man in his mid-thirties whom I will call John. John came to the emergency room one night complaining of very severe chest pain typical of the pain involved in a heart attack. I admitted him to the hospital and ran many tests — all of which turned out normal. Two weeks after his discharge he came to my office one evening in obvious agony with the same pain. I suspected that he was a satanist receiving the worst end of a fight, but did not at that point have a clear revelation from the Lord. As I had already run all the tests available to me at the hospital in which I practiced, I sent him to a large city nearby to be further evaluated by cardiologists there. They admitted him to the hospital there and ran further tests. They also did what is called a cardiac catheterization where dye is injected into the arteries of the heart to see if there is any blockage to the blood flow there. Again, all was normal.

When John returned to see me after this complete evaluation, he was most discouraged because he was still incapacitated with frequent episodes of the chest pain. With the Lord's guidance, I sat down and talked with him and challenged him directly with the fact that I thought he was a satanist and that his chest pain was the result of demonic fighting between himself and someone else. He was shocked. So shocked, in fact, that he didn't even bother trying to deny that what I said was true. I talked with him extensively, sharing the gospel with him and telling him that his only hope was Jesus Christ. Unfortunately, this young man wanted power at any price. Despite everything that had happened to him he was still determined to stay in Satanism. He acknowledged that he knew his pain was caused by demonic fighting. Finally, he moved out of state to get away from the other stronger satanist and to establish himself in a new coven to try to grow in power there. I often pray for that young man and wonder what happened to him. How sad to see such a life wasted because of the lust for power!

The various types of emotional problems that can be caused by demons are endless. But again, we cannot assume that ALL emotional disorders are demonic in origin. I have seen some very sad cases of Christians who have been greatly damaged by others telling them their problem was demonic, when they were having a purely natural human reaction to the stress in their lives. Let us never forget that we ARE human beings, once we become Christians we do not become some sort of super-being no longer susceptible to weaknesses and reactions to stress.

I think we should discuss here one of the most common problems afflicting the human race — **DEPRESSION**. Much is written about depression in the Bible.

> "Why art thou cast down, O my soul? and why art thou disquieted in me? hope thou in God: for I shall yet praise him for the help of his countenance. O my God, my soul is cast down within me: therefore will I remember thee from the land of Jordan, and of the Hermonites, from the hill Mizar."   Psalm 42:5-6

There are a multitude of references in the Psalms and other places to depression. This battle is real, and we are very human! I am so thankful that the Lord included such scriptures in the Bible. Look at the following verses:

> "Awake, why sleepest thou, O Lord? arise, cast us not off for ever. Wherefore hidest thou thy face, and forgettest our affliction and our oppression? For our soul is bowed down to the dust: our belly cleaveth unto the earth."   Psalm 44:23-25

If any true born-again believer tries to tell me that he has never felt the emotions expressed in the above two sections quoted, I would have to say that either he has never taken a stand for the Lord and thus become involved in spiritual warfare, or he is lying!

Look at the great honesty with which Paul the apostle wrote:

> "For we would not, brethren, have you ignorant of our trouble which came to us in Asia, that we were pressed out of measure, above strength, insomuch that we *despaired* even of life: But we had the sentence of death in ourselves, that we should not trust in ourselves, but in God which raiseth the dead."
> II Corinthians 1:8-9

There are many, many causes of depression. Unfortunately, too many people involved in deliverance ministries say that *all* depression is demonic. I think this is because we humans always are looking for the easy way out of any situation. If all depression is demonic in origin the solution is simple, cast out the demon and presto, the depression is gone! It has been my experience that the majority of cases of serious depression that I have seen have **not** been the result of a demon of depression indwelling the person.

The most frequent cause of serious depression that I have seen is a direct result of an almost complete lack of mind control. (Please see a more detailed discussion of mind control in Chapter 16.) God's word clearly tells us that we are to take captive every thought to make it obedient to Christ. (II Cor. 3:5.) Seriously depressed people (including Christians) almost never obey this direct command from the Lord. They allow any thought to stay in their mind which Satan and/or his demons chose to put there. They never stop to evaluate how accurate their thoughts are with the reality of their situation, or with the situation in the light of God's word. They accept all thoughts as being from themselves, in short, they are *lazy!* They have allowed their minds to slip into lazy passivity and in such a state they come under tremendous emotional torment by demonic forces.

The fight to regain control of your mind is one of the most difficult battles you will ever engage in, but it will be well worth the effort. I saw many cases of depression in my medical practice because word quickly spread that I was a Christian physician. I can say that in every case of depression I saw, except the few that were a direct result of demonic infestation, dramatically improved with the institution of the steps toward mind control listed in chapter 15. Please note how David was doing this in Psalm 42 where he says " . . . I will yet praise the Lord . . . " He was using his will to overcome the depressive thoughts in his soul (mind) and declaring that he would praise the Lord. Praise plays a very important part in overcoming depression. Please note my own experience as described near the end of Chapter 14.

Other common sources of depression are a major loss, such as of a loved one, physical illness and weakness, big adverse changes in life circumstances and, of course, from pure exhaustion — especially in people involved in spiritual warfare. Those of us involved in spiritual warfare need to be continually *sensitive and obedient* to the Lord's leading in this area. When the Lord commands you to stop and rest you had better obey no matter how unnecessary you may think the request at the moment, or you will no doubt get shot down quickly. By this I mean, you will suffer either serious physical or emotional difficulties, (especially in the area of relationships with other people) or you may fall into error and be deceived because you can no longer be as alert as you need to be. Too many people forget that they are still human with human weaknesses and limitations. If we let the Lord guide us in these areas we will avoid much difficulty.

Some of the most powerful demons I have ever encountered have come into a person as a result of incest within a family and the various sexual perversions — especially sadomasochism which has become so popular today through heavy metal Rock music.

These powerful demons often are of a class of demons that are able to inhabit all three areas of the human at once — body and soul and spirit. Let me give you an example of this.

I received a call one afternoon at my office from a minister in a nearby city. He asked if I was "The doctor involved in a deliverance ministry." On receiving my affirmative reply, he said that he had a young woman that must be seen that day. I agreed and they came at the end of my office hours that evening.

Jane (not her real name) was a 25 year old young woman who had been married two years. Her husband was a very intelligent young man slightly older. Both had committed their lives to Jesus about a year prior to their marriage and had attended this church regularly. They had been involved in counseling with the minister and assistant pastor because Jane was completely frigid. They had not been able to consummate their marriage.

Three days prior to coming to me the pastor and some other members of the church had correctly discerned that the problem was demonic and had attempted to deliver her. They had been unsuccessful, and as a result, for the 48 hours prior to coming to me, Jane had completely lost her mental function. She babbled nonsense constantly, could not control her bodily functions or eat or drink. She did not know who she was or where she was.

They were all very frightened because her husband had received a call from her very domineering parents that day and was told that they were coming up the next day to take Jane home with them and " . . . put her in a mental hospital where she belonged." Placement on a psychiatric ward was the *last* thing Jane needed at that point. Treatment with all sorts of strong drugs and possibly electroshock therapy would have only caused more harm. What a mess! The legal implications of the situation were stupendous and my overwhelming desire was to tell them all to leave! But, I was impressed that her husband had been committed enough to remain in an unconsummated marriage for over two years and I could see that he was desperate. So I told them I needed 20 minutes or so to seek the Lord's will as to what I should do.

I went upstairs by myself and fell on my knees before Father to earnestly seek His will in prayer. Almost immediately He gave me a complete peace that He was willing to deliver Jane. Then He revealed to me that Jane was possessed by one of the powerful demons that inhabit all three areas of a human being at once. These people had not realized this and therefore had been unsuccessful in their attempts to deliver Jane. They had stirred up the demon and he was methodically proceeding to kill her before she could be delivered. The Lord opened my spiritual eyes and let me see what was going on in her body. Her brain was ripped and torn as if something with huge claws had attempted to shred it. Other areas of her body were in the same condition. The Lord instructed me to anoint Jane with oil and hold my hands on her head and pray until He had delivered her. He also specifically instructed me that in this particular case that I was not to permit any of the others to touch her.

When I returned to my office I tried to explain to them the characteristics of the demon and why they had been unable to cast it out. Then I proceeded as the Lord had instructed, sitting on the arm of Jane's chair, hands on her head. Immediately the battle was on. First I had to gain control of the rather minor demon that was babbling through her mouth continuously and causing her to be so restless. As soon as the Lord took him out Jane became quiet. She was still completely confused, however. Several other minor demons tried to obstruct and move Jane away from me, but they were quickly cast out. The last one went out screaming:

"You think you're so smart, you'll never get Yurashuha out! He's too strong and he's been there too long!"

"How did Yurashuha get in?" I asked curtly. The demon laughed, "That's easy stupid, he came in while her father had sex with her when she was a child." The Lord had previously revealed to me that that was the doorway through which this powerful demon had entered Jane.

It is well known in medical circles that traumatic sexual assaults in childhood is one of the most common causes of frigidity in women in later life — especially incest. We were taught in our courses in psychiatry in medical school that the percentage of these women ever successfully helped is dreadfully low.

258

After about 20 minutes or so, the pastor and the others with him left saying they could not spare any more time. I must admit I was rather relieved. It was a memorable experience for me. As I sat there, hands on Jane's head, praying and praising the Lord, I felt His power being channeled through me and flowing down my arms and hands. I became so hot, especially my arms and hands, that I was very uncomfortable. Afterwards Jane complained that my hands were so hot that they had burned her head and she had what looked like almost first degree burns on her scalp. These disappeared in an hour or so. The battle raged and I held that position for a little over two hours. As always, the Lord was faithful, and at last the demon lost his hold and came out screaming profanities.

Immediately when the demon was out a great change came over Jane, she became almost completely alert and oriented again. A slight amount of intermittent confusion remained and because of this her husband was doubtful that she was completely delivered. I explained to him about the damage that had been done, telling him that it would take some time to heal all of the physical damage. I did go ahead and do a bunch of medical tests over the next few days both for their peace of mind, and to be sure I wasn't missing anything. Each day saw a big improvement in Jane's condition. All the tests came back normal just as I had expected. It took about a month for Jane's complete recovery. The last I saw them was about three months after Jane's deliverance. They were very happy and Jane's husband joyfully told me they were now having a normal sexual relationship and that Jane was expecting their first child. I cannot thank the Lord enough for His tremendous work in the lives of that young couple!

Satan's kingdom is vast beyond our comprehension. We must daily walk in complete dependence on the Lord for wisdom and guidance. No two people are alike, and every attack by Satan is different. We are not smart enough to begin to figure out Satan's deceptions on our own. It is continually my prayer that the Lord will give us wisdom because this battle is real and if we are not in touch with our "Captain," we can cause great harm to those we are trying to help.

Jane's case brings me to a point that, sadly, many deliverance ministers tend to forget. Isaiah chapter 42 says it best in the prophetic description of Jesus:

> "Behold my servant, whom I uphold; mine elect, in whom my soul delighteth; I have put my spirit upon him: he shall bring forth judgment to the Gentiles. He shall not cry, nor lift up, nor cause his voice to be heard in the street. A bruised reed shall he not break, and the smoking flax shall he not quench: he shall bring forth judgment unto truth. He shall not fail nor be discouraged, till he have set judgment in the earth: and the isles shall wait for his law." Isaiah 42:1-4

> "My little children, let us not love in word, neither in tongue; but in deed and in truth." I John 3:18

I have seen many, many people remain undelivered or only partially delivered because of the lack of love on the part of the deliverance ministers. I challenge everyone in any way involved in a deliverance ministry. *Just how much do you love* the person you are trying to deliver?? Do you love them enough to sit patiently and work patiently for several hours at a time, perhaps in more than one session in order to see them delivered?

Do you love them enough to take them into *your own home* for a time if necessary to continue the battle? Do you love them enough to take the time and effort to take them to a *private* place for deliverance to avoid embarrassment for them? Do you men have enough love to sink your pride and leave the room when it comes time to deal with certain sexual demons in a woman and let just women do the deliverance in that case? Also vise versa for men. Or would your pride prevent you from even hearing such a request from the Lord?

Jesus would not break a bruised reed. Love always protects.

260

Why then should you not think about and seek in every way possible to protect a person being delivered from the often intense embarrassment involved? They have trauma enough without adding to it. Deliverance of the deeper and more powerful demons is usually *not* something that can be accomplished in 5-10 minutes up at the altar in front of the whole church, or in front of TV cameras. Our God is a God of love and compassion. If you do not have His love and compassion for every person you deal with then you are *not* fit for a deliverance ministry. If you are "too busy" to take *time* with individuals, then you should not attempt to be involved in a deliverance ministry.

The same principles apply in the area of healing whether the source of the illness is demonic or purely physical. James chapter 5 and Mark chapter 16 *do not* give time limits.

> "And these signs shall follow them that believe . . . they shall lay hands on the sick, and they shall recover."   Mark 16:17-18

> "Is any sick among you? Let him call for the elders of the church; and let them pray over him, anointing him with oil in the name of the Lord: And the prayer of faith shall save the sick, and the Lord shall raise him up . . . "   James 5:14-15

Why are we humans always in a hurry? Why do we usually think God works in a hurry? Does not the Bible itself from cover to cover demonstrate to us that God *never hurries?* I will tell you plainly why we are always in a hurry — *selfishness*. Our time is the last thing we want to give up. How many people go forward to the altar in faith, asking the elders to pray for their healing and are not healed? We would be staggered if we knew the percentage, but the world's low regard for the church should give us a good indication. In Acts we find that the world regarded the church very differently then they do now:

> "And great fear came upon all the church, and upon as many as heard these things. And by the hands of the apostles were many signs and wonders wrought among

261

> the people; (and they were all with one accord in Solomon's porch). And of the rest durst no man join himself to them: but the people magnified them."
>
> Acts 5:11-13

Elders, are you willing to tarry in love and in prayer 30 minutes, an hour, two hours, if necessary in order that someone can be healed? God is so powerful He can heal instantly and sometimes does. But often, because of His great love and compassion He does not do so because of the pain and trauma that would be caused by so much cellular rearrangement in a short time. How many people go unhealed because the elder praying for them is so selfish with his time that he is unwilling to tarry in prayer while the Lord works?

> "And Jesus rebuked the devil; and he departed out of him: and the child was cured from that very hour. Then came the disciples to Jesus apart, and said, Why could not we cast him out? Jesus said unto them . . . this kind goeth not out but by prayer and fasting."
>
> Matthew 17:18-19 & 21

Does not much prayer and fasting take both time and love? God does not choose to heal or deliver in the same way everytime. If He did, we would soon depend upon the method rather than upon God. If we are selfish in the area of time, we will not be able to discern the Lord's guidance in this area. God's work must be done in God's time, not ours!

There is another area regarding healing that few are willing to discuss, let alone put into practice in a practical way. Let us look at Isaiah:

> "Is not this the fast that I have chosen? to loose the bands of wickedness, to undo the heavy burdens, and to let the oppressed go free, and that ye break every yoke? Is it not to deal thy bread to the hungry, and that thou bring the poor that are cast out to thy house? when thou seest the naked, that thou cover them; and that thou hide not thyself from thine own flesh? Then shall thy light break forth as the morning, and thine

262

> health shall spring forth speedily: and thy righteousness
> shall go before thee; the glory of the Lord shall be thy
> reward."   Isaiah 58:6-8

> "Bear ye one another's burdens, and so fulfill the law
> of Christ."   Galatians 6:2

In light of these scriptures and others, I am absolutely convinced that the reason why there are so few miraculous healings in the Christian church today is because of the selfish refusal by God's people to bear one another's burdens.

> "This is my commandment, that ye love one another,
> as I have loved you. Greater love hath no man than
> this, that a man lay down his life for his friends."
>   John 15: 12-13

Did you ever stop to wonder just how you could lay down your life for a brother or sister other than going out and stepping in front of a gun to get shot instead of him? There are many other ways! Look at all the ways God lists in Isaiah 58:6-8 quoted above. What about bringing someone into your house to live with you? That really hits! People like to keep the privacy of their homes. Our homes belong to God and are for His use. This means that we no longer have any right to our "privacy" because there are people out there who need to be brought into our homes. Very few Christians ever hear the Lord's request asking them to take someone into their home because they are so selfish in this area.

Are you willing, when a brother is sick to say "Lord let me share my brother's burden, let me literally have some of his weakness and/or pain so that you can heal him more quickly." *Yes* we pray for healing and God heals, *Yes* we rebuke Satan, *but* are we also willing to share the burden? You see, dear ones, I think that this is how we can lay down our lives for each other and I think that as we do this, then God will be set free to do many more miraculous healings. In Isaiah 58 the Lord tells us that when we do these things that ". . . thine health shall spring forth *speedily* . . ." (verse 8). God certainly has all power in heaven and on earth! He has the power to heal and raise the dead in *every* case, but I firmly believe that in many cases He is hindered from acting freely because of our selfish unwillingness to share one another's burdens and "so fulfill the law of Christ." (Gal. 6:2)

Not long ago a brother in Christ with whom I work daily, injured his back. The injury was so severe that he was ordered to stay completely down in bed by his doctor. I knew that he was greatly needed at work and as I prayed for his healing I told the Lord that if it was within *His will*, I was willing to share my brother's back injury. I forgot all about my prayer as I became engrossed in the activities of the day.

Later that day as I started to jump up from a chair, in a hurry as usual, I fell back in surprise. My back was so painful that I could hardly move! Immediately I asked the Lord what had happened and He quickly reminded me of my prayer that morning. The Lord was allowing me to share in my brother's injury. That evening this brother called into work rejoicing that he was able to be up on his feet, although he still had pain.

Over the next five days the Lord completely healed his back, much to his doctor's astonishment. Let me tell you, not once during those five days did I forget to pray for my brother! Everytime I tried to move I remembered to pray because of the pain I was sharing. I also became completely pain free as the Lord healed my brother. This is a practical example of what I am talking about. I know from my medical training that healing can be a painful process. I believe that often the Lord must slow down the healing process because of the pain it involves. If we are willing to share, the healing can be accomplished much more quickly.

This warfare is real and the wounds are real. We've got to be willing to help one another. When someone is speaking or someone is in deliverance, let someone else sit back and say "Lord let me share that person's burden."

Let me give you an example. I had a beautiful dear young woman come to my house a couple of months ago with whom I spoke at length. She had been involved in witchcraft and had come out and had been completely delivered. She has what I call a "gentle heart." She is a very gentle loving person. Because of her involvement in witchcraft, Satan is going to hammer her the rest of her life. This is the way it is with everyone who has once served Satan in such a way — this is real life. This young woman was being terribly battered and she is not a physically strong person. She is strong in the Lord, but she is in personality a gentle person. She has so much gentle love in her heart for other people.

Now some people are just naturally more a fighter than others. God has such a range of ministries. This young woman is *not* by nature a fighter and she is having to spend all of her time and energy just "hanging in there" against the demonic attacks. This young woman was created to be a minister of gentleness and love, not a fighter.

I was so upset after talking with her, my heart just broke and I went before God the Father in tears about her, and asked "Father, WHY? People with gentle hearts like this are so rare and their love is so needed amongst your people, why does she have to spend all her time and energy battling?" His answer was "Because my people are unwilling to share her burdens." If the people in her church were willing to share her burden she would be set free to minister gentleness and love because she wouldn't have to fight so much. Those who God has raised up with the personalities and strength to fight would be fighting the battles for her and she in turn would be ministering with the gifts God has given her and there would be a sharing and great blessing for all. Then pretty soon Satan wouldn't be attacking her so hard any more because he would find out that such attacks were useless. It's not that she doesn't have the power of Christ to withstand these attacks, she does, but we need to share.

This is a wear-and-tear warfare! Let us learn to share each other's burdens, this is what being part of a body, the body of Christ, is all about.

CHAPTER 19

Straight Talk To Those Who Want To Come Out Of The Occult

REBECCA TALKS:

I want to speak directly to those reading this book who are involved in the occult (i.e. Satanism) and want to leave. What I have to say to you will seem harsh, but it is the honest truth based on God's word. There is *no* easy way out. Jesus is *not* an easy escape route. Jesus has all power and authority over Satan and his demons and that power can be available to you, but *you* chose to serve Satan, and Satan does not give up his servants easily. This is just a plain fact. You will have to fight to be free. Your only hope is to fight with the power and authority of Jesus Christ. But the battle is *real.* Leaving occult involvements is an all-or-nothing thing. You cannot partially or gradually leave Satanism. You must make up your mind to totally leave it once and for all. If you try to go back you will probably be killed and you will never have another chance to leave. This is serious business.

> "For *it is impossible* for those who were once enlightened, and have tasted of the heavenly gift, and were made partakers of the Holy Ghost, And have tasted the good word of God, and the powers of the world to come, *if they shall fall away, to renew them again unto repentance;* seeing they crucify to

themselves the Son of God afresh, and put him to an
open shame."   Hebrews 6:4-6

Once you have tasted of the power and goodness of Jesus
Christ and His salvation, if you turn back to the occult you
will *never* be able to repent again, and you will spend an
eternity in the most agonizing torment in Hell.

"Jesus saith unto him, I am the way, the truth, and the
life: no man cometh unto the Father, but by me."
                                John 14:6

There is only *one* way to come to God the Father and be
set free from Satan's kingdom, that is by Jesus Christ. If
you want to break free from bondage to Satan you can do it
only by making Jesus your Lord and Savior and *total*
Master. You cannot serve Jesus and Satan at the same
time, and if you are not totally serving Jesus, then you
ARE serving Satan. All you need to do is speak out and ask
Jesus to forgive you, wash away all your sins with His precious blood shed on the cross, and ask Him to take complete control of your life. The demons in you and around
you will do *anything* to keep you from doing this, but
they cannot stop you.

"Let every one that nameth the name of Christ depart
from iniquity. [evil]"   II Timothy 2:19b

You *must* make a complete and total break with *all* evil. I
am well aware that this will be a most difficult thing to do,
as nearly everything you have has been given to you by
Satan. You *must* give up all your powers of witchcraft —
this especially includes your ability to communicate with
the spirit world. You must ask the Lord to take away *all* of
your powers, and take them away so completely that even
should you rebel and try to get them back you could not.
You must ask the Lord to sever between your soul and
spirit so that you completely and forever lose your ability to
communicate with Satan and his demons, or use your own
spirit body. You cannot use your witchcraft, even to protect
yourself.

"For the word of God is quick, and powerful, and

268

> sharper than any two-edged sword, piercing even to
> the dividing asunder of soul and spirit, and of the joints
> and marrow, and is a discerner of the thoughts and in-
> tents of the heart. Neither is there any creature that is
> not manifest in his sight: but all things are naked and
> opened unto the eyes of him with whom we have to
> do."   Hebrews 4:12-13

You cannot hide anything from God! You must make a total break with everything evil. If you are living with others still involved in Satanism such as in a commune, you must get out, no matter what the cost. You must understand that you cannot continue to even associate with friends or relatives who persist in serving Satan. You will come under heavy influence and attack especially by family members remaining in Satanism.

> "But when they persecute you in this city, flee ye into
> another . . ."   Matthew 10:23

Once you have asked Jesus Christ to forgive you and cleanse you and to become your Lord and Master, you will have His power and authority over the demons within you and around you.

Don't try to fool yourself. Just because you have asked Jesus to save you the demons didn't politely say "good by" and hop out of you. *You* asked them in by serving Satan, now the Lord expects YOU to take up the power and authority available to you in the name of Jesus and kick them out. You must understand that the demons inside you are committed to killing you even if the satanists don't get to you physically.

Don't let the demons control you. *You* must now control them. Rebuke them out loud in the name of Jesus and command them to come out of you and leave you in the name of Jesus.

> "And these signs shall follow them that believe; in my
> name shall they cast out devils . . . "   Mark 16:17
> "Behold, I give unto you power to tread on serpents

and scorpions, and over all the power of the enemy . . ."
Luke 10:19

You *need help.* Pray and ask the Lord to lead you to Christian brothers and sisters who are able and willing to help you, but be careful. Satan has many servants in the Christian churches and there are many Christians who are not fully committed to the Lord. Seek the Lord's confirmation and guidance before you trust anyone. You will most likely need help to be able to obtain complete deliverance from the demons within you. Complete deliverance IS possible — don't let anyone tell you otherwise. Seek complete deliverance as quickly as possible. As you seek the Lord earnestly, He will hear you and will help you.

You *must* read and study and learn God's word. *Obedience* to God is an absolute necessity.

> [Jesus said] "If ye love me, keep my commandments."
> John 14:15

> [Jesus speaking] "If ye keep my commandments, ye shall abide in my love; even as I have kept my Father's commandments, and abide in his love."
> John 15:10

> "Not every one that saith unto me, Lord, Lord, shall enter into the kingdom of heaven; but he that doeth the will of my Father which is in heaven."
> Matthew 7:21

Your best protection against Satan's attacks is instant obedience to God's commands — not only those commands found in the Bible, but also those given to you by the Holy Spirit directly. You must understand that you are basically a rebellious person or you wouldn't have been involved in the occult in the first place. Satanism attracts people because they want power to control their own lives and the lives of others. The issue of the mastership of Jesus will be an area in your life where Satan will attack hard. He will put all sorts of questions into your mind such as "Why should I always have to do everything the Lord's way? It's *my* life after all." No it isn't. Don't ever forget, you have been bought with a terrible price — the sufferings of Jesus on the cross.

You belong to the Lord now. The scriptures are very clear on this matter:

> "For rebellion is as the sin of witchcraft, and stubbornness is as iniquity and idolatry." I Samuel 15:23

You *must* study and memorize God's word. This is your safeguard. God himself will give you the understanding of the scriptures. Don't accept anything anyone else tells you without checking it out with the scriptures and asking the Lord about it.

You will probably experience a total change in your life circumstances — especially financially. Don't forget, everything you have you received from Satan, it all belongs to him and he has the legal right to take it away from you. God is absolutely just with Satan as well as with us. But take courage, the riches the Lord will give you will be worth far more than anything Satan could possibly give to you.

> "Lay not up for yourselves treasures upon earth, where moth and rust doth corrupt, and where thieves break through and steal: But lay up for yourselves treasures in heaven, where neither moth nor rust doth corrupt, and where thieves do not break through nor steal: for where your treasure is, there will your heart be also." Matthew 6:19-21

The truest treasure you can ever have is a personal knowledge of God. Ask Him to reveal Himself to you.

Jesus asked Peter, and asks each one of us today this pointed question:

> " . . . lovest thou me more than these?" John 21:15b

The mastership of Jesus is absolute:

> "He that loveth father or mother more than me is not worthy of me: and he that loveth son or daughter more than me is not worthy of me. And he that taketh not his cross, and followeth after me, is not worthy of me." Matthew 10:37-38

You will be directly challenged by Satan on this issue. Are you willing to put the Lord Jesus Christ before everything and everyone else? If Jesus does not come before your loved ones, then your hopes of escaping Satan are empty. Satan will use your loved ones to keep you in bondage. Let me give you an example of what I mean.

We had the privilege of working with a beautiful negro couple whom we will call "the Blacks." They were both in their late 20s, were very intelligent, and had reached a fairly high position within The Brotherhood locally. They committed their lives to Jesus and refused to serve Satan any longer. We advised them to move out of state, but they were understandably hesitant to do so as Mr. Black had a very good paying job. They had two children, a girl four years old, and a boy two years old. They experienced a terrible test of their commitment to Jesus.

About 6 months after they came out of Satanism, Mr. & Mrs. Black and their 4-year-old daughter were kidnapped by The Brotherhood. They were taken to a meeting where their little girl was literally skinned alive before their horrified eyes. They were told repeatedly that the torture of their daughter would be stopped only if they both renounced Jesus Christ and proclaimed Satan as Lord and agreed to serve Satan again.

Despite the unspeakable anguish they experienced as they were forced to watch their beloved child being tortured and hear her screams of agony, they held firm. They had put Jesus first in their lives and would not deny His Lordship. Finally their little girl died and they were released by their captors. A week later, their son became violently ill. He was hospitalized and seen by the leading specialists in the area — all to no avail. He died within 48 hours, the doctors never did find out what was wrong with him. He was obviously killed by witchcraft. Again, Mr. & Mrs. Black stood firm and continued to serve Jesus.

Shortly after the double tragedy they moved out of the state. We stayed in touch with them occasionally. Two years later, Mrs. Black gave birth to twins, a boy and a girl. Mr.

Black was studying to become a minister.

You may be saying, "How can this be, why didn't the Lord protect their children once they became Christians?" This is not a game! When you make that complete commitment to Jesus Christ you give everything to Him. You may be sure Satan is going to petition the Lord for everything you committed to the Lord just as he did in Job's case. Father may give Satan permission to take what he petitions for.

> "For my thoughts are not your thoughts, neither are your ways my ways, saith the Lord. For as the heavens are higher than the earth, so are my ways higher than your ways, and my thoughts than your thoughts."
>
> Isaiah 55:8-9

GOD IS GOD. We cannot begin to understand His thoughts or the reasons why He does what He does. Terrible as it was, the sacrifice the Blacks made to serve Jesus pales to nothing when compared with what Jesus sacrificed and suffered for us on the cross. Jesus tells us plainly:

> "Fear none of those things which thou shalt suffer: behold, the devil shall cast some of you into prison, that ye may be tried; and ye shall have tribulation ten days: be thou faithful unto death, and I will give thee a crown of life." Revelation 2:10

> "And fear not them which kill the body, but are not able to kill the soul: but rather fear him which is able to destroy both soul and body in hell." Matthew 10:28

Let me make one thing very clear. This battle is *very real and deadly*. I am well aware that many will strongly disagree with me and flatly refuse to accept what I am going to say. But, I, on my part, must speak as my Master, Jesus has commanded me, regardless of opposition.

Any Christian entering true spiritual warfare and *any* Christian serving Jesus Christ who was once a servant of Satan, must expect persecution, suffering, and battle wounds. *And*, you will probably *not* receive immediate relief or healing for any of these.

273

> "Yea and *all* that will live godly in Christ Jesus *shall* suffer persecution."   II Timothy 3:12

Just how much are you willing to suffer for the Lord? (I am speaking of suffering physically, mentally, emotionally, spiritually and financially.) What price do *you* put on a soul? What price are *you* willing to pay to bring about the salvation of a soul, or to refuse to serve Satan and honor the Lord Jesus Christ who set you free from bondage to Satan? Jesus was willing to pay a very big price — unbelieveable suffering and death!

> "Who, [Jesus] being in the form of God, thought it not robbery to be equal with God: But made himself of no reputation, and took upon him the form of a servant, and was made in the likeness of men: And being found in fashion as a man, he humbled himself, and became obedient unto death, even the death of the cross. Wherefore God also hath highly exalted him, and given him a name which is above every name: That at the name of Jesus every knee should bow, of things in heaven, and things in earth, and things under the earth; And that every tongue should confess that Jesus Christ is Lord, to the glory of God the Father."   Philippians 2:6-11

But, people will say, "In Christ we have victory, not defeat." That is true. Indeed the purpose of this whole book and our lives is to declare that victory. But that victory is not always instantaneous in our physical world of time. There is often much struggling and battling and suffering to be done first. Ultimately, in the end, we will have complete victory in Jesus, every tear will be wiped away by God Himself and we will spend all eternity in one long joyous celebration of that victory.

In the meantime, when we are in the middle of suffering that is beyond our ability to endure, what is our hope? How do we cope? Often in such a situation eternity seems so nebulous and far off that the thoughts of it bring little comfort. How often have I been given the trite answer, "Oh, don't worry, God won't let you have more than you can bare!" That is wrong and a misquotation of the scripture. The scripture being referred to is:

> "Wherefore let him that thinketh he standeth take heed lest he fall. There hath no temptation taken you but such as is common to man: but God is faithful, who will not suffer you to be tempted above that ye are able; but will with the temptation also make a way to escape, that ye may be able to bear it."
>
> I Corinthians 10:12-13

There is a vast difference between temptation and suffering. Paul wrote very clearly in II Corinthians 1:8:

> "For we would not, brethren, have you ignorant of our trouble which came to us in Asia, that we were pressed out of measure, above strength, insomuch that we despaired even of life."

Consider the following scripture:

> "Wherefore when we could no longer forbear, we thought it good to be left at Athens alone; and sent Timotheus, our brother, and minister of God, and our fellow laborer in the gospel of Christ, to establish you, and to comfort you concerning your faith: That no man should be moved by these afflictions: for yourselves know that we are appointed thereunto. For verily, when we were with you, we told you before that we should suffer tribulation; even as it came to pass, and ye know."
>
> I Thessalonians 3:1-4

So what is the help, or hope, or answer? I speak out of my own experience, having been for more than three years in the midst of suffering and under pressures far beyond my ability to endure with no relief in sight. I know beyond a shadow of a doubt that I will inherit a "Crown of Life" and have great joy throughout eternity. But in all honesty that does not ease my hurt much now. I have no "pat" answer. All I can say is that as I firmly place my feet on "The Rock" (Jesus Christ), and day by day, with many tears, ask the Lord to give me His strength and grace to continue standing, I experience the reality of those beautiful verses which say:

> "Blessed be God, even the Father of our Lord Jesus

275

> Christ, the Father of mercies, and the God of all comfort; Who comforteth us in all our tribulation, that we may be able to comfort them which are in any trouble, by the comfort wherewith we ourselves are comforted of God. For as the sufferings of Christ abound in us, so our consolation also aboundeth by Christ."
>
> II Corinthians 1:3-5

As I continue to stand firm, the Lord helps me carry the suffering and pressure and grief so that I am not overwhelmed unto death; so that I can continue with the work which is given me to do, having the full assurance that:

> " . . .for I know whom I have believed, and am persuaded that he is able to keep that which I have committed unto him against that day." II Timothy 1:12b

Often we will find ourselves in a position where we have done all that we know to do and yet the situation continues to seem hopeless. Then we must remember Paul's wise counsel in Ephesians:

> "Wherefore take unto you the whole armor of God, that ye may be able to withstand in the evil day, and having done all, to stand." Ephesians 6:13

Simply standing, holding our ground in Christ Jesus and waiting on Him is the hardest thing we will ever have to do. So let us stand my dear brothers and sisters in Christ. Let us stand together with the knowledge that:

> "Though I walk in the midst of trouble, thou wilt revive me: thou shalt stretch forth thine hand against the wrath of mine enemies, and thy right hand shall save me. The Lord will perfect that which concerneth me: [will fulfill his purpose for me] thy mercy, O Lord, endureth for ever . . . " Psalm 138:7-8

No matter what happens, the great, incredible God of the universe has a purpose for *you*. For *YOU!* You, as an individual and He *will* fulfill it. All the forces of Satan and his vast army cannot stop God from fulfilling His purpose for you. Many things you do not understand and will never understand while here on this earth. Whatever the outcome may be — be it life, or death, or continued suffering to the end — this you can know and rest in: day by day, somehow, someway that you may not understand, God *is* fulfilling His purpose for you and His love for you endures forever!

Don't give up! The Lord *will* set you free from bondage to Satan. *Only* the Lord can set you free — you are not stronger than or more intelligent than the demons! You cannot do anything yourself, but *Jesus can and will!*

Jesus came to set the captives free!

CHAPTER 20

Definitions

REBECCA TALKS:

Perhaps it would be well to give definitions of some of the most commonly used occult terms. The list here could be very long, but we have chosen to limit it to only the most commonly used terms the Christian is likely to come across.

FAMILIAR OBJECTS

These are objects to which demons cling. Anything used in the worship of Satan or in serving Satan is legal ground for demons. In other words the demons have a right to cling to or use such objects. Let us look at a couple of scriptures that pertain to this.

> "The graven images of their gods shall ye burn with fire: thou shalt not desire the silver or gold that is on them, nor take it unto thee, lest thou be snared therein: for it is an abomination to the Lord thy God. Neither shalt thou bring an abomination into thine house, lest thou be a cursed thing like it: but thou shalt utterly detest it, and thou shalt utterly abhor it; for it is a cursed thing."   Deuteronomy 7:25-26

> "What say I then? That the idol is any thing, or that which is offered in a sacrifice to idols is any thing? But I say, that the things which the Gentiles sacrifice, they sacrifice to devils, and not to God: and I would not that ye should have fellowship with devils."
>   I Corinthians 10:19-20

These two scriptures show that the idols represent demons. The passage in Deuteronomy clearly shows that all such things used in the service of Satan are an abomination unto the Lord, even the gold and silver on them cannot be used — it must all be destroyed. God has a purpose for every command. He did not want the Israelites bringing such "demonically contaminated" objects into their homes because of the effect they would have on them. God warned them that they would also become "a cursed thing." Why? Because the powerful influence exerted by the demons would cause them to fall into demon worship themselves.

The seriousness of God's concern about these objects used in Satan's service is demonstrated over and over again in the scriptures. Read the story of Achan in Joshua chapter 7. God commanded the Israelites not to take any spoils from the city of Jericho. The entire city of Jericho was involved in worshiping and serving Satan. But Achan took some of the articles from the city. God told Joshua:

> "Israel hath sinned, and they have also transgressed my covenant which I commanded them: for they have even taken of the **accursed thing,** and have also stolen, and dissembled also, and they have put it even among their own stuff." Joshua 7:11

As a result of Achan's actions the entire army of Israel was defeated in their next battle. This is a very solemn warning to us. If we have not cleaned out our homes as well as our lives, we will be defeated every time we try to fight against Satan.

Common *familiar objects* include: any occult object used in the practice of the occult arts, any Rock & Roll records, tapes, posters, T-shirts, etc., any material from occultic role-playing fantasy games, any artifacts of Eastern religions such as the little statues of gods people buy as souvenirs while traveling, any rosaries or objects used in the practice of Catholicism, any articles used in the practice of Masonry, any literature or tapes on the occult or pagan religions, and so on — the list is nearly endless. All such materials must be destroyed. I think the Ephesians set an excellent New Testament example for us in Acts:

> "And this was known to all the Jews and Greeks also dwelling at Ephesus; and fear fell on them all, and the name of the Lord Jesus was magnified. And many that believed came, and confessed, and shewed their deeds. Many of them also which used curious arts [occult arts] brought their books together, and burned them before all men: and they counted the price of them, and found it fifty thousand pieces of silver."
>
> Acts 19:17-19

There is another type of *familiar object* as well. Satan's servants can call up demons and attach them to specific non-occult objects, then present the object as a gift to someone, there-by placing the demon directly into their home without their awareness of what has happened. The purpose of these demons is to exert a strong demonic influence to produce such things as marital discord, strife amongst family members, illness, depression, difficulty praying, difficulty reading the Bible, and so on. These objects usually do not need to be destroyed. A simple anointing with oil and prayer asking the Lord to sanctify and cleanse the object is usually sufficient. This is according to the principle God gave Moses in Exodus 40:9ff:

> "And thou shalt take the anointing oil, and anoint the tabernacle, and all that is therein, and shalt hallow it, and all the vessels thereof: and it shall be holy."

> "Whoso boasteth himself of a false gift is like clouds and wind without rain." Proverbs 25:14

Christians must be alert and very cautious about receiving any gift from someone they do not know well enough to know where he/she stands with the Lord. This is an area where we must be very sensitive to the Lord's guidance.

FAMILIAR SPIRITS

> "There shall not be found among you any one that

> maketh his son or his daughter to pass through the
> fire, or that useth divination, or an observer of times,
> or an enchanter, or a witch, or a charmer, or a consul-
> ter with *familiar spirits,* or a wizard, or a
> necromancer."   Deuteronomy 18:10-11

A *familiar spirit* is a demon with whom a witch has developed close communication. Such demons are used in many ways. In our times, a *familiar spirit* is used primarily for spying and information gathering purposes. For instance, the term a "witch's familiar" is often used in reference to some animal. In this instance the demon is placed within the animal and the witch can then, through her communication with that demon, both control the animal and see and hear everything the animal sees and hears. Also, a witch may astral project her (or his) own human spirit into an animal and then control the animal for her own use. People in the occult often form a very close link with an animal or bird that is used in this way. Traditionally witches are thought to use black cats. This is a lie spread by Satan's servants for the purpose of misleading people. Witches can and do frequently use cats for such purposes, but they prefer pure white cats, because white stands for purity.

An incident with a familiar spirit happened in my own office just recently. I am very much an animal lover. I have a couple of cats who love to ride in the car and I usually take one or both to the office each day. Normally we keep them closed in an area where they do not come into contact with the patients. That particular evening, one of my last patients was a fairly powerful local warlock. I do not think that at that point he had any idea I knew his true identity.

Somehow, that evening Joshua, my cat, got loose and came into the room where the patient was. I grabbed him up before the patient had the opportunity to touch him saying:

"I'm sorry, Joshua got loose somehow, I hope you don't mind cats?"

"Not at all, in fact we have a cat ourselves whom we love

very much."

As I carried Joshua out of the room the Lord revealed to me that I was too late. The patient had succeeded in putting a familiar spirit demon into him. One second, that's all it took!

After all the patients were gone, I was sitting in my personal office talking with two friends. The change in Joshua was remarkable. Normally he is an extremely calm and quiet cat. But as we sat talking, he paced continuously from one to the other of us, looking up at each one of us as we talked. I explained to the others what had happened. The patient was using the cat's eyes and ears to monitor all that was going on. I picked up Joshua and looking directly into his now glaring eyes said:

"Now you listen to me, Jimmy (the patient's name). Your master Satan is a liar. He is *not* stronger than Jesus. Jesus Christ *is God* and He died on the cross for you as well as me. Jesus is the one you should be serving, not Satan. Now I'm going to prove to you that what I am saying is true. We are going to cast your familiar spirit out of this animal with the power of Jesus Christ. *If* Satan is as strong as he says he is we should not be able to do this."

I then took some oil and anointed Joshua and we joined in prayer asking our Lord Jesus to cast out the demon. Again, the change was immediate. The glare left his eyes, he stopped struggling and with a big sigh lay down and promptly fell asleep.

If you have pets, always be alert to the possibility of their having familiar spirits, but please be sure to briefly share the gospel before casting out the demon or asking the Lord to remove the human spirit. Usually you will not know if you are dealing solely with a human spirit or with a demon, and whenever possible you want the satanist involved to hear the gospel. We daily pray for special shielding of our animals.

282

Animals are usually easily cleared because they do not sin, therefore Satan has no legal ground in them in the same way he does humans. However, they have been affected by the curse of sin. The scriptures make this very plain.

> "For we know that the whole creation groaneth and travaileth in pain together until now."   Romans 8:22.

In the end, all of creation, including the animals, will be made new through Jesus Christ to remove the curse of sin.

> "For it pleased the Father that in him [Jesus] should all fulness dwell; And, having made peace through the blood of his cross, by him to reconcile *all* things unto himself; by him, I say, whether they be things in earth, or things in heaven."   Colossians 1:19-20.

In Biblical days, the term *familiar spirit* seemed to refer more to a witch simply consulting with a demon. A most interesting example is found in I Samuel 28. Saul was at the end of his career. He was so far in rebellion against God that he decided to seek out a woman who consulted with familiar spirits to find out how the battle of the next day would end. The really interesting thing in this story is the fact that Saul asked the woman to use her demons to call up the dead spirit of the prophet Samuel. Obviously the woman didn't hesitate to do so, expecting her demon to come up and masquerade as Samuel. But God actually sent Samuel! Verse 12 of chapter 28 tells us that when the woman saw that the **real Samuel** was there instead of a demon she cried out and was terrified.

The many seances that are held to supposedly contact the dead are all lies. These witches cannot actually contact the dead. This scripture shows us that they only use demons who masquerade as the dead person. Satan can kill humans physically, but he cannot control their spirits and souls after death. Jesus said:

> "But I say unto you my friends, Be not afraid of them that kill the body, and after that have no more that they can do. But I will fore warn you whom ye shall fear: Fear him, which after he hath killed hath power

to cast into hell; yea, I say unto you, Fear him."

Luke 12:4-5

"The fear of the Lord is the beginning of wisdom . . ."

Proverbs 9:10

Our Lord clearly tells us not to fear the physical death that Satan can cause, but to fear rather God, who is able to cast the soul and spirit into hell after death. I believe that these scriptures and others clearly show that Satan and his demons have *no* control whatsoever over peoples' souls and spirits after they have died. One other scripture that is particularly pertinent to this is found in Revelation.

"[Jesus speaking] I am he that liveth, and was dead; and, behold, I am alive for evermore, Amen; and have the keys of hell and of death."   Revelation 1:18

SPELLS, INCANTATIONS, HEXES & CURSES

All of these accomplish the same purpose — that is, to summon a demon or demons to perform a given action. Frequently incantations are in poetic form, they are multitudinous and have been passed down from generation to generation. They are usually spoken aloud (remember, demons cannot read the human mind), but often are spoken by the witch's spirit into the spirit world which is not audible to the physical ear.

The term "Placing a spell, hex, or curse on someone," refers to the act of calling up a demon and then sending it to the person to perform certain influences or damage. ALL spells, etc., are accomplished by demons, even the so-called "good" ones such as those stimulating love in a person, etc. Another term used especially in some other countries is "bewitched," that is, someone who is under the influence or control of demons sent by a witch.

The more powerful witches do not have to use long and complex incantations. They simply communicate with the demons directly in the spirit world, or through their "guiding spirit."

GUIDING SPIRIT

A guiding spirit is usually a powerful demon specifically asked by a witch to come and dwell in him/her for the purpose of giving them all sorts of occult skills and powers and increased communication with other demons. Mann-Chan was Elaine's guiding spirit. He ruled her entire life. He gave her the many abilities detailed earlier in the book.

FETISH, TALISMAN, AMULET

These three terms all mean about the same thing. They refer to objects, most often worn or hung over the door of a home, which are supposed to bring protection and/or good fortune to the owner. Talismans are most often for the purpose of bringing "good luck."

Amulets and fetishes are frequently made to protect a person from a particular enemy, such as another witch. In these cases, something from the enemy (usually hair) is incorporated into the amulet or fetish. These vary greatly in composition, but the power involved is the same in *all. Demons!* The Lord has no such objects! The Christian's power is *only* through our Lord Jesus Christ and His finished work on the cross. Any Christian who accepts or uses such things is directly using demons. It is amazing how many Christians accept such things as a crucifix or even a Bible as being a protection in just the same manner amulets or fetishes are used. This is in absolute contradiction of God's word.

MARKS

Marks are called different things in different areas of the world. A mark is in essence an identifying object. When a witch wishes to send out a demon against another person, the demon does not automatically know who that person is. The quickest, most effective way is to present to the demon some identifying object or mark, such as the person's hair, fingernail clippings, etc. Articles of clothing are sometimes used, but are not as effective as part of the person. These marks serve to identify the person just as fingerprints do.

We have, on a number of occasions, had problems when satanists have tried to kill our pets with witchcraft. On these occasions, we have noted that the whiskers have been cut off of our cats and dog on only one side. We have lost some pets from demons afflicting them with illness, but we continually remain alert to this possibility and pray for them and anoint them with oil asking the Lord for special shielding for them. The whiskers taken from our animals were the "mark" or identifying object the witches gave the demons to use to identify our animals.

HAGSTONES

These are most commonly a form of onyx, but may be made up of any crystal or gem. The purpose of a hagstone is communication. They are frequently worn as a piece of jewelry. Special incantations are used over these stones along with various ways of rubbing the stone, etc. to summon the necessary demon or demons to take communication to another person. Often the demon will cause the stone to glow with light to signify his presence.

FORCES AND POWERS

White witchcraft is full of references to forces and powers. As an example, look at the following quote from a book on White witchcraft called *Ritual White Magic Tape Instruction Book*, by Dick Stephens (Valley of The Sun Publishing Co, 1985).

> "Magic works in accordance with natural laws and harnesses and employs those forces. It is a means of making us into better, wiser people and is an extension of our consciousness. The ultimate aim of magic is for the practitioner to create his own reality. And you are about to open the door to this incredible power that can assist you to do exactly that." p. 3.

Many other descriptions for this same thing are used, but ultimately all white witchcraft comes down to "uniting the person with the forces of the universe." Of course what these authors always neglect to say is the fact that these so called powers and forces *are demons,* and the "extension of our consciousness" or "altered state-of-mind" are really the establishing of communication with the spirit world.

To the unwary reader it all sounds so good and harmless, but be warned, it *is* witchcraft and as such is an abomination to God.

In Conclusion

Elaine and I join in earnest prayer asking the Lord of lords and King of kings, our beloved Jesus Christ, to open your spiritual understanding to all that we have attempted to say in this book. Remember this, no matter what happens to you in battle, or as a result of entering into spiritual warfare, even if you are despairing of your very life; you will *always* be in the center of our God's love and guardianship. Psalm 116:15 assures us: "Precious in the sight of the Lord is the death of His saints." God jealously guards your life.

In closing we wish to commit this book, with all the love our hearts can hold, into the hands of the One whom we love above everything else: God the Father, God the Son, and God the Holy Spirit. May all love, and glory, and praise, and honor, and thanksgiving be given to Him for ever and ever! Amen.

Please come quickly, Lord Jesus!